JORDAN

Walks, Treks, Caves, Climbs & Canyons

Their Majesties King Hussein and Queen Noor in Wadi Rum. Photo: Palace

JORDAN

Walks, Treks, Caves, Climbs & Canyons

By
Di Taylor and Tony Howard

Sketches by
Mary Hartley and Peter Hall

Maps, photos and Wadi Rum rock art
by the authors

Cicerone Press
Milnthorpe, Cumbria, U.K.

© Di Taylor & Tony Howard 1999
ISBN 1 85284 278 4

Other Cicerone Guide by Tony Howard:
Treks and Climbs in Wadi Rum, Jordan

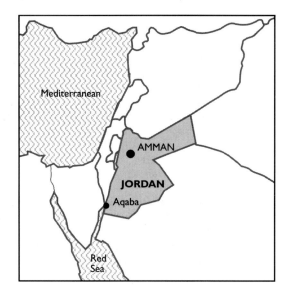

Advice to readers
The authors and publisher cannot accept any responsibility for loss, injury or inconvenience arising from the use of information contained in this guide.

Readers are advised that whilst every effort is taken by the authors to ensure the accuracy of this guidebook, changes can occur which may affect the contents. It is advisable to check locally on transport, accommodation, shops etc. Also please be aware that paths may alter or be eradicated by road-building, land-slip, flash-floods or even change of ownership.

The publisher and authors would welcome notes of any changes.

Cover photos
　　　Front: The Canyon of Wadi ibn Hammad (R47)
　　　Back:　The Mujib Siq (R44)

Foreword by H.M. Queen Noor of Jordan

I have watched with vicarious pleasure over the past 15 years, as Tony Howard and Diana Taylor have been trekking, climbing and leading safaris in the deserts of Wadi Rum. More recently, they have spread their explorations to other areas of Jordan. They have taken others with them, but their love of the land and landscape is such that they wanted to share it with a much wider audience. The result is this book, the first to present to the world the walks and other adventures to be had in the little known but infinitely varied scenery of our land. I am sure that connoisseurs of travel from all corners of the globe and many Jordanians as well will find this book fascinating.

In these pages, you will discover travels to suit every taste: gentle walks amongst ancient 'Roman' olive groves, and rambles over dales as green and beautiful as any in England, or down valleys that rival the Swiss Alps in their kaleidoscope of spring flowers. There are walks through canyons as impressive as the world-renowned Siq of Petra, but previously only known to the Bedouin people, or treks, camel and horse rides, even four wheel drive journeys along the ancient Caravan Routes used for bringing incense and spices from Arabia.

If you have the skills, you can descend into the recently discovered cave of Zubia hidden in the oak forests of the north, or the dark chasm of the Mujib Siq in the mountains of Moab, abseiling through waterfalls to the Dead Sea four hundred metres below sea level. In the south in Wadi Rum, you can climb to the spectacular Rock Bridge of Burdah, brought to the world's attention by the authors after their Bedouin friends showed it to them back in 1984. You can even make the ascent of Jebel Rum following a route up the rock more than 2,000 years old, or scramble to the summit of the highest mountain in Jordan, Jebel um Adaami, in a remote part of the desert near Saudi Arabia. And in the quiet and wild mountains, canyons and valleys around Petra the experienced trekker can discover true wilderness.

As Patron of the Royal Society for the Conservation of Nature, I am particularly pleased that the authors have included walks and treks in the beautiful Dana and Mujib and other Nature Reserves in this book, helping to support these precious but little known areas, while introducing them to the outside world. In Wadi Rum, too, their efforts have been directed toward benefiting the local people and encouraging them in their effort to protect the desert and mountain habitat for future generations. The thoughtful Introductory notes on environmental and cultural awareness are especially relevant in these areas, but are useful throughout the country.

This book demonstrates that ours is a land well worth discovering, where you will find a wealth of natural beauty and warmth of welcome rare in this day and age. I am pleased to add my welcome to Jordan and to wish you a safe and pleasant journey as you explore our ancient trails and scenic wonders - even if you never leave your chair.

Thanks to all concerned

Numerous friends have accompanied us on our explorations, enjoying the excitement and new discoveries and paying the sometimes inevitable price of being rained on, snowed on, sunburnt, dehydrated or absolutely worn out at the end of some very long days. In particular we would like to thank Wilf Colonna, Mick Shaw, Al Baker, Bernard Domenech, Sami Sabat, Hanna Jahshan, Qusai Shaath, Claud Zoumot and Paul and Mandy Taylor.

In Wadi Rum we are forever indebted to Haj Atieeq and his sons Sabbah, Dayfallah, Eid and Mazied, also to Hammad Hamdan and his sons (a list of whom would fill this page!), Mohammed Eid and his brothers, particularly Sabbah Eid and, of course, the youngest rebel of them all Atieeq Auda and his mentor on the mountains, Sheikh Kraim. Still in Rum we must thank Samir Farouqa of the Tourism Ministry, and Ali Hillawi and Atta at the Rest House for their hospitality, also Alfie at The Bedouin Cafe and all the wives and sisters of our Bedouin friends for the innumerable mensefs, the excellent Bedouin bread and for making us part of the family.

Elsewhere, The Royal Society for the Conservation of Nature made it possible to fill in the blanks on our map by welcoming us into their Nature Reserves and by providing knowledgeable guides and much appreciated hospitality. In particular we must thank Khaled Irani, Qusai Ahmad, Tariq abul Hawa and the guides and staff of the Dana Reserve. Also Adnan Budieri of Eco-peace and Birdlife International, who shares their offices and, like Khaled, has been a long time supporter of our work.

In the Petra area, Mr Kamel Mehadine and Mr Suleiman Farajat of The Petra Authority provided helpful advice whilst Wendy at Petra Moon Travel, Ismael at La Bedouins Tours, Khalil of Petra Caravan Tours and Nyazi of Nyazi Tours went out of their way to be of assistance with information on southern Jordan.

The Ministry of Tourism has also been of continued assistance to us: Mr Nasri Atalla supported not only our original explorations in Rum, but also those elsewhere in Jordan when he was Director of Tourism. His interest in our work to the present day has been tremendously encouraging. For currently assisting with our work we are also indebted to H.E. Mr. Akel Biltaji, The Minister of Tourism and Antiquities.

For the success of our two visits in 1998 we are also particularly grateful to our good friend Sami Sabat who not only provided his house for our base but also gave us additional back-up transport competently driven by Walid whenever we needed it, making life so much easier, whilst his mother and brother made sure we were well looked after in Sami's absence. Also in Amman, Rami Khouri of Al Kutba gave his support when the project looked like faltering as well as his encouragement over the years and provision of archaeological information. We were also very pleased to make the acquaintance of Hanna Jahshan and Qusai Shaath of Cheval and Outdoors Unlimited who freely provided endless coffees as well as office facilities and enthusiasm.

Back home, Christine Evans helped with some French translations, whilst Mary Hartley and Peter Hall of Sansome and Hall, Architects, Milton Keynes, have done a superb job not only by providing the vast majority of the drawings which so enhance the book, but also by helping with typing so we could meet our deadlines. Meanwhile StJohn Armitage provided new and, as always, interesting historical information on our Bedouin friends in Wadi Rum, whilst M.C.A. MacDonald provided translations of Thamudic inscriptions.

Even closer to home, Suzanne and Dave Cummins of the Dave Cummins Partnership gave us essential assistance when lost in the complexities of our computer whilst Troll provided equipment and clothing for our travels in the equally complex mountains and canyons of Jordan. For getting us there we are indebted to Royal Jordanian Airlines and to Emma Bodossian at their London office, for her always helpful, friendly and invaluable assistance over the years.

Finally, we would like to thank Lt. Colonel Omar Damra and the Royal Jordanian Air Force for the wonderful helicopter flight over the canyons of Moab near the Dead Sea, arranged with the approval of Her Majesty Queen Noor of Jordan without whose support this guidebook could not have been written. We are also deeply indebted to Her Majesty for kindly contributing the Foreword, also to Dana Toukan at the Office of H.M. Queen Noor for her constant help and reliable efficiency and for smoothing the way whenever the going became difficult; and to Salameh Awamleh, our 'Palace Driver', who happily and willingly accompanied us to more places in Jordan than he ever knew existed - we hope he enjoyed it as much as we did!

To all the above and to everyone in Jordan we are indebted for fifteen years of fascinating adventures in a beautiful country with wonderful people. We trust this book will be some small recompense.

Thanks, it's been great!

Di Taylor and Tony Howard. November 1998.

n.o.mads

NEW OPPORTUNITIES FOR MOUNTAINEERING, ADVENTURE AND DESERT SPORTS
Greenman's Farm, Greenfield, Oldham
OL3 7HA ENGLAND.

Tel & Fax: + 44(0)1457 873231
e-mail : tony & di@n-o-m-a-d-s.demon.co.uk

Permissions
We thank the following copyright holders for permission to quote from their books:

Al Kutba	*The Antiquities of the Jordan Rift Valley*	R.G. Khouri
Alpine Club Library	*Mountains in the Desert*	C. Longstaff
Fawzi Zayadine	*The Journey of Sultan Baibars*	F. Zayadine
Harper Collins	*Portrait of a Desert.*	G. Mountfort
Iris Davies (née Service)	*Call of the Wild*	R. Service
Methuen	*In the Steps of the Master*	H.V. Morton
Seven Pillars of Wisdom Trust	*Seven Pillars of Wisdom*	T.E. Lawrence

Many of the other quotations used in this book are now out of copyright whilst other authors, publishers or copyright holders proved impossible to trace despite our very best efforts. We thank them here for their works which gave us the inspiration to seek out little known places.

Have you gazed on naked grandeur where there's nothing else to gaze on,
Set pieces and drop-curtain scenes galore,
Big mountains heaved to heaven which the blinding sunsets blazon,
Black canyons where the rapids rip and roar?
Have you swept the visioned valley with the green stream streaking through it,
Searched the Vastness for a something you have lost?
Have you strung your soul to silence? Then for God's sake go and do it;
Hear the challenge, learn the lesson, pay the cost.

From 'The Call of The Wild'   Robert Service.

CONTENTS

PREFACE *Page*
    Foreword by H.M. Queen Noor al Hussein 5
    Thanks to all concerned 6
    Permissions 7

INTRODUCTION
About this book 12
    Traveller's Trails 12
    The people and places that inspired it 12
Environmental and cultural awareness 14
    Culture clash 14
    Cultural Tips for Traveller 14
    The environment - a plea 15
    Environmental tips for the traveller 16
The Royal Society for the Conservation of Nature 18
    Essential information for visitors to RSCN reserves 19
    Visitor code 20
    Visitors' enjoyment and safety 20
    How to make a booking 20
Bird watching in Jordan 21
    What sort of birds might you see? 21
The lie of the land 22
    Geographic and historical boundaries 22
    North Jordan 22
    The Mountains of Moab 23
    South Jordan 23
On the move 23
    Where to go 23
    Going there 25
    Getting in 26
    When to go 26
    On the road 26
    Getting your head down 27
    Camping 27
Other things worth knowing 28
    Holidays and Holy days 28
    Communication breakdown 28
    Money matters 29
    Food and drink 29
    Clothing and equipment 30
    Mountain biking 31
    Guides 32
    Maps 32
    Maps in this guide 32
    Be prepared! 33
    Help! 33

	Page
About the routes	34
Route descriptions	34
Grading of walks and treks	35
Grading of canyons	35
Grading of scrambles	35
Grading of climbs	36
Grading of caves	36

LET'S GO!

North Jordan	38
The Jordan Valley	39
The Northern Highlands	42
The North Eastern Desert	59
The Capital Area	62
The Mountains of Moab	67
Madaba Area	68
The RSCN Mujib Nature Reserve	73
The Kerak Area	88
South Jordan	94
The Tafileh Area	95
The RSCN Dana Nature Reserve	103
Shaubak Area	111
The Petra Area	115
The Hisma	153
Wadi Rum	154
Wadi Araba	179

MAPS

1. RSCN Nature Reserves featured in this book	18
2. The Hashemite Kingdom of Jordan	23
3. Areas and route locations	24
4. **Jordan Valley and the Northern Highlands**	38
5. The Yarmuk Gorge area	44
6. Zubia Cave approach	47
7. Zubia Cave	48
8. Wadi Yabis	50
9. Ajlun to Pella	54
10. Sami's Cliffs, Ajlun	57
11. The Capital area	63
12. **The Moab Area**	67
13. Wadi Zerqa Main & Wadi Wala	71
14. The RSCN Mujib Nature Reserve	74
15. Wadi Wala and the Hidan Gorge	79
16. The Mujib Gorge	85
17. Wadi ibn Hammad	90
18. Wadi Numeira	92

		Page
19. **South Jordan**		94
20. Selah, Buseira and Dana area		99
21. The RSCN Dana Nature Reserve		104
22. Dana to Feinan		107
23. Dana, Feinan, Shaubak area		109
24. The Petra area		116
25. The Petra Basin		119
26. Petra, northern approaches		129
27. Petra to Jebel Harun		138
28. Petra, southern approaches		140
29. Wadi Sabra area		145
30. Wadi Rum cental area		155
31. RSCN Wadi Rum National Park		158
32. Jebel Rum		160
33. Wadi Shelaali and the Rest House area		161
34. Lawrence's spring, Wadi Shelaali		162
35. The Thamudic Way, Jebel Rum		164
36. Sheikh Hamdan's Route, Jebel Rum		167
37. Hammad's Route, The Traverse of Jebel Rum		169
38. Jebel um Ishrin area		171
39. Rakabat Canyons, Jebel um Ishrin		172
40. Barrah Canyon		173
41. Jebel Burdah and the Rock Bridge		176
42. Wadi Rum, southern area		178
43. Wadi Araba and Humeimah areas		180

APPENDIXES

Relevant Reading		184
Background reading		184
Guidebooks		184
Some useful Arabic / English words		185
Topographical words		185
A few other useful words		185
Glossary		186
Index of routes and locations		187

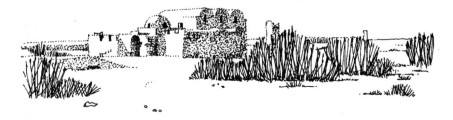

Qasr Amra, North Eastern Desert.　　　　　　　　　　*Peter Hall*

INTRODUCTION

ABOUT THIS BOOK

Travellers' Trails

" *The time has surely come when the world will 'discover' the real Jordan and the charm of its proud but hospitable people. When it does so it will find a country more rich in historical heritage than Egypt of the Pharaohs, with more archaeological treasures than Greece and a scenic magnificence rivalling the Grand Canyon and Yosemite.* "

Portrait of a Desert. Guy Mountfort. 1965.

There are no truly 'new' adventures in this book but other than some of those in Rum and Petra, hardly any have been previously documented; it is, in fact, largely a book of 'travellers' trails', some having their origins in Iron Age times and even beyond that, as ancient man spread across the land making his home in sheltered valleys and leaving dolmens and forts to guard the heights.

Stone tools from the Palaeolithic Era possibly dating back 250,000 years were left in Jordan by primitive man as he wandered the hills and valleys hunting large game animals now only found in Africa. There are excavated settlements dating back 10,000 years. The Edomites, Moabites, Amorites and Ammonites settled these lands around 1,200BC. Moses and the Israelites reputedly passed through the mountains and deserts of Jordan about this time though experts differ on exactly when.

The Nabataeans ruled here from 500 B.C. to 100 A.D. controlling the trade routes and their precious silks and spices from the Orient and distant Arabia Felix. The ubiquitous Greeks and Romans left their imprint as did the Byzantines and the soldiers of Islam, the forces of Saladin, and the invading Crusaders. Hardly changed by time and the swirl of events, the wandering nomadic tribes of Bedouin settled or passed through on their migrations, in search of grazing and hunting. Their black tents still adorn the windswept plateaux, the open deserts and the hidden green valleys, moving with the seasons. Travellers like el-Bakr, Burton, Burkhardt, Doughty, Musil and Lawrence have journeyed through the land, documenting their tales of adventure.

It has been fascinating to read these stories of discovery and to follow in their footsteps and those of the shepherds who still wander Jordan's quiet hills and valleys. We hope you too will share in the delights of treading these ancient and modern 'travellers' trails'.

The people and places that inspired it

We have endeavoured to give not just the basic directions necessary to follow the routes but also to portray something of the history and unexpected variety and beauty of the land they pass through. We have quoted liberally from the poetic and romantic writings of those earlier travellers in the nineteenth and early twentieth centuries who inspired us on our explorations and took us to some quite unexpected places.

For most people there is something uniquely special about trekking in Jordan which Louis Golding identified in 1938 in his book 'In the Steps of Moses the Conqueror' where he wrote *"It is idle to compare phenomena like the Wadi Mojib and the Wadi Hasa and the Grand Canyon at Colorado in terms of figures and say this is the most impressive because it is the deepest and the broadest. Each is a unique experience, compounded out of its own elements of colour and proportion. There is, however, the element of the spiritual significance one rather than another may hold for the onlooker."*

Remarkably little has changed in the wilder parts of Jordan: the Bedouin are just as likely to appear unexpectedly from nowhere as sixty years ago when Louis Golding observed *"Every now and then the totally uninhabited landscape would yield up a sudden crop of Bedouin who would hasten up to us to find out what we were all about."* The inhabitants of the deserts and mountain valleys are fortunately less war-like these days than they were at the turn of the century when tribal squabbles were still common and guns and daggers seemed de rigueur. Thompson, in 'The Land and The Book', 1859, describes the Bedouin as *"land-pirates"* though most considered them to be as hospitable as they are now. Charles Doughty's description, in his classic two volumes of Arabia Deserta, of his arrival at an encampment in the late 1800's is typical and timeless: *"The sun was setting and the camels wandered in of themselves over the desert, the housewives at the tent milked the small cattle. By the ruins of a city of stone they received me, in the eternity of the poor nomad tents, with a kind hospitality."*

The eagle, vulture and lammergeir still fly overhead on the warm winds, the ptarmigan and sand grouse still disturb the air with their noisy flight. Mongoose, porcupines, snakes, wolves and hyenas still lurk in shaded corners of the mountains, canyons and deserts; fleet-footed gazelles are still to be found in the remote deserts and shy ibex still lock horns amongst the rocky tops despite illegal hunting which still continues.

Of course, the cities and villages of Jordan have grown in size, paths have sometimes become driveable tracks; tracks have become roads; roads have multiplied. The Desert Highway, only a rough road twenty years ago, is becoming a motorway. Even so, 'off the beaten track' you will find not only a contrasting land of harsh yet sometimes surprisingly delicate beauty but a people who will welcome you with a warmth of custom that has its roots in the not-so-distant hard life of the desert.

Be as good to this land and its people as they will be to you and perhaps it is not too altruistic to hope that both you and they, and thereby the world, will be a little better for your journey.

Rum Inscription

ENVIRONMENTAL AND CULTURAL AWARENESS

Culture clash

"A good holiday is one spent among people whose notions of time are vaguer than ours."

J.B. Priestley

We are all too frequently astonished at the lack of awareness of many tourists concerning the impact of their actions on the cultures and environment of the places they visit: girls riding camels or sitting in Bedouin tents dressed in beach wear; picnic boxes and drink cans discarded from 4-wheel drive vehicles or left at campsites, toilet paper left protruding from beneath stones, names carved on the rocks. The list is a long one and gives our hosts a very poor impression of our society.

One of the great joys of travel is meeting people from different countries - if we want to be accepted by them it is up to us to behave in a way that is acceptable to them. Make yourself aware of other people's customs and traditions, and act accordingly. Keep the generally good reputation of trekkers and climbers.

Cultural Tips for Traveller

The notes below are a modified version of a check-list from The Ecological Centre, Leh, Ladakh, India, the original source being confirmed by Tourism Concern as from "A Third World Stopover - The Tourism Debate" by Ron O'Grady.

☺ Travel in a spirit of humility and with a genuine desire to learn more about the people of your host country. Be sensitively aware of the feelings of other people thus preventing what might be offensive behaviour on your part. This applies very much to photography - do not take photographs of people without first asking for their permission.

☺ Instead of the western practice of "knowing all the answers", cultivate the habit of asking questions, listening, observing and learning, rather that merely hearing and seeing.

☺ Realise that often the people in the country you visit have time concepts and thought patterns different from your own. This does not make them inferior, only different.

☺ Instead of looking for that "beach paradise", discover the enrichment of seeing a different way of life, through other eyes.

☺ Acquaint yourself with local customs. What is courteous in one country may be quite the reverse in another. People will be happy to help you.

☺ Remember that you are only one of thousands of tourists visiting this country and do not expect specific privileges.

☺ If you really want your experience to be a "home away from home", it is foolish to waste money on travelling.

☺ When you are shopping remember that "bargain" you obtained possibly because of the low wages paid to the maker or because the poorest merchant may sooner give up his profit than his dignity.

☺ Do not make promises to people in your host country such as sending photos when you get home unless you intend to carry them through.

☺ Spend time reflecting on your daily experience in an attempt to deepen your understanding. It has been said that "what enriches you may rob and violate others".

☺ Enjoy yourself, but remember that an extravagant display of wealth is insensitive to local people who may have to manage on much less money than you have. Nevertheless, respect and accept genuinely given hospitality - do not taint your hosts by offering money when none is required but discreetly establish first what is expected.

The environment - a plea
"The true servants of the most gracious are those who tread gently on the earth."
The Qu'ran. Sura 25, verse 63

This book has been slowly taking shape since 1984 when we were invited by Jordan's Ministry of Tourism to assess Wadi Rum in South Jordan for its rock climbing and adventure tourism potential. With the help of the local people who were still, at that time, predominantly semi-nomadic Bedouin, we quickly identified Rum's huge potential for climbing, trekking, and camel safari. This led to the publication of 'Treks and Climbs in Wadi Rum' in 1987, followed by 'Walks and Scrambles in Wadi Rum' in 1993.

Whilst all this was going on, we made increasingly more trips into Jordan's other mountain areas, finding a wild and beautiful country unspoiled by tourism. In 1985 we walked through Wadi Dana from what was then a ruined village with few inhabitants - it has since become one of Jordan's first Nature Reserves with tremendous work having been done by Jordan's Royal Society for Conservation of Nature (RSCN), not only to identify the indigenous flora and fauna, but to ensure that the village was restored to its original state and the inhabitants helped by bringing traditional work into the area such as agriculture and crafts. It is one of Jordan's success stories. On that same trip of ours, back in 1985, we returned to Petra via Wadi Siyyagh, from the wilderness of Wadi Araba. This was another astonishing journey for us, discovering waterfalls, deep pools and palms where the maps showed only desert and rocky ravines.

Other exploratory trips in the following years were equally or even more astounding: the spectacular Siq of Tibn: the oasis of Sabra, the 'Grand Canyon' of Mujib, the hill top ruins of Selah, the Cave of Zubia. The list goes on: all 'new', all exciting and beautiful, all different. Coupled with the treks and scrambles we were still discovering in Rum with the help of our Bedouin friends, such as that to Jebel Adaami, Jordan's highest mountain, we soon realised we had a unique collection of adventures which deserved publication.

The dilemma for guidebook writers is, however, a real one: do we say nothing and hope these places will stay 'undiscovered' and pristine, or do we tell all and risk the hidden jewels being destroyed so that others can share our discoveries and the local people can benefit from their visits?

Our experience in Rum has been salutary. In this day and age, it is extremely rare that a truly 'new' area such as Rum was, is revealed in a guidebook and we have had fourteen years to see the changes that have taken place, partly as a result of our work. This has given us cause for considerable soul-searching: the bad news is, that despite our advice in the guidebook places like the Rock Bridge and the summit of Jebel Rum have been vandalised by graffiti. Some of the ancient rock art has gone the same way. Four-wheel-drive tracks now cover most of the desert, destroying fragile ecosystems. Litter can be found at popular tourist sites. Here and there a few rock-climbers' safety bolts have appeared in unsightly places visible from the desert.

The good news is that the local people have benefited tremendously and are co-operating with the RSCN in the creation of a new reserve, to protect the area. The damage to the rock art and desert has reached a point where others are finally becoming concerned and are supporting efforts to stop it. The destruction could be contained and the worst of the damage could be removed. Thousands of people have had wonderful, memorable experiences in the desert and mountains, and many have struck up lasting friendships with the Bedouin to the benefit of all.

We have to hope that the result of the inevitable growth of visitors has perhaps been less destructive than it may otherwise have been had we not taken great care to stress the cultural and environmental considerations in our books. Even so, we are tremendously concerned about the damage that has happened, and are working actively with the local people, the RSCN and others to eradicate and reduce it.

In actual fact, we believe that most of the damage has come from the uncontrolled growth of *mass* tourism (from Jordan itself, as well as from abroad), rather than from the relatively small numbers of, hopefully, 'aware' trekkers and climbers. Tour Guides, usually from outside the area and often sadly lacking in environmental awareness, are also responsible. Nevertheless, we cannot be complacent - few of us are entirely blameless and we should be aware at all times that our actions will inevitably impact on the environment and cultures of the places we pass through. It is up to us all to make our impact a positive one. We consequently hope that readers of this guide will act in a way that will be a credit to them.

You should find little or no litter on the trails in this book, no new way-markers, no toilet-paper, few signs of fire other than perhaps a few burnt sticks left by shepherds enjoying their regular cups of 'shai'. The people you will meet will inevitably be welcoming and friendly. Please do everything you can to keep it this way. Have fun, take care and tread gently!

Environmental tips for the traveller

"The world is green and beautiful and Allah has appointed you as his stewards over it. He sees how you acquit yourselves."
Sayings of The Prophet Mohammed.

Below is an amalgam of the International Union of Alpine Associations (UIAA) Mountain Code, The British Mountaineering Council's conservation booklet - Tread Lightly, and the Himalayan Tourist Code published by Tourism Concern, sponsored by The Independent and Rough Guides publications:

By following these simple guidelines, you can help preserve the unique environment of the places you pass through.

  Δ **Observe restrictions and access agreements** negotiated by National Mountaineering Federations, (or, in Jordan's case, Nature Reserves and other RSCN zones), and avoid any actions which might endanger access.

Δ **Limit desertification - make no open fires** and discourage others from doing so on your behalf.

Δ **Remove litter, burn or bury paper** and carry out all non-degradable litter. Keep campsites clean. Graffiti are permanent examples of environmental pollution.

Δ **Keep local water clean and avoid using pollutants** such as detergents in streams, wells or springs. If no toilet facilities are available, make sure you are far away from water sources, and bury waste. Burn toilet paper or use water instead.

Δ **Do not disturb nesting birds or other wildlife** and respect sites of geological or other scientific interest. Plants should be left to flourish in their natural environment - do not take cuttings, seeds and roots. It is illegal in Nature Reserves and bad practice elsewhere.

Δ **Do not disturb livestock or damage crops or vegetation.**

Δ **Avoid actions which cause unnecessary erosion** (such as taking shortcuts on footpaths). Wear lightweight boots or trainers and tread carefully, especially in descent. Do not leave unnecessary waymarks.

Δ **Rock climbers should respect established mountain traditions** in ethical matters such as the use of chalk, pitons or bolts etc. Avoid indiscriminate or excessive use of fixed equipment.

Δ **Help your guides and porters to follow conservation measures.**

For information on tourism and its effects on others, contact:
Tourism Concern, Stapleton House, 277 - 281 Holloway Rd., LONDON N7 8HN
Tel: 0171 753 3330 fax: 0171 753 3331, e-mail: tourconcern@gn.apc.org

For information on mountain tourism and the ethics and responsibilities of trekkers and climbers, contact:
The British Mountaineering Council, Burton Rd., Manchester M20 2BB, ENGLAND
Tel: 0161 445 4747   Fax: 0161 445 4500, or your National Mountaineering Body.

For information on environmental action in Jordan and the Middle East, contact:
Friends of the Environment - an independent non-profit making NGO encouraging the younger generation to take an active part in conserving and improving their natural environment:
PO Box 840795, Amman 11184, JORDAN   Tel: 009626 5514430, Fax: 009626 5514431
e-mail: foes@nets.com.jo and foejord@go.com.jo

EcoPeace - a consortium of Egyptian, Israeli, Jordanian and Palestinian environmental, non-governmental organisations, all working jointly to promote sustainable development in the Middle East Region:
2 El Akhtal St., East Jerusalem, 97400, PO Box 55302, ISRAEL
Tel: 00972 2 6260841 / 3 Fax: 00972 2 6260840, e-mail: ecopeace@Netvision.net.il

For archaeological info. contact:

> Friends of Archaeology, P.O. Box 2440, Amman 111181, JORDAN
> Tel/Fax: 009626 696682, e-mail: foa@nets.com.jo

For information on Jordan's Nature Reserves contact:

THE ROYAL SOCIETY FOR THE CONSERVATION OF NATURE

The following information was kindly supplied by the RSCN:

Jordan is blessed with a wide range of climates, resulting in an unusually large number of different habitats and great biological diversity for a country of its size. However, many of these are extremely fragile, and can be easily disrupted.

There are substantial local climatic variations, largely due to the extensive differential in heights from the lowest point at the Dead Sea, 400 metres below sea level, to the high mountain tops at around 1800 metres. Other contributory factors include the different soil types (rich agricultural soil to desert sand) and the varying rainfall levels from a mean annual rainfall of 50 mm. in the eastern badia to nearer 800 mm. in Ajlun. Run off from the mountains is high and much water soaks into the valley floors. Consequently, the vegetation there is much denser than would be expected from the low rainfall. All of these lead to multiple wildlife habitats, and complex ecology.

The difference in habitats creates a wonderfully varied and beautiful country, with many different species of flora and fauna. It also creates an environment that needs to be carefully protected.

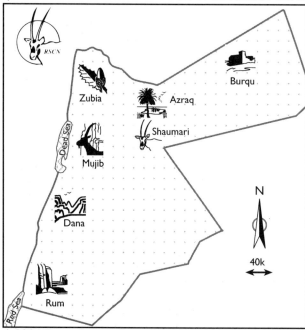

1. *RSCN Nature Reserves featured in this book*

The Royal Society for the Conservation of Nature, founded in 1966, has set up a system of wildlife reserves as part of its environmental protection scheme. Its mission is to protect wildlife habitat in Jordan and to promote an understanding of the natural environment.

The established nature reserves of Jordan offer visitors a chance to experience some of the country's most beautiful landscapes, including the spectacular sandstone cliffs and wild valleys of Dana, the flowing streams of Mujib, the oak woodlands of Zubia, the desert grassland of Shaumari and the marshes of Azraq.

Negotiations are currently underway to add Wadi Rum to this list as a special Reserve with its own unique regulations. Whether you enjoy hiking, bird watching, archaeology or simply a quiet picnic, RSCN's nature reserves offer something for all people who love nature and wild places.

With RSCN nature comes first, so it is able to offer visitors to their reserves special experiences and benefits:

⊛ **Beauty without crowds** In order to protect the environment within the nature reserves, the number of visitors allowed to enter each day is limited and cars are required to park outside, so you can get a real chance to experience the wonders of nature in peace and quiet.

⊛ **A chance to learn about nature** RSCN offers trained guides to accompany visitors who can tell them all about the wildlife, landscape and history of the area.

⊛ **A chance to explore unspoiled landscapes** There are hiking trails in all the reserves which enable visitors to discover the beautiful places and experience the special character of each reserve. Some can be self-guided, others need a tour guide.

⊛ **A sense of adventure** For small groups seeking a challenge, adventure treks can be arranged in the more dramatic and remote wild places of Jordan.

⊛ **Specialist tours** A number of these are being developed on interesting topics like bird watching and botany to cater for those visitors with a thirst for more in-depth knowledge. Adventure trekking is also being offered.

⊛ **A way to support the conservation of wildlife** All the money visitors contribute through entrance fees, accommodation charges and buying crafts is used to further the work of RSCN and help it protect the wildlife and wild places of Jordan.

⊛ **A way to help local people** RSCN has a policy to employ local people where possible and to try and create opportunities for them to earn income from the nature reserves. Tourism is one of the main ways by which local people can improve their standard of living.

Essential information for visitors to RSCN reserves

The RSCN is a non-profit making organisation. The income it receives from visitors is used directly to support its conservation work. There is an entrance fee to all reserves and a charge is made for guided walks, visitor centres and accommodation. An RSCN guide must accompany every tour.

Every reserve has regulations to protect the environment which must be respected by all visitors. They include no casual fires and no radios and loud music. There are daily limits on the number of people allowed in each reserve, so all visits should be booked in advance to avoid disappointment. All bookings should be made through the RSCN or nominated tour operators.

RSCN nature reserves are for people who like nature. There is no 5-star luxury accommodation but the facilities are clean and simple and the service friendly and efficient. Some of the reserves are not suitable for bus tours or large groups. Check before you book.

Visitor code

RSCN welcomes all visitors to its nature reserves but to ensure that these special places are protected for future generations, we ask visitors to respect all regulations, and particularly to:

Obtain a valid permit before entering the reserve

Leave vehicles in designated parking places

Protect all nature. (Don't hunt or collect flowers, rocks, fossils or archaeological artefacts)

Camp only at official sites

Keep to permitted hiking trails and access routes

Enjoy the sounds of nature. (Don't use radios or instruments or play noisy games)

Leave nature's beauty for others to enjoy. (Don't damage trees or rocks)

Refrain from making open fires (firewood collection damages trees and shrubs and many animals make their home in dead wood)

Keep the reserve clean. (Don't leave litter or pollute watercourses)

Please dress modestly and ask permission before taking pictures of local people

Respect their cultures and traditions and you will be rewarded with their warmth and hospitality

We ask all tour operators to make sure that potential visitors are made aware of these regulations.

Visitors' enjoyment and safety

For a day trip to a nature reserve, visitors are advised to bring water, hats and comfortable walking shoes. A camera, binoculars, wildlife identification guides and a picnic lunch will also enhance their visit.

For overnight camping trips (applicable to all reserves except Dana), visitors will also need sleeping bag or blankets, food, a camping stove, pots for cooking and garbage bags. Tents are available for rent at the RSCN. Other useful items are a flash light, a compass, matches, waterproof clothing and first aid kit.

Group rates and special tours can be discussed and arranged by contacting the head of the Tourism Unit - see below.

How to make a booking

When you have decided which reserve you want to visit, contact RSCN to make a booking by telephone, fax or mail. The address and contact numbers are as follows:

The Royal Society for the Conservation of Nature

PO Box 6354, Amman 11183, JORDAN

Tel: 00962 6 5337931/2   e-mail: rscn@nets.com.jo

Ecotourism Unit Direct Line, Tel: 00962 6 5337610   Fax: 00962 6 53347411

The RSCN Headquarters are about 10 - 11k from the 3rd Circle in Amman. If the taxi driver doesn't know it, head out for 2k to the Regency Palace Hotel, passing it on your right, continuing along past Jordan University and uphill for 8k from the Regency, past the roundabout with the steel sculpture to the Jubeiha Circle. Turn right here then right again a short distance up the road at the next circle, then right again 50m down a small road. The RSCN building with its Oryx head logo is on your left.

BIRD WATCHING IN JORDAN

Jordan sits at the junction of three continents, Europe, Africa and Asia, and you often see birds from each of these regions in the same general area. There is a remarkable variety of habitats from rugged mountains and evergreen woodland to scrubby steppe and hot deserts. Each of these has its special complement of birds.

Jordan's great Rift Valley is a 'bottle neck' on the main route for birds migrating from Eastern Europe and Russia to Africa. At certain times of the year the skies over the Rift Valley are full of circling birds-of-prey.

Jordan's culture is exotic and its people renowned for their friendly welcome. You can bird watch in the ruins of the ancient Nabataean city of Petra, or in the stunning landscape of Wadi Rum, the favourite of Lawrence of Arabia, or many other uniquely beautiful and unusual places.

Bird watching tours in Jordan are organised by the Royal Society for the Conservation of Nature. By joining one of their tours, you are helping to finance the conservation of the country's finest nature areas. You may do so directly via the address above, or via any Travel Agency including:

Discovery, P.O. Box 3371, Amman 11181, JORDAN
Tel: 00962 6 5697998, fax: 00962 6 5698183   e-mail: discovery@discovery1.com

For additional information, contact the RSCN or Bird Life International:

P.O. Box 6354, Amman 11183, JORDAN
Tel: 009626 5337931/2, or 5347733, fax: 009626 53347411, e-mail: birdlife@nol.com.jo

What sort of birds might you see?

The eastern part of the country consists mainly of desert habitats and contains the Azraq wetland. While the wetland itself holds aquatic species and is packed with migrants in spring, its surroundings support characteristic desert birds, such as the Temmiinck's Horned Lark, Desert Lark, Hoopoe Lark, Desert Wheatear and Trumpeter Finch. In winter, Cranes and Imperial Eagles roam across this area. While walking around the Desert Castles, Thick-billed Lark and Red-rumped Wheatear can be spotted.

In the west, the highlands contain typical Mediterranean habitats, usually surrounded by open steppe country. In the wooded areas, (e.g. Ajlun, Rumeimin, Zubia, Dibbin, Salt, Dana), Palestine Sunbird, Upcher's, Orphean and Sardinian Warbler can be found, while the more open, steppe habitats typically contain Spectacled Warbler, Long-billed Pipit, Black-eared Wheatchat, Shrike and Linnet.

The rift valley margins on the western side of the highlands and the wadies cutting into and crossing the mountains, many of which are described in this book, often hold a wide range of birds as they represent the cross-roads of four bio-geographic zones. Wadi Shu'eib and Wadi Mujib contain perennial watercourses which are home to the beautiful Smyrna Kingfisher, whilst the magnificent rocky gorges of Wadi Rum, Dana, Mujib and Petra are the sites to find Griffon Vulture, Bonelli's Eagle, Hume's Tawny Owl, Blackstart, different Wheatears, Scrub warbler, Sinai Rose Finch, House Bunting, Tristram's Grackle and Fan-tailed Raven, just to mention a few.

Last but not least, the Dead Sea area and Wadi Araba contain mainly Arabian and African species:

Sand Partridge, Bar-tailed Dunns, Hoopoe Larks, Little Green Bee-eater, Blackstart and Arabian Warbler can be found here.

THE LIE OF THE LAND

"Sometimes I have seen the desert referred to as a dead land without life, a barren waste or a landscape of the moon. Nothing could be further from the truth, for the desert is in reality indescribably beautiful with its pure air, its distant blue horizons and its rolling hills and valleys covered with shrubs. There is a magical fascination about the desert which fills one with a wild elation".
A Soldier with The Arabs. Glubb Pasha. c1930.

Jordan is generally perceived as a 'desert country'. Don't be deceived! There are, of course, vast and generally arid deserts to the east and north-east, bordering Saudi Arabia, Iraq and Syria. The southern end of the Dead Sea Valley, down below sea level, can be as hot and dry as almost anywhere on the planet but elsewhere Jordan has different stories to tell: the desert of Rum in the south-east is a land of great isolated steep walled 'jebels' rising like battleships from coloured sands which are dotted with vegetation and, after the spring rains, carpeted in flowers.

The hills which bound the east side of this extension of the Rift Valley run the full length of the country. Whilst increasingly arid to the south, they and their upper plateaux are riven by beautiful gorges and canyons often concealing rivers. Oak forests, junipers and small green fields cultivated by Bedouin or local farmers give an unexpected Mediterranean charm to these otherwise seemingly inhospitable and wild hills.

At the northern end of the Dead Sea, this great valley, now the Jordan Valley, is lush and green with year round crops of fruit and vegetables. The hills above are generally less rocky than their southern counterparts with thick forests and pine woods sheltering rich carpets of spring time anemones and other flowers, which appear as winter's snow melts or the spring rains finish.

Amongst this vast varied landscape, archaeological sites abound; 10,000 year old pre-historical settlements, great tumuli, castles, fortresses, abandoned villages, lost cities and Biblical sites. We need hardly mention the world renowned Petra, or the magnificent Islamic hilltop fortress at Ajlun, the great Roman city of Jerash, King Herod's fortress at Mukawir, the Crusader castle of Kerak, the tomb of Aaron, brother of Moses, on a hill top high above Petra. The list is endless.

The journeys in this book follow trails ancient and modern through this wonderful landscape and often far from the nearest road. They are journeys of discovery both of nature's wonders - deserts, mountains, canyons, caves and hot springs, and of the history of man.

Ahlan wa Sahlan: Welcome to Jordan, its land and its people.

Geographic and historical boundaries

East of the River Jordan and its southern continuations, the Dead Sea and Wadi Araba, the mountains explored in this guide are divided by three steep gorges with perennial rivers. These districts correspond roughly with the Kingdoms of the Old Testament. They are described in this book as follows:

North Jordan

Amman and the north. It includes the modern district of Ajlun (the Biblical Land of Gilead), which lies between the Yarmouk River marking Jordan's border with Syria, and Wadi Zerqa (the Jabbok of Biblical times). The area abounds with famous Greek and Roman ruins as well as castles from the Crusader period and Iron Age remains. For the purposes of the book, we have divided this into The Jordan Valley and Northern Highlands. The region between Zerqa and Amman was originally the land of the Ammonites and is described as The Capital Area. The oases in the north-eastern deserts are also covered and the whole of this area is easily accessible from Amman.

The Mountains of Moab

This, (once the Biblical land of Moab and consequently with a considerable number of important sites from that period), is nowadays mostly part of the district of Kerak and extends from the hills immediately north of the Mujib Gorge to Wadi al Hasa. Amman is the base for the region north of Mujib, otherwise the town of Kerak with its magnificent Crusader Castle is centrally located.

South Jordan

The District of Ma'an (the land of the Edomites and later the Nabataeans) stretches south from Hasa to the Gulf of Aqaba. There are numerous Biblical, Nabataean and Roman sites especially in the Shara Mountains around Petra and down in Wadi Araba. The northern part of this area is the Tafileh Area; moving south from here, we pass through the Dana Area then the Petra Area. South and east of here is the great expanse of the Hisma, and the south eastern desert including Wadi Rum, whilst to the west the barren Wadi Araba extends from the Dead Sea to the Red Sea. Bases for exploration of this area are commonly Dana, Wadi Musa (Petra) and Wadi Rum or Aqaba.

ON THE MOVE

Where to go

As outlined above, this book sets out to cover all of Jordan's mountains though in reality there are other huge blanks on the map when it comes to treks and other aspects of adventure tourism. We have, for example, been told of interesting walks between archaeological sites in the great basalt deserts of the north east and of others in the eastern deserts or in the mountains north of Aqaba which may not be so harsh as they first appear. If you visit these areas and find anything new and exciting or interesting, let us know. Alternatively, if you want to experience the many

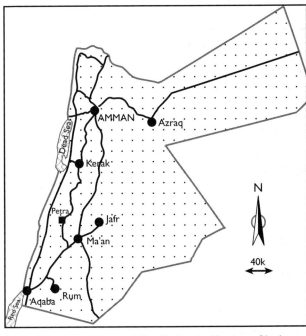

2. The Hashemite Kingdom of Jordan

23

excellent trips that are already 'on the map' then you need look no further than this book.

The routes are described from north to south. Generally, those in the north are in a greener, kinder environment requiring the least experience. Most are in the vicinity of sites of antiquity and many can be reached from Amman and done in half a day, returning to the city in the evening.

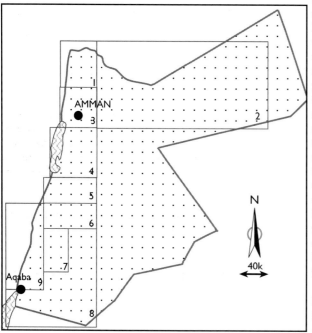

Moving south, there are still some short walks to be done, but the big canyon walks of the Mountains of Moab in central Jordan are the pièce de résistance of this area - you should not consider them unless you are an experienced walker and you should not go alone. These treks do however offer truly spectacular and often unexpected scenery and are very rewarding for those wanting real adventures and having the skills to extricate themselves if things go wrong: anything can happen, broken ankles, snake bites, flash floods, even hyenas!

In southern Jordan around Dana and Petra there are options for everyone with small walks and multi-day treks starting from places like the Dana campsite or the town of Wadi Musa, outside Petra. Specialist adventure travel companies offer guiding to some very remote areas, usually in the company of local Bedouin, even treks on foot or by horse or camel from Petra to Rum. Whatever you are looking for, spectacular and beautiful scenery, wilderness adventure, wild-life or archaeology, you will find it here in abundance.

3. Areas and route locations

North Jordan

1. Jordan Valley & Northern Highlands	R1 - 17
2. North Eastern desert	R18 - 19
3. The Capital Area	R20 - 25
The Mountains of Moab	
4. The Mountains of Moab	R26 - 50
South Jordan	
5. Tafileh Area	R51 - 58
6. The Dana Area	R59 - 70
7. The Petra Area	R71 - 103
8. The Hisma	R104 - 115
9. Wadi Araba	R116 - 118

Last but by no means least is Wadi Rum, the land of Lawrence of Arabia, a mountain desert *par excellence*. Here you will find awe-inspiring treks and climbs, 4-wheel drive journeys and camel and horse safaris amongst scenery unsurpassed anywhere in the world. A group of two or more can walk and climb alone if they have the skills and equipment though many prefer to hire local Bedouin guides for a real desert experience. Wherever you go you are sure to find adventures the equal of any with the unique ambience that only Jordan's land and people can offer.

Going there
There are mumerous travel guides with advice on international travel (see Relevant Reading in Appendixes). Suffice it to say that British Air now fly to Jordan from London, whilst other airlines fly from Manchester to Jordan via major European cities. Royal Jordanian Air fly daily from London, Paris and many European cities to Amman, and on to Aqaba. Their UK address is:

Royal Jordanian Airlines, 32 Brook Street, LONDON WIY IAG, ENGLAND
Tel 0171 878 6333, Fax 0171 629 4069.

There are also inexpensive charter flights to Eilat in Israel, which is right next to Aqaba. If you search around, you will also find comparatively inexpensive fares to Jordan. Prices vary between £200 to £400 but have to be considered against the inconvenience of, for example, flying via Moscow, or having to take various taxi and bus rides to get from Eilat Airport which is about 60k from Eilat, then having to pay an Israeli exit tax before entering Jordan and getting another taxi to Aqaba.

Take the most convenient way and you can be in Jordan in 6 hours and on the hills the next day. Go a cheaper way and it may well take one or two days. Such is life!

For British travellers, tourist info. is available in the UK from:

The Jordan Tourist Board, Unit I, Blades Court, 121 Deodar Rd, LONDON SW15 2NU
Tel: 0181 877 0554

Travellers from the UK could also contact any of the following:

Freelance Travel Ltd., Mere House, Dedmere Road, Marlow, Bucks SI7 IPB
Tel: 0118 934 1398. Fax: 0118 934 268.
e-mail: jasSmith@compuserve.com.

The Imaginative Traveller, 14 Barley Mow Passage, Chiswick, LONDON W4 4PH
Tel: 0181 742 3113. Fax: 0181 742 3045

Arabica Travel Ltd, PO Box 26119, LONDON SW8 4RZ
Tel: 0171 640 2332. Fax: 0171 627 3748
e-mail: arabica@annal.dircon.co.uk

For climbing and trekking holidays from the UK in Wadi Rum, contact:

High Places, Globe Works, Penistone Rd., Sheffield S6 3AE
Tel and Fax: 0114 275 3870   e-mail: highpl@globalnet.co.uk

Or, contact any of the Jordanian Adventure Travel companies listed in the section on Southern Jordan, or Jordan's Ministry of Tourism at:

PO Box 224, Amman IIII8, JORDAN
Tel: 009626 464231I/4 Fax: 009626 4648465   e-mail mota@amra.nic.gov.jo

Getting in

On arrival in Jordan you will need a visa. You can get it beforehand from the Visa Dept. at the Jordanian Embassy which for the UK is at:

6 Upper Phillimore Gardens, London W8 7HB (visa info: 0891 117 1261)

Or, you may buy it at the airport or other point of entry to Jordan. The cost varies with your nationality - for UK citizens the price is 23JD whereas for the Irish it is 11JD and for the French it is only 6JD. The visa allows a fourteen days stay.

To stay longer you will need a Visa Extension. This is simply and freely obtained from the Police Station at Aqaba (just above the bus station), or from that in Amman. Finding the Amman Office is not so easy; the best thing to do is to ask a taxi driver to take you downtown to Markhaz am Muhajireen or to the Tourist Police Office at the 8th circle, open between 10.00 a.m. and 1.00 p.m. There is also a Police Station in Wadi Musa, next to the roundabout at the top of town that can, in theory, extend your visa but apparently they sometimes ask for medical certificates, so don't ask there on the last day as you may have to go to Aqaba instead. Elsewhere, it is done whilst you wait and shouldn't take more than fifteen minutes, but beware of being caught out by holidays.

If entering from Israel you should be aware that an Israeli stamp or even a Jordanian or Egyptian stamp from an Israeli border crossing point may preclude entry to countries such as Syria.

When to go

There was a time when travellers chose only to visit Jordan in autumn and spring. April is undoubtedly our favourite month: water is at its most plentiful and the land is green and carpeted with flowers in the pine-woods of the north and, if you're really lucky, in the deserts of the south. Springtime is definitely the best time to wander amongst the flower-filled northern meadows, forests and valleys, and to discover your own short walks in this generally gentle terrain. However, it may not be the time for trips into the great canyons such as Mujib and Hidan which are prone to flash floods from rain in the distant hills.

These days, apart from the hotter summer months of July and August, travellers seem to be taking to the trails throughout the year. Suffice it to say that in the hills north of Amman there may well be snow in the winter months and there will inevitably be some rain almost anywhere in Jordan from early November through to the end of March or even early April, especially in the north. (A few years ago it even snowed in Aqaba!)

Winter also has, of course, short days and really it's not the best time to go though there are climbers and trekkers in Wadi Rum right through this time of year. The best seasons are spring and autumn, late March through to the end of May, and late September to mid-November. If you are considering any canyon trips, remember, people are killed by flash floods in these inescapable places. Go there when the weather is fine. In places like Hidan and Mujib, especially their exit canyon, whilst late spring should be OK, the safest time of all is late summer and early autumn, when the water is low, and before the winter rains.

On the road

Transport in Jordan is generally good. From Amman airport, there are regular JETT (Jordan Express Tourist Transport) bus services to Abdali bus station in Amman leaving every 30 - 40 minutes from 6.00 a.m. - 10.00 p.m., and every 2 hours through the night. The cost is 1JD plus 0.25JD for bags. Or, of course, you can take a taxi.

Getting around in Jordan, public transport costs are likewise much less than in Europe, for example 4JD from Amman to Aqaba. JETT and other private operators such as Alpha and Petra, with hostesses and air-conditioned buses, go to major places like Aqaba or there are public bus services, 'service-taxis' and regular taxis. The private buses are fast, punctual and efficient, though it is usually necessary to book in advance.

The regular bus services, on the other hand, do not require booking and although there are usually plenty of them, they tend to go when they're full, stop frequently and arrive at their destination after a rattling and often dusty journey. However, they are very cheap and you may well meet lots of friendly Jordanians en route.

Service-taxis also ply regular bus routes on a similar basis. They are a bit more expensive but they'll get you there quickly - you may wish you'd gone on a bus - it all depends on the driver! Private taxis: you're in control, if he drives too fast you can ask him to slow down and you can go when and where you want but, as always, it costs; establish the price first! Alternatively you can always hire a car - prices start from 25JD / day. Fuel prices are considerably lower than European prices:

Diesel	0.16JD / L	Petrol Super	0.22JD / L
Petrol Regular	0.13JD / L	Petrol Unleaded	0.35JD / L

The costs of public transport, vehicle hire and accommodation are well covered in general travel books to Jordan such as Lonely Planet's 'Jordan and Syria, A Travel Survival Kit.'

Getting your head down

As with all things in life you get what you pay for: you can find small hotels in most towns for as little as 3-5JD a night. Generally speaking they will be adequately clean, though not always. If you move up nearer the 10 - 15JD bracket you may even get a shower and TV and perhaps even breakfast. Beyond that, anything goes - the sky's the limit and if it turns you on you can live in the lap of luxury in ultra modern hotels some of which such as at Taybet Zamman, a tastefully converted old village high above the Petra mountains, have won international awards.

Elsewhere, in places like Wadi Rum and Wadi Dana there are official campsites with prices ranging from 1JD a night to 8JD dependent on location and facilities. Or, of course, out in the deserts and mountains you can camp or bivouac for free.

Camping

The official situation seems to be confused! In Wadi Rum, camping is allowed anywhere. In the RSCN Nature Reserves, camping is only permitted in the RSCN tents on their campsites. In Petra, camping (or sleeping in the 'caves') is not permitted in the old city of Petra or its immediate vicinity. However, in the outlying areas of Petra, sleeping out seems to be allowed except on the top of Jebel Harun which is a holy place.

In other parts of Jordan, camping does not seem to be a problem although professional travel companies need Permits and it is possible that individual trekkers and campers would be moved if they camped near roads and villages. The official position seems unclear, but if you camp in remote places it is highly unlikely that you will have any problem with officialdom, whose main concern is for your safety in times of Middle East instability even though Jordan always seems to be a haven of peace.

OTHER THINGS WORTH KNOWING

Holidays and Holy days

Ramadan commemorates the revelation of the Qu'ran to the Prophet Mohammed. During this time nothing is allowed to pass the lips, including smoking, from dawn till dusk. It lasts for 28 days and follows the lunar calendar moving back about 11 days each year. During Ramadan it may not be quite so easy to get guides, or to shop, or carry out normal business as most Jordanians observe the fast.

Ramadan is followed by the Holy day of Eid el Fitr to celebrate the end of fasting. The next Holy day is Eid el Adha which marks the time of The Haj, or pilgrimage to Mecca when many businesses may be closed for four days.

Dates are roughly as follows and depend upon the sighting of the moon from Mecca:

Start of Ramadan	Eid el Fitr (end of Ramadan)	Eid el Adha
08.12.1999	07.01.2000	16.03.2000
27.11.2000	26.12.2000	05.03.2001
16.11.2001	15.12.2001	24.02.2002
Prophet's Birthday		
25.06.1999	14.06.2000	03.06.2001

There are also traditional Christian holidays celebrated by the Christian community.

Other holidays are:

1st May	Labour Day
25th May	Independence Day
10th June	Army Day
11th August	King Hussein's Accession to the Throne
14th November	King Hussein's birthday

Otherwise, Jordanians work a six day week (though a five day working week is currently being debated). At the moment, the only day off is Friday when banks, offices and many shops are closed.

Communication breakdown

Jordanians, of course, speak Arabic but English is the second language and many speak it very well indeed. Most have at least enough English to offer advice and have a simple conversation. However you should try to speak a few words of Arabic - it always helps even if it's only 'Hello' (Marhaba), "How are you"? (Kayf - halik) and "Very well thanks" (Quais el Hamdulillah, or more easily Quais or Quaisa if you're female). "Thanks" (Shokran) is another useful and often needed word. Have a try, the worst you can do is make someone smile! Most travel guides have a section with key words and phrases or you can get pocket guides to Arabic such as Berlitz or Penguin or the BBC Language series supported by tapes. (Also see 'Useful Arabic - English words' in the Appendix at the end of this book.)

The daily English newspaper is the Jordan Times, also the leading European and American papers can be bought in Amman and Aqaba and the international hotels. Radio Jordan (in English) with news, interviews, weather forecasts and a variety of music is broadcast on MW 855 KHz, FM 96.3 - 99 MHz. Jordan TV also has quite a lot of English and French programmes whilst satellite TV with programmes such as CNN News can be seen at the larger hotels and at many households, even in Wadi Rum which not too long ago was a Bedouin encampment! International phone calls can be made at a reasonable price from Tele-communication Offices in Amman and Aqaba and some of the other larger towns as well as, of course, from hotels though that is more expensive.

If you get withdrawal symptoms away from a computer, there is a new Internet Cafe in Amman, called Books@Cafe. It has the usual Net facilities as well as a book and music shop and reading room. To find it, head down to the 1st Circle and continue along Rainbow Street, in old Amman, past the British Council. Continue past the sign for two craft centres - Jordan River Designs and the Bani Hamada House. Books@Cafe will be found a little further on, down the hill and along the last street to the right before the T-junction. The British Council, mentioned above, halfway along Rainbow Street, also has computer facilities and a useful library of books on Jordan.

Money matters
The unit of currency is the Jordanian Dinar (JD). In 1998, 1JD was worth £0.85 sterling (ie. £1 was 1.18JD).

The Dinar is split into 1000 fils or 100 piastres - make sure you have some small currency including coins on you everywhere outside major cities as change always seems to be in short supply.

Credit Cards are increasingly acceptable, but still mostly confined to the larger international hotels, shops and restaurants, or businesses dealing with tourists on a regular basis.

Money can be changed at Amman airport (near the visa office), and in all major cities at money exchange offices and most banks. Check around, prices do vary a little and if you're changing a lot it can be worthwhile. (The airport exchange rate is not the best.)

Food and drink
For lightweight provisions (dehydrated foods), as well as fresh foods, the major towns generally have a huge selection. In the bigger towns there are also super-markets and off-licences selling alcoholic drinks. The smaller villages have less choice but you can usually find bread, veg. (usually, though not always, fresh), powdered milk (usually in very large cans), tinned fish and other foods, biscuits, tea, coffee, sugar and bottled water. Quite often you will find a small shop selling fresh eggs and chickens (killed for you on the spot). A vegetarian diet is the cheapest! The best place to shop for fresh fruit and veg. is always in the local markets.

The larger towns also have a good choice of restaurants and cafes of all standards serving International or local Arabic foods, with a range of prices to match. The more expensive ones are also likely to sell alcoholic drinks. Many of the smaller villages also have at least one street cafe for locals and these are always friendly places to eat in as well being inexpensive.

Most of the best cafes and restaurants are listed in travel books, but there are a couple of quite new ones in Amman: Books@cafe is mentioned above, the Cafe is upstairs and serves a good selection of coffees, sweets and meals either inside, on the balcony or in the garden. Prices are 'European' but the ambience is nice. The other, which is also upstairs, is the Eco-Tourism Cafe with its balcony overlooking the street. It is above the road leading up town from the King Hussein Mosque and not far from the 'back-packer hotels' of Venicia and Cliff. Not much Eco-Tourism, but plenty of old-style ambience and a chance to meet other travellers and soak in the life of down-town Amman.

In other areas popular with tourists such as Wadi Musa outside Petra you will find numerous eating places and shops. In Wadi Rum there is a 'Bedouin Cafe' as well as the restaurant and bar at the Rest House and at least three small grocery shops and a chicken shop. There is also good drinkable water on tap in Rum, so there is no need to buy bottled water. Indeed, the tap water throughout Jordan is usually drinkable but most people prefer to buy bottled spring-water. Other tourist sites such as Um Qais, Pella, Ajlun, Jerash, Kerak etc. all have their own restaurants. Some are excellent and most tend to be a bit pricey. Nevertheless, it will cost you less to eat in Jordan than it does in most parts of Europe. If you eat in street cafes and buy local produce for your treks, it will cost you far less.

Remember that during Ramadan most food shops and cafes are closed during daylight hours, smoking is frowned upon and alcoholic drinks are banned at this time except in some international restaurants.

Clothing and equipment

Jordan can be cold at night, especially in the north or on the mountains (it may even snow in mid-winter!), so have some warm and preferably windproof clothes. Waterproofs can be useful in north Jordan in the winter, but otherwise are rarely necessary: it seldom rains for long periods, though the occasional storm can be very severe, bringing waterfalls down the mountains and flash-floods through the canyons. If you get caught out in a storm, it can be quite exciting - shelter under a rock and keep out of the canyons and narrow gullies or 'siqs'.

Conversely the lack of water can be an ever present problem. If you are returning to base at night then you can manage on 1 - 2 litres a day. If you are camping you should allow 4 - 5 litres a day. If you expect to get water from wells you may need to carry 6 or 7m of strong, thin cord.

For most of the routes in the book, except in mid-winter, lightweight clothing, with a fleece jacket, windproof top, sunglasses and sun hat will be adequate. Shorts and vests are fine up on the mountains, weather permitting, though on a hot day you may suffer sunburn and will lose precious body moisture quickly and without noticing, leading to speedy dehydration. Whatever you wear remember to dress with respect for local traditions if you want to be welcomed into Bedouin camps or the houses of local people.

Trainers or modern lightweight trekking boots are all that's needed for footwear; even modern 'trekking sandals' can be worn on easier walks but you could regret it if you disturb a scorpion or, worse still, a snake! (Although we've seen plenty of snakes - mostly Palestinian Vipers and the much more venomous Horned Viper - we've never heard of anyone being bitten.) Additionally you will need a comfortable 40 - 50 litre sack, a lightweight sleeping bag and tent and the usual camping gear, including a Swiss knife or similar, a head torch with spare batteries and a cooking stove, though it may be possible to cook on a small open fire when trekking. However, remember, wood is a scarce commodity and should be used sparingly if at all and never in Nature Reserves. (If sleeping in a Bedouin camp they will be happy to cook and provide blankets.)

Whether or not you feel that using wood for fires is environmentally acceptable is another matter. When only a few people pass by, burning a little wood may not seem a problem; when the number of trekkers gets into the hundreds, it becomes an environmental disaster. At the moment, in some places, a minimalist fire that's adequate for cooking, the ashes of which are covered over after, is possibly OK. If you find that unacceptable, you'll need a multi-fuel stove, or a Gaz stove. Either of these options, of course, means extra weight. (Cylinders can be bought in Amman supermarkets, and in Wadi Musa and in Aqaba in the street below the veg. market. The standard French blue cylinders cost around 1.5 to 2JD. There are also red cylinders which will fit the stoves but do not last as long.)

Whilst it is possible to do all but the hardest routes in this book without any specialist equipment, ropes etc., if required, can be provided by one or two of the more experienced Bedouin guides and specialist trekking companies. You should, anyway, always have your own small first aid kit and water bottle with you. It's also always worth having a compass even though good maps are difficult to get. Hopefully the maps in this guide will be adequate for this selection of routes though a local guide with knowledge of the area is always worth having and usually good company.

A few of the trips in this book are considerably more serious undertakings than the rest. For example, if you're crossing Jebel Rum, descending the whole length of the Mujib Gorge, climbing at Ajlun or exploring Zubia Cave you're going to need additional specialist kit. Whenever extra equipment is required it's mentioned in the route description - ignore this advice at your peril!

Mountain biking
Mountain biking is a very new sport in Jordan as it's only in the last few years that groups have been visiting the country to explore the old hill and desert routes by bike.

Some of the routes described in this book would be possible by mountain bike and we are aware of ways which have already been used by French and Italian bikers. For example some of the 4 w.d. tracks between villages above the Jordan Valley like those down from Zubia to Kufr Abil and Pella. In the Mountains of Moab the route from Libb or Main down Wadi Zerqa Main and down to Hammamat Main is possible. Just south, the old track from Mukawir to the Dead Sea has been done on mountain bikes although it is now in the Mujib Reserve and is not yet a 'designated trail'. There are also other routes in the Wadi Hasa and Tafileh areas.

South again, the 4 w.d. tracks from Mansourah below Shaubak Castle can be followed to Beidah (Little Petra) and down into the hot depths of Wadi Araba and south below Jebel Harun. Finally, bikers have also done the desert track from Wadi Rum to Aqaba. There are many more old tracks that could be followed - the best way would be to link up with a local company who knows the terrain and can offer back-up.

Whilst we cannot recommend any one company, we are aware that Nyazi Tours, La Bedouina and Petra Moon (see the section on South Jordan for addresses) have all worked with mountain bike groups.

Guides

Guides are recommended for many of the routes in this book as the terrain they pass through is off the beaten track and sometimes quite complex so that inexperienced parties could well have problems. Of course, many visitors to Jordan are experienced enough to do any of the routes in this book without guides. Others come to Jordan with qualified climbing and trekking guides from Europe or elsewhere to lead their party and there are now an increasing number of Jordanians who are capable of guiding many of the treks and easier scrambles in this book. In the RSCN reserves, guides are compulsory as the routes are inside conservation areas with fragile environments.

If you are going on a scramble where a rope is recommended, for example Wadi Siyyagh in Petra or the harder scrambles in Wadi Rum, you should check that your guide has a rope and any other necessary equipment and knows how to use it. Three Bedouin from Rum have been on training courses in the U.K. Other Bedouin of Wadi Rum and Petra are also very good natural climbers and are rapidly acquiring the necessary guiding skills for mountain terrain. There are also a number of local people and travel companies elsewhere in Jordan who are approved as Trek and Safari Guides. Details will be found in the relevant sections of this guide.

Guiding fees whether for safaris, treks or mountain climbs can vary from 20 to 100JD per day or maybe more dependent on the size of the group, the difficulty of the route and whether vehicles, camels or horses are involved. Information relevant to each specific area is in the section dealing with that part of Jordan.

Maps

Although there is a 1:50,000 map series to Jordan (code K 737) it is both out of date and very hard to get copies of. If you want to try, you should contact:

The Royal Geographical Centre, PO Box 20214, Al Jbeha, Amman
Tel 009626 5345188, Fax 009626 5347694

The relevant map numbers are given at the beginning of each section.

The Royal Geographical Centre also produce and sell tourism maps such as the 1:750,000 road map of Jordan, whilst Travel guides such as Lonely Planet and Rough Guide have some road and town maps. Maps of this type can be also be obtained from the Tourism Ministry, large hotels or book shops. You could also contact specialist map suppliers in Europe.

There are sketch maps of Wadi Rum in the two Rum trekking and climbing guides and also a larger scale map to Rum (1:38,500) obtainable in book shops; unfortunately the area covered by the latter is inadequate for most purposes as it only covers the central area of Rum. The 1:50,000 maps covering the whole Wadi Rum area are on display on the Rum Rest House wall.

Maps in this guide

The combination of maps and route descriptions in this book should be adequate to find and follow the routes though route finding skills will inevitably be needed for the more complex treks and climbs due to the inevitably small scale of the maps and consequent limited information.

In particular the 'contour' lines are there simply to give an idea of the general inclination of the

Wildlife - clockwise:
Ibex, Blue Sinai lizard, Horned viper, Baby tortoise, Tree frog

Some flowers of Jordan

The walk to the Crusades Caves of Al Habis Jaldak, visible in the cliff face beyond. R8

Caves of Jordan
Above and right: Zubia Cave. R13
Below: Outside the Roman copper mines of Umm el Amad, Feinan. R69

North Jordan

Top: In Wadi en Nuheir, en route to Pella from Ajlun Castle. R15, option b.

Centre: Ancient 'Roman' olive groves, Wadi Yabis. R14 & 15

Left: The Natural Bridge over Wadi Hamra, Pella. R3

North Jordan

Left: Ajlun Castle, the start of the track to Pella. R15

Above: View of Sami's Main Cliff (R16) from Wadi Muzeirib en route from Ajlun Castle to Pella. R15

Below: Getting up 'Saladin's Nose', Sami's cliff, Ajlun. R16

Right:
The idyllic campsite on the trek between Ajlun Castle and Pella. R15

land rather than to define any specific altitude, though approximate maximum and minimum heights are shown. The scale also is always approximate.

Be prepared!
Some of the walks in the guide are easy low level strolls (sometimes so low they go below sea level!) taking only a couple of hours or so. Others are more serious undertakings of two or three days or even more, sometimes crossing complex terrain, perhaps with no reliable water sources and always with inadequate maps when compared to European ones. In fact, it may well be that you have no maps at all other than those in this book! On top of that, there are often only disconnected shepherd's paths or sometimes none at all! Furthermore, it's likely to be hot and, because of the water situation and the amount of camping gear and food you have with you, you may well be carrying around 15 kg. If you're trekking between hoped for water sources you could be in for a long day and you need to be prepared for the worst.

Key to Maps	
———	Roads
– – – ·	Tracks
············	Walks & Climbs
	Wadies
	'Contours'
———	Borders
	Lakes & Seas
	RSCN Nature Reserves
	Deserts
●	Towns & Villages
■	Sites of Antiquity
▲	Mountains
○	Caves
△	Campsites
●	Other relevant places

You also need to be self-sufficient as on some of the routes in this guide you may well be far from any villages and the only people you may meet are Bedouin shepherds. If you have an accident or get lost it will be up to you to get yourself out, always bearing in mind that there is no official Mountain Rescue Service in Jordan. As always, what you carry will be a compromise between weight, comfort and safety. Your pack should, anyway, always include a First Aid Kit and other items such as water purifiers (not necessarily essential, but worth having with you), sun creams, insect repellents etc. (see 'Clothing and equipment').

Be aware that as well as mosquitoes which can sometimes be a nuisance it is also possible (despite tents with mosquito nets) to be bitten by minute sand flies which may carry Leishmaniesis. The result is unsightly scabs which appear three or four months later and take another eight months or so to disappear, possibly leaving a small scar. To avoid sand flies it is always best to sleep away from water and vegetation. It is, apparently, also possible to get malaria in Jordan and though we have never taken any anti-malaria tablets, insect repellent creams are probably a wise precaution if sleeping out near wadies and pools. There is also said to be bilharzia present in some rivers, especially near and below agricultural areas, which makes it a wise precaution to leave footwear on when wading through rivers.

Help!
Despite the above note on rescue facilities the Royal Jordanian Air Force have carried out a number of helicopter rescues from the mountains of Wadi Rum and Petra.

If you need assistance in Petra, go to the Visitor Centre or Emergency Centre which is near the Forum Hotel, or phone them:

Petra Visitor Centre	**03 215 6020**
Petra Emergency Centre	**03 215 7161**

In Wadi Rum, three local Bedouin, Sabbah Atieeq, Sabbah Eid and Atieeq Auda have had some rescue training in the UK, though as yet there is no rescue equipment available to them. However, they and any climbers at the Rest House Campsite should be able to help. In emergency, go to the Police Post or to the Tourist Police at the Rest House whose phone number is:

Wadi Rum Tourist Police   03 201 5661

Outside these areas you will have to get to the nearest Police Post or place with a phone and ask for assistance. It may take time though everyone will be as helpful as possible. There are good hospitals in Aqaba and Amman, with medical centres in most towns.

As mobile phones now work in most parts of Jordan outside Wadi Rum and the deeper mountain valleys and canyons leading down to the Rift Valley, it is now possible to phone directly for help in emergency. (Even these difficult communication areas may soon be opened up.) Please don't abuse the system.

Useful emergency numbers are:

Rescue Police	192
First aid and ambulance	193
Civil Defence Emergency	199
Emergency (mobile phones only)	112

One more thing, let someone know not only where you're going, but when you expect to be back and having made this commitment, don't go somewhere else and do check in on your return!! Think twice before going caving - there are no specialist mountain, canyon and cave rescue teams in Jordan.

ABOUT THE ROUTES

Route descriptions

Each route introduction commences with comments on its special features, attractions and risks and concludes with details of any special equipment and / or skills needed, whether or not guides are particularly advisable, the grade of difficulty, distance covered with altitude changes and the time required for an average party. The approach is then described before giving details of the route followed by, if necessary, the return.

The terms 'true left' and 'true right' apply when looking *down* a mountain, canyon, wadi or valley, whereas directions to go 'left' or 'right' apply to the *direction of travel*, whether in ascent or descent. Compass points are abbreviated to NSEW, for north, south etc, whilst route numbers in the text and on the maps are prefixed by R.

Distances and heights are in metric, as is altitude, (abbreviated to alt). They are quoted in kilometres (k) or metres (m) and are as accurate as possible given the difficulties of obtaining good maps (or any maps) to most parts of Jordan. Four wheel drive is abbreviated to 4 w.d. and times in hours and minutes are shown as hrs and mins.

The term 'exposed' indicates that the climbing or scrambling is above a steep drop, needing a 'head for heights' and use of a safety rope and associated equipment should be considered. The routes in this guide are predominantly those travelled by the authors. A few are based on notes supplied by others and in this case the words 'Not checked by the authors' appear in the route introduction. Anyone doing any routes in this book and having useful comments to make, or anyone with details of new routes should send their notes for inclusion in future editions of this guide, to either:

Cicerone Press, 2 Police Sq., Milnthorpe, Cumbria, LA7 7PY England, or

n.o.m.a.d.s. Greenman's Farm, Greenfield, Oldham, OL3 7HA England

Grading of walks and treks

Easy walk No difficulties such as scrambling on rock or scree, no exposure to heights, no steep ascents or descents and no serious route finding problems. Probably not more than half a day.

Moderate trek Altitude differences may be considerable, though more often than not in a downhill direction! Some easy scrambling may be necessary and experience in route finding is required. Usually not more than one day but could be combined with other routes to make a multi-day trek.

Serious trek These routes pass through remote areas, sometimes with unreliable water sources and require a degree of self-sufficiency and experience in wilderness terrain. There could be considerable ascent and descent and route finding experience is essential. Inexperienced parties should take a guide. Although they are mostly described in stages between water sources, the complete routes generally take two or more days.

Grading of canyons

Easy canyon Ascents or descents of canyons where the water is usually shallow. There may be a little scrambling but otherwise the route should be straightforward. As always in canyons, flooding must be borne in mind. Less than a day.

Moderate canyon Ascents or descents of canyons with normally flooded sections, possibly waist deep; scrambling over boulders is likely and the possibility of flash-floods should be considered. Some route finding may be necessary. Not more than one day unless combined with other routes.

Serious canyon Technical 'canyoning' routes with long sections of flooded canyon and waterfalls which must be passed using abseil techniques. Swimming also necessary and flash-floods can be a serious risk. Inexperienced groups will need a qualified guide. Less than a day (unless Access Restrictions are eased on the whole Hidan Gorge!)

Grading of scrambles

Easy scramble Otherwise straightforward, the route has quite a lot of ascent or descent, sometimes on easy rock or scree. Probably less than half a day.

Moderate Scramble Generally, scrambles through rocky canyons or to summits requiring a 'head for heights' and some confidence on easy rock up to Grade 2. Safety rope and associated equipment sometimes advisable and the knowledge to use it for ascent and descent. Not more than one day.

Serious Scramble These routes are serious mountaineering challenges. They involve a considerable amount of scrambling as well as rock climbing up to Grade 3 which any fit person should be capable of. Route finding ability, ropes and other equipment are necessary, also a thorough knowledge of rope safety techniques or a qualified guide to accompany you will be essential for anyone not familiar with rock climbing and mountaineering. Not more than one day. (But the routes on Jebel Rum could be extended to two.)

Grading of climbs

Modern grades for rock climbing go from 1 to 8, in increasing difficulty. The hardest Bedouin routes, originally climbed without ropes or equipment, have some moves of Grade 5. Whilst there are a few true rock climbs in this guide, the routes described are mostly long and serious scrambles up Bedouin routes or through rocky canyons with moves of up to Grade 3 rock. These routes may require a knowledge of climbing equipment and how to use it and can be serious undertakings since big falls are possible.

Where relevant, rock climbing grades are noted both in the route introduction as well as in the actual description and are shown in brackets, for example (Grade 3).

Rock Grade 1 The point at which hands are required for balance or safety.

Rock Grade 2 Generally friction slabs or steeper rock with good holds.

Rock Grade 3 The point where the climbing becomes more technical.

Rock Grade 4 Apart from the descent of Hammad's Route on Jebel Rum and a few climbs on the recently discovered limestone cliffs in North Jordan, there are no routes in this guide with moves above Grade 3. Routes of Grade 4 and above are for experienced rock climbers only and require special equipment. Each grade is divided into three categories in increasing order of difficulty, which may be shown as, for example, 5a, 5b, 5c, or 5-, 5, 5+. The rock climbing grades used in this book follow the French system. Anyone climbing in Jordan will find full details of comparative rock climbing grading systems in the guidebook to 'Treks and Climbs in Wadi Rum', in which area the majority of Jordan's climbing is.

Grading of caves

Advice from a British Caving guide: "When planning a caving trip think of the return journey and remember that caving grades only apply to fit, competent and properly equipped parties; novices in particular will find caves harder than indicated and for most systems there must be sufficient and competent cavers in the party."

Currently only one route in Jordan demands some knowledge of speleology. Whilst it is only grade 1 on a commonly used British scale for grading the difficulty and seriousness of caves, which goes from 1 to 5, that does not mean it can be taken lightly - we'll say it again: there are no cave rescue teams in Jordan! Just in case more caves are found in Jordan, here is a brief résumé of cave grades:

Easy Cave. Grade 1. No rope-work or technical difficulties. Route finding may present problems for the uninitiated.

Moderate Cave Grade 2. This grade includes small pot-holes. Ropes may be required for ascent and descent. Possibly quite long.

Serious Cave Grade 3 or more. Definitely experienced cavers only.

Be aware that if you enter an 'active-cave', that is, one which still has (or could have) water running through it, it will be subject to flood hazard. If in doubt, don't!

Do not attempt any routes in this book without either adequate experience and equipment or a qualified guide, especially routes involving canyons, climbs and caves.

Now, let's go ...

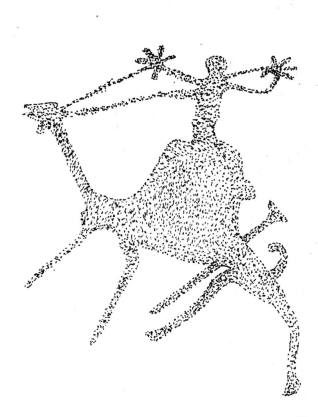

Rum inscription

For the purposes of this guide this is the area north of and including Amman. It is divided into the sub-sections of The Jordan Valley, The Northern Highlands, mostly around Ajlun, The North Eastern Desert and The Capital Area.

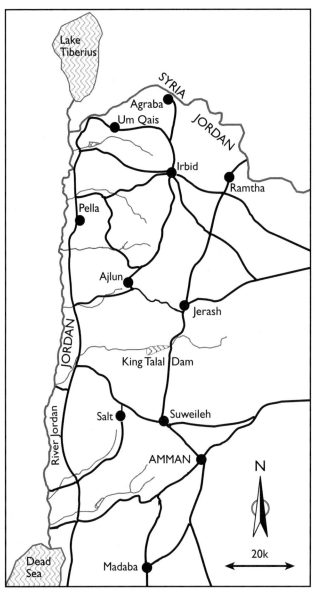

4. Jordan Valley and the Northern Highlands

Accommodation and transport

With private transport you can visit anywhere in the north from Amman and be back the same day, and that's usually the best way to do it. With local public transport, although there are regular services from Amman, it is not so easy though, as always in Jordan, it's cheap - you can get most places in the north for less than 1JD.

There are obviously an abundance of hotels in Amman from five star luxury to downtown 'backpacker' hotels like The Venicia and The Cliff which are almost next door to each other and cost about 5JD per person or 2JD on the roof. There are other hotels near the King Hussein mosque which are even cheaper than that!

There doesn't seem to be much accommodation in the Jordan Valley itself; the only place we know of is at Pella where there are some very pleasant apartments in an olive grove not far from the Rest House, costing 15JD a double for self-catering - ask the Rest House manager. Otherwise you have to go to Ajlun, Irbid or Um Qais in which places you can find a bed for upwards of 5 or 6JD.

Or, of course in places like Yabis, you could camp. Out E there is accommodation at the Azraq oasis and RSCN Reserves with prices varying from 3 to 30JD.

Guides

This area has not yet really been developed for adventure tourism so not many trekking companies are aware of the routes at the moment. No doubt this situation will change quickly once the adventure travel companies which are mostly based in South Jordan (see that section of the book) become more familiar with the region north of Amman! Right now the only person we know of who has done any of the routes in this area and who is hoping to start a Travel Company in 1999 is:

Hanna Jahshan, Outdoors Unlimited, PO Box 9177, Amman 11191, JORDAN
Tel: 00962 6 552 7230 Fax: 009626 552 0240   e-mail: hjahshan@go.com.jo

The RSCN also have trails in their eastern Reserves for which they provide guides.

Otherwise, call at the Tourism Ministry which is not far from the Third Circle in Amman for information on other Travel Companies. (For address see Intro.)

Maps

The following 1:50,000 topographical maps of the K 737 series (from the 1960s) cover this section of the guide. Permission is unlikely to be given, but enquire at the Jordanian Royal Geographical Centre. (See notes on 'Maps' in Intro. chapter.)

3155 - III,	3155 - II:	Um Qais area
3154 - IV,	3154 - I:	Ajlun, Zubia, Yabis & Pella
3154 - III,	3154 - II:	Salt & Talal Dam
3153 - IV,	3153 - I:	Amman & S. Jordan Valley

THE JORDAN VALLEY

"Archaeological surveys have identified Stone Age flint tools, hunter-gatherer camps and small settlements in the foothills immediately above the valley floor, indicating a human presence in the foothills for the past half a million years"

Antiquities of The Jordan Rift Valley. Rami G. Khouri. 1988.

The Jordan Valley is the northern end of the Rift Valley. It connects the Dead Sea with Lake Tiberius (The Sea of Galilee) and descends from 200m below sea level at its northern end to 400m below at the Dead Sea, the river forming the border between Jordan and the West Bank. Being in a politically sensitive area there are frequent check points so you should carry your passport though, as always, everyone is friendly.

To reach the valley from Amman, head out of town past the Amra Hotel (sixth circle) and continue down hill to the seventh circle. Go left here for the Dead Sea, otherwise, continue on to the eighth. Turn right here to Suweileh which is reached in 9k. Turn left at the roundabout and continue towards Salt. Ignore the Salt exit (20k from sixth circle), and continue down to the Jordan Valley passing a check point after another 21k. Turn right 1k beyond, at the Deir 'Alla junction, close to which the Zerqa River reaches the valley.

The 3,500 year old Tell or mound of Deir 'Alla stands above the north end of the town. Pottery sherds from the nearby Chalcolithic settlement date back 6,500 years.

Go right here, N along the Jordan Valley, passing the Jerash turn-off at 54k from Amman and reaching the village of Kureiyima at 56k with its cliffs and caves above to the E and the scenic Wadi Haramiya passing through it:

1. Wadi Haramiya (Valley of Thieves)
This valley can be followed for 5 - 6k to the E to the Jerash road and, according to locals, a trail leaves it to Ajlun, with its Islamic fortress, 16k to the NE and 1100m above. Not checked by the authors.

Continuing up the Jordan Valley for a further 6k (26k from Deir 'Alla and 72k from sixth circle, Amman, but signed '80k Amman' on the opposite side of the road), and just past one of the frequent check points, is the entrance to Wadi Yabis, just after crossing the East Ghor Canal.

Wadi Yabis
This is the Biblical Yabesh of Gilead where the Prophet Elijah was reputedly born around BC900. It is a truly beautiful valley descending 20k from the forested uplands to the warmth of the Jordan Valley and offering some excellent walks and treks. There is an ancient Tell nearby from that period.

2. Lower Wadi Yabis from the Jordan Valley
If you don't get the opportunity to walk down this particularly scenic valley from its source high in the mountains (R14), it's worth walking up a short way from the Jordan Valley, especially in spring. Flowers are everywhere and there's also plenty of bird-life with many large white egrets. Map 8.

Easy walk
Distance optional, say 1 - 2k, ½ - 1 hr for return journey.

Approach Follow a small road on the NE side of the East Ghor Canal for less than 0.5k, leaving it to drive up a track into Wadi Yabis. The track ends at the river 3k from the Jordan Valley road.

The Route Simply follow the river up the valley, crossing as and when necessary to eventually finish on the true right (N) side. You should be able to see the cliffs which conceal the waterfall at the head of the valley.

Follow your footsteps back, or scramble to the top of the small hill on the right (N) for a view of the Jordan Valley.

Back on the main road, a further 5k up the valley brings you to the Pella sign. Turn right for 3k to reach Pella nestled in the mouth of Wadi Jirm.

Pella
"Pella may prove to be the richest archaeological site in all Jordan ... work shows that the Pella area has been the scene of human activity for nearly a million years, and the main tell itself has been inhabited almost without interruption for the past 6,000 years."
Antiquities of the Jordan Rift Valley. Rami G. Khouri. 1988.

There is an excellent two day trek to Pella from Ajlun - see R15. Whilst there, apart from the site itself there are some natural features worth a visit:

3. The Natural Bridge and Hot Springs of Pella

"Near Fahil [Pella] there is a remarkable natural bridge and a hot spring with a temperature of 103°F. The bridge is thirty feet wide and about a hundred feet high and nearly three hundred feet long; its single arch is thirty feet high formed by the rock itself."

Palestine Past and Present.
L. Valentine. c1918

These natural features are 2k N up the road from the Rest House above the antiquity site. The Bridge is a huge natural arch

Pella

Peter Hall

spanning Wadi Hamra. There was once an old road crossing it, now unusable for vehicles (although our driver was keen to have a go!), but crossable on foot without problem. A dirt track made by bull-dozers descends into the wadi E of the Bridge. Bull-dozers also attacked the hillside opposite in a fruitless 'gold-rush' a few years ago, destroying the scenic beauty of the area at the same time.

The Hot Springs are directly under the bridge and there is a 'hammam' or bath in a small building by the wadi 100m to its W. Just upstream a 4 w.d. track winds NE for 3 - 4k to Juffein and Deir abu Said, en-route to Um Qais. The main valley itself goes for 8k up to Kufr Rakib 500m above and 5k W of the Zubia Cave. Neither route checked by the authors.

4. Wadi Khusheiba

Just past half way from the Rest House to the Bridge, about 0.5k before the Bridge, the winding road has a hairpin bend in the narrow and pretty little valley of Wadi Khusheiba. **Do not go up this valley as we were told there were still uncleared land-mines in it. It could be a rumour, but ...**

5. Jebel Sabarta from Pella

This oak covered hill is ESE of Tell Hism, the small hill just S of Pella. It has a ruined Hellenistic fortress on its summit (309m) and can be visited from Pella or included in the Ajlun - Pella Trek via Kufr Awan. (R15. option d.) It is particularly pretty in the spring when the hollyhocks and yellow flowered mimosa are in bloom. You can also see Ajlun high to the E and Mt. Tabor rising from the Jordan Valley to the W. Map 9.

Easy walk
4k up and down, climbing 300m. Allow 2hrs for the round trip and more to enjoy the site.

The route Take the obvious path from the ruins of Pella. Only visually checked by the authors. Information from Pella Rest House Manager.

Beyond the Pella turn off, the Jordan Valley road continues N 23k to North Shuna where the road to Irbid forks right. It is then another 19k up to Um Qais, the last section of the road being above the impressive Yarmuk Gorge.

THE NORTHERN HIGHLANDS

" ... we pass to the plain of the Yarmuk. This plain has been the scene of great historic battles. Here, Chedorlaomer defeated the giants; here Israel conquered Og, King of Bashan. Across it marched the armies of the Assyrians; and on the banks of the Yarmuk was fought in A.D. 636, a most desperate battle, between the Greeks and Moslems ... the Battle of Yarmuk decided the fate of Palestine; for it was only retained by the Crusaders for a period of a hundred years, and it was never, even then, wholly free from these earlier conquerors, who left their faith in Mahomet firmly established among the people."

Palestine Past and Present. L. Valentine. c1918.

North Jordan is a great area to spend a few days with a hire car and a tent or, if you prefer, there are the above mentioned hotels. There are numerous opportunities for short walks of an hour or so, and also possibilities for longer treks of a day or more, necessitating a return journey by taxi or bus to collect your vehicle unless you can make other arrangements.

6. Walks near Um Qais

Um Qais, which is 150k from Amman and 30k NW of Irbid, is the site of Gadara, a city of the 'Decapolis', flourishing around the time of Christ but dating from at least 300BC. It is situated on a headland with superb views N and W over the Yarmuk Gorge to the Golan Heights, the Sea of Galilee, Tiberius and Mount Tabor on the far side of the Jordan Valley. The site is well documented in all the travel guides, though it seems that few people wander far beyond the old town and Rest House.

To escape the visitors, walk out W from the Rest House along the old Roman Road, The Decumanus Maximus, to find an ancient Mausoleum below ground level on your left. The road continues, out through the old West Gate and out onto the headland beyond, above the Jordan Valley, its original destination being Tiberius.

Below the car park on the S side of the Antiquity Site is the head of Wadi um Qais. We have not had time to explore it, but a track is marked on the 30 year old map SW down the valley for 5k to the head of the Wadi el Arab Dam which is 2k E of North Shuna in the Jordan Valley. Its S side is a popular picnic site with a small restaurant and is easily reached by road from North Shuna. If there is a path down from Um Qais to here, it would make a pleasant 7k walk.

7. The Yarmuk Gorge

"The Yarmuk is the dividing river between Bashan and Gilead. It flows through a magnificent gorge, and is called by the Arabs Sheriat el-Mandhur, from the tribe of Arabs who pasture in its valley. It falls in a series of cascades into the immense gorges through which it winds, till it enters the Jordan below Gadara."

Palestine Past and Present. L. Valentine. c1918.

At some future date this may well make a good adventure tourism trip. Right now, it's politically out of the question! About 20k NE of Um Qais, the gorge passes below:

8. The Crusader Caves of Al Habis Jaldak

Reputedly one of the strangest Crusader sites in the Middle East. These man-made caves known as Cava de Suet by the Crusaders are well worth a visit if you're in the area, the walk to them being enhanced by some great views of the Yarmuk Gorge and a big waterfall up a side valley on the Syrian side. Map 5.

Easy walk (with a little scrambling).
2k for the return journey. Allow 1hr (or more if you climb up to the caves).

Approach The caves are 25k N of Irbid (120k N of Amman). Take the road N out of Irbid (signed Um Qais) for 8k, to where the Um Qais road forks left (NW). Continue straight on for about another 7k past Khureiba and at a cross roads with narrow roads going left and right, take the left road down hairpins past the spring in the pretty little valley of Quweiliba which is filled with pomegranate trees. (See R9.)

Just beyond, up the hill, take the signed turn right to Harta which is reached in 3k. Continue through Harta to the roundabout. (There is a small cafe about 100m before the roundabout, on the right.) Continue on across the roundabout with the scenic Wadi um Irsheid below to the left (W). After 4k the road descends into a dip. To get to the Crusader Caves, turn off the road here into an olive grove. (If you miss this point, the road runs up on the left side of a small hill, then up a longer hill to Agraba high on a shoulder overlooking the Yarmuk Gorge.)

Leave your vehicle at the olive grove, just beyond which an old military observation post on a rocky mound gives fine views of the Yarmuk and Syria to the N and Wadi Habis to the SE. The Crusader Caves are visible 1k away in the cliff at the head of this Wadi.

The Route To reach the caves, scramble down right, into the gap, and down to small paths which contour round the valley SE to the cliff; in the spring this hillside is carpeted with flowers and falcons skim the crag.

Once at the cliff, the going becomes rather less pleasant as the flat area at its foot is covered in goat-muck! The shepherd who lives nearby will be pleased to tell you about the 'Christians' who lived in the caves and may well invite you for tea in his own cave just up the hill.

To enter the caves It is actually possible to climb up to the caves which are about 10m up through what appears to be a natural chimney in the cliff at the left end of the goat-ledge. (It looks about Grade 3, and a rope might be advisable, but when we were there in mid-March '98, the goat muck was soaked by the previous three days of rain and snow and clung so thickly to our footwear it made climbing impossible!)

Just 3k E of the caves is:

9. Wadi Quweiliba, Abila and Wadi es Sijn

This very pleasant area is 2k E of Harta (see R8) and has relaxing walking to an interesting archaeological site. Map 5.

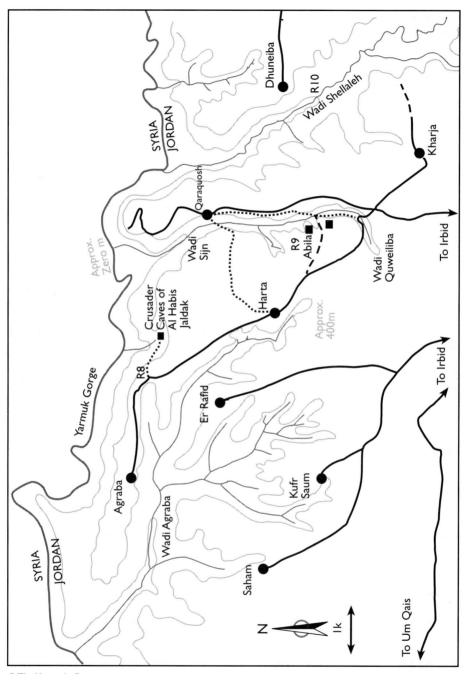

5. The Yarmuk Gorge area

Easy walk
Anything from 2.5k - 11k. 1 - 4hrs

Approach Take the road N from Irbid for 15k turning left into Wadi Quweiliba (see above). Here you have two choices:

a. Drive another 2k towards Harta and take the track back right for 2k to the ruins of Abila (the track is rough towards the end).

b. Leave the car at the spring of Ain Quweiliba where the road crosses the valley bottom.

The Route Taking option b, walk down alongside the pomegranate groves for 1.5k to the ruins of Abila which are on the hill to the left (W). There are actually two mounds, the most southern has many standing columns hence its name Umm el Amad "mother of columns".

From Abila it is possible to continue the walk N down the wadi on paths in the bottom or a 4 w.d. track on its E side for another 2.5k rising up E to Qaraquosh.

If you were to continue a further 3k down Wadi Sijn you would reach the road in the bottom of the Yarmuk Valley. This may be off limits. There would certainly be military checkpoints down there. Ask before going.

Alternatively there are tracks rising SW from the wadi, passing through the olive groves and orchards of Zawiyya, reaching Harta after 3k.

From Harta or Qaraquosh you would need to return to your car at Ain Quweiliba by road - either way about 4k. It would certainly be possible to arrange a lift back from Harta. Ask at the cafe.

If you have your own transport, it is easy to continue 3k N from Qaraquosh to the viewpoint above the Yarmuk Gorge on a peninsula between Wadi Sijn and Wadi Shellaleh.

10. Wadi Shellaleh to the Yarmuk Gorge

It is also worth driving out further E via Kharja, first 2k SE through orchards on the narrow road from the Quweiliba cross-roads (see R8), then on E for another 2k to the lip of Wadi Shellaleh. This huge river gorge extends 20k S from the Yarmuk with numerous villages along its upper edges and 4 w.d. tracks descending and rising between them as well as following the gorge itself - good mountain bike country! There are also rumoured to be caves here. Map 5.

The whole area is particularly beautiful in the spring when the hillsides and orchards are full in bloom.

Now, moving S and back to the W edge of the Northern Highlands, above the Jordan Valley, we come to an altogether different kind of terrain:

The RSCN Zubia Nature Reserve

The Zubia Nature Reserve is located in the Ajlun Highlands, around a long valley known as Wadi Ain Zubia. It consists of Mediterranean type hill country, dominated by open woodlands of oak and pistachio. The Reserve was established in 1988 in an area known as Burqush, where a captive-breeding programme for the Roe Deer was initiated. It was later moved to Eshtafeena, an area NW of Burqush.

The Eshtafeena area (12 sq.k) is now considered the official nature reserve. The rich greenery of Zubia has made it a popular spot for picnickers and walkers. Visitor services, however, are few at present. A Ranger Station at Eshtafeena has been constructed and there is a wilderness campsite located near the station with two hiking trails leading from the campsite. The Zubia Cave is just outside the Reserve.

Entrance Fee
For non-Jordanians, 3JD, for Jordanians, 1JD.

Camping
There is a primitive wilderness campsite located near the Ranger Station. It is a large area enclosed by oak and pistachio trees, with grassy spots to pitch tents. The campsite will contain 7 large tents and can host a maximum of 30 visitors per night. Camping permits are required for all overnight camping in the reserve. Permits and rental tents can be obtained at RSCN headquarters in Amman. For details, contact the RSCN.

Walks at Zubia
Two hiking trails have been designated in the Eshtafeena area, beginning at the Zubia campsite. Guided hikes can often be booked at the RSCN headquarters. (Details from RSCN.)

11. **Zubia Village overlook trail**   *Easy walk, 5k, 2hrs round trip.*

12. **Zubia Scenic viewpoint trail**   *Easy walk, 3k, 1 - 2hrs round trip.*

Stop press. Nov.'98. There have been some delays in establishing the Zubia Reserve. Contact the RSCN for the latest details.

Just on the edge of the reserve is:

13. The Zubia Cave
Going down! Rumour has it the cave goes 3k to water. There is also supposed to be another cave nearby where "a shepherd lost all his goats". Both these stories may well be true, but we never found more than 200m or so of passages in the Zubia Cave, nor have we found another one, but anything's possible in the caving world!

The cave, which is home to bats and in which we found some old pottery, is situated in a very nice part of Jordan on the edge of the forested valley of the RSCN Zubia Nature Reserve at an altitude of 800m. Unfortunately although its discovery is only recent, people have been going in and destroying the cave formations, presumably in the mistaken belief they are valuable. This is a tragedy since they have taken hundreds of thousands of years to form and it has obviously been a well decorated cave, so please respect what is left of them and support our request to the RSCN to gate the cave and keep the key at the nearby Ranger Station.

There has been substantial roof-fall in the cave a very long time ago (indicated by stalagmites forming on the collapsed roof), perhaps during some of the earthquakes that shook the Jordan Valley around 1,500 to 2,500 years ago? Some of the original stalagmites over 2m thick are actually cracked through. The roof-fall, tumbled blocks and numerous columns make for sometimes difficult going and quite complex terrain - make sure you can find your way out again!

If you go to Zubia, please respect the cave environment and the bats and other creatures which live there and please do not damage the formations or add to the painted arrows: that's not the way to route find in caves! Finally, if you discover any new passages, don't get lost and do let us know! Maps 6 and 7.

Special equipment and skills Good torches are essential; head torches are the best. Carry spare batteries and make sure you have power for at least 3hrs. Otherwise old clothes and trainers are all you need. If you suffer from claustrophobia or don't like bats flapping past your head, Zubia Cave is not the place for you!

Guide recommended for non-cavers The only adventure travel co. who have currently been in the cave are Outdoors Unlimited of Amman (address, see North Jordan intro.).

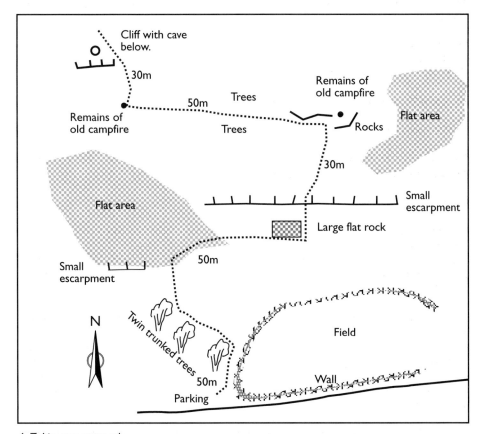

6. Zubia cave approach

Easy Cave
500m round trip. Allow 2hrs or more if you want to explore all the 'squeezes'. You never know, you might get lucky and find another 3k of passages!

Approach Before going to Zubia Cave you should check with the RSCN to see if a gate has been fitted to keep out vandals who are smashing the cave formations. The cave is not yet a part of the Zubia Nature Reserve, but enquiries are being made.

The cave is approx. 43k by road from the Jerash visitor centre and 2k W of Zubia village on the opposite bank of Wadi Wara. From Jerash take the road NW to Suf, 9k, then Ibbri, another 7k. 2k after Ibbri go for 7k (passing Khirbet Afara) to a signed turn to Zubia on the left. After 3k, the Zubia road goes straight on. Take the left fork here and after about 1k another small road goes right to Zubia. Pass this and go another 3k to where a small road forks right along a wooded hillside above a wadi. Follow this, ignoring another small road which goes right, for about another 3k until the last large wall is reached on the right side of the road. Go to the far NW end of this wall and park up. (Just beyond, the road starts to descend on the left side of the hill.) You are now a couple of hundred m from the cave which is down the slope to the NE at the foot of a 3m cliff with quite a clear path the last few m (see map).

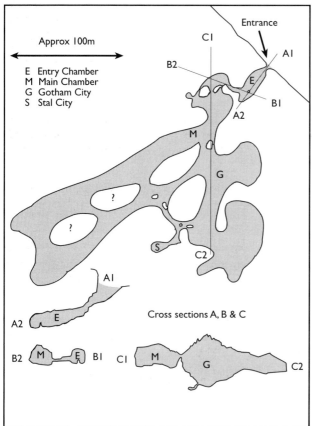

E Entry Chamber
M Main Chamber
G Gotham City
S Stal City

Approx 100m

Entrance

Cross sections A, B & C

7. Zubia Cave

(A further 2k down the road a dirt track goes right for 0.5k to the RSCN Zubia Forest Reserve Ranger Station on a headland. It is recommended to call here first to advise them of your intentions - and don't forget to let them know you have come out safely afterwards!)

The Route Enter down a 3m drop, then a 1m drop. The head high Entry Passage then leads gently down to a squeeze through to the right for 5m to enter the Main Chamber. Here, life gets more confusing and the enclosed sketch is simply that - what cavers call a 'Grade 1 Survey', an indication of the rough layout of the cave; don't expect to route find with it!

The Main Chamber opens out

almost immediately. Much of the floor is covered by ancient fallen blocks whilst the roof rises to about 10m, with bats roosting in the highest chamber, Gotham City. This is reached by going 50m or so diagonally left past stalagmites of various sizes (some quite large, 3m or so high).

Beyond Gotham City there are a number of passages, some with quite large formations. A narrow passage split by stalagmites along its centre goes back right to the Main Chamber. A tight squeeze goes left from this passage and down a tube for 5m before opening out briefly into the prettily decorated Stal City - perhaps the cave vandals didn't get in there yet? There are also some squeezes under some of the blocks forming the cave floor, but they all seem to close after a few m. Further into the Main Chamber there are more large stals. and arches dividing the chamber into different passages, but we found no way on. Is there an elusive on-going system? Surely there must have been one at one time?

Back outside in the sun, and continuing S, we come to:

14. Wadi Yabis
A botanical banquet and downhill walker's dream! One of the prettiest and most varied walks in Jordan, especially in the spring-time. There are optional starts and the walk can be split into two sections, the easier and more pastoral upper valley with its gardens, orchards and ancient olive groves, but also some dramatic rock scenery, then the lower ravine plunging down to the Jordan Valley where the going gets rougher and the precise route is sometimes less obvious. Bird life is plentiful with eagles in the higher reaches, the olive groves and gardens full of bird song, sunbirds in the pomegranate trees and egrets in the lower valley. Maps 8 and 9.

Moderate trek
12k, descending from 500m above sea level to 180m below with almost no ascent - 4hrs from the Ishtafeina road (option 2b) or from the end of the track through Halawa, or 5 - 6hrs if you walk from the centre of Halawa all the way out to the Jordan Valley road at 250m below sea level.

Approach Wadi Yabis descends into the Jordan Valley about 80k N of Amman (see R2). Its descent can be started from various points:

The north side:
Option 1. From Zubia Cave (R13) Cross to the SW side of the road and pick up a track going slightly E of S down rolling wooded hills and crossing Wadi ez Zalana after 3 or 4k, before rising up for 2k to the village of Irjan on its S side. Wadi ez Zalana is the head of Wadi Yabis. Not checked by the authors.

Option 2. From Ajlun There are two approaches:
a. Take the road N then NW from Ajlun for about 5k to Ishtafeina, then 4k down the hilltop ridge road leading NW towards Kufr Abil, but turn right after 4k at Ba'un and go NE for 2k to reach Irjan (see above).
b. Alternatively, continue along the road from Ishtafeina, to cross Wadi Yabis 5k after Ba'un and 6k downstream of Irjan.

The south side
Option 3. Halawa from Ajlun Take the road to Ishtafeina, then turn left (SW) and follow the

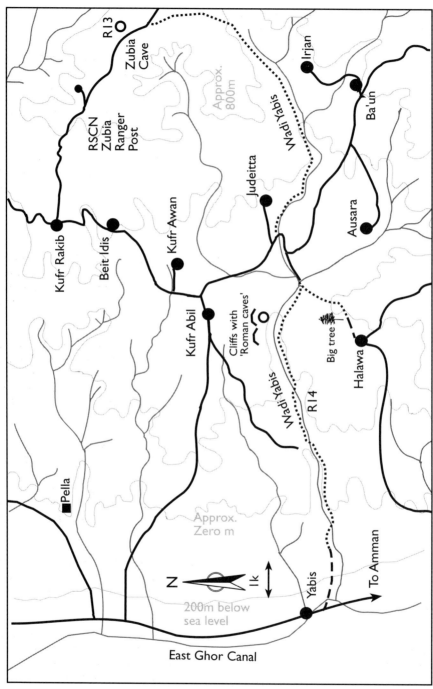

8. Wadi Yabis

road for about 15k to the village of Halawa which is on a hilltop 7k W of Irjan and 2k above Wadi Yabis on its S side, 8k downstream of Irjan.

Option 4. Halawa from the Jordan Valley This is useful if you have a driver to drop you off at the start and meet you again at the end of the walk. From Deir 'Alla in the Jordan Valley, it's about 21k N to the new Halawa turn off, or 26k to the lower end of Wadi Yabis. If you have two vehicles you will want to leave one here first, at the lower end of the wadi (See R2), from where it is then necessary to go 5k back S down the Jordan Valley to Halawa junction which you passed earlier. This small road goes NE up into the hills arriving at Halawa after 10k.

In the small hill-side town of Halawa, go 2k NE up a small road passing right of the mosque and up a hill between houses towards a very tall, slender tree prominently visible on the hill beyond. The small road becomes a track and stops after 2k on a saddle just S of the tree, at an altitude of about 500m.

The Route Dependent on the start, there are obviously various initial stages:

From Zubia or Irjan (Options 1 and 2a, see above) Descend into Wadi ez Zalana which joins Wadi Ba'un after 2k to become Wadi Yabis; at this point the valley bottom is choked with trees, and there are small cliffs on the hilltops above. Small paths continue along both sides above the tree-line and descend Wadi Yabis for 4k to reach the Ajlun - Ishtafeina - Kufr Abil Road. (This section only visually checked by the authors, but looks nice). 6k.

From the point where the road crosses Wadi Yabis (reached directly by **Option 2b)** take a narrow lane SSW on the left bank of the stream and through well tended gardens and orchards of figs and pomegranates (their beautiful red flowers in blossom in mid-May). After about 2k the lane turns into a path which descends to meet the confluence of the Yabis with Wadi Naum near some ruins and ancient olives. (See R15.) This point can also be reached from Halawa which is on a hilltop to the SW (see below).

From Halawa (Options 3 / 4) From the end of the driveable track, a donkey-track continues down the hill to some olive groves from where the orchards in the upper reaches of Wadi Yabis can be seen below. Go through the groves on small paths to find a path which continues down slightly left (N) towards the gardens, passing by a well concealed Bedouin house built into a small cliff. Wadi Yabis with its olive groves and gardens 300m above sea level are reached in less than ½hr, 1k from the start of the donkey track. Here are the ruins at the junction of Wadi Naum and Yabis - see alternative approach options and R15.

The way on is now obvious and easy. Follow a good path initially down the side of the river through the ancient olives groves - some trees have trunks in excess of 5m circ. and are reputed to date back to Roman times which may well be true. The orchards and gardens are over the river and the area is particularly pretty.

Continue along, following the river (cross to the right side as the gardens end as it's easier going for a while). After 15mins some cliffs will be seen above on the right (N), riddled with caves, one in particular is huge. They are known locally as 'The Roman Caves', but we have no other information and haven't been up to them. (The cliff with the big cave in is about 20m high and might give good rock climbing.)

51

After a while, change over to the track on the left bank for the easiest progress and continue down past ancient olives and small cliffs in a truly beautiful 'Derbyshire' dale. In less than Ihr from the confluence of the rivers, another wadi enters from the left (4k from the start of the walk). Immediately beyond, the river enters a scenic canyon. Follow the path down to emerge after 20mins into a siq with more 'Roman Caves' to the left. Beyond is a building. Less than 2hrs from the start (6k, alt I10m above sea level).

(This building can be reached by a dirt road from Kufr Abil 4k above to the NE and it is consequently possible to do this section of the walk without continuing down the more serious path beyond, to the Jordan Valley. In this case it would be better to start by option 2b, which is 4k down the road from Kufr Abil en-route to Ishtafeina, commencing the walk through the gardens of the upper Wadi Yabis.)

Now, back at the building, continue the walk down the valley, having crossed to the left bank again by the bridge. The river now flows between bamboo and pomegranate trees which, in mid-May, were in full bloom, their scarlet flowers attracting sun-birds. There were also many butterflies in the area. The river then passes between white cliffs then, after about Ik, starts to descend between more cliffs into a siq. At this point, the track rises up the left bank to a rocky shoulder above the gorge with the first view of the Jordan Valley beyond. Follow the path along precariously above the deep gorge to the next shoulder; just beyond, the path splits. Take the right fork, descending the rocky hillside above the river which can be seen plunging over a big waterfall where it descends cliffs at the head of the valley.

The track continues along the left side, sometimes quite steeply above the chasm, at one stage supported by an ancient wall as it skirts beneath a small cliff. Now, becoming less evident, the track continues past a lone tree and above small crags (don't go too low) eventually descending across easier terrain to reach the river at a point opposite the obvious good path on the right bank where the valley opens out 1½hrs (3k) from the building, 3½hrs (9k) from the start.

The rest of the way is easy, following the track along the right side of the river for about Ik to reach the 4 w.d. track in the valley bottom (where you can be met by car). Otherwise, you will need to continue along the track for another 3k to reach the Jordan Valley road.

Return If you don't have a vehicle, there are bus services down the Jordan Valley to Deir 'Alla, then on to Amman, or N up the valley to N Shuna and Irbid or Um Qais.

Overlooking Yabis and the other approaches to the highlands from the Jordan Valley is the castle above:

Ajlun
"*Passing on to Ajlun we pitched our tents in a grove of fine old olive trees just above a beautiful clear stream, and all the population came out to sit in rows in front of our tents and enjoy a hearty stare at us.*"
With the Bedouin. Gray Hill. 1890.

The classical hill top Islamic fortress of Qal'at er Rabad dominates Ajlun. It was built in 1184 by Izz ad Din, the nephew of Sal ad Din and has great views of the surrounding area including much of the following route:

15. Ajlun Castle (Qal'at er Rabad) to Pella (Tabaqat Fahl)

Another spring-time floral feast, walking on rolling hills carpeted in multi-coloured flowers including the wild black iris, through forested uplands, green valleys, and orchards. There is also plenty of historical interest as the walk goes from an Islamic castle to ancient Pella of Greek origin built on a site with signs of occupation by primitive man dating back 250,000 years! The route also passes through 'Roman' olive groves whilst the campsite is at an idyllic spot next to abandoned Ottoman ruins. It is also not without its wild-life, birds are everywhere: amongst others, we saw eagles on the heights and a pair of flashing turquoise Rollers near Pella; we also saw two tortoises making a lot of noise doing what comes naturally, as well as a snake and a wolf!

There's a bit of road work along the way, but really only country lanes so they don't detract from the ambience of the walk and anyway they can be mostly avoided by taking alternative routes. We had a great two days of easy walking with numerous offers of 'shai', and were treated to a 'Bedouin breakfast' near Ajlun and a major meal in the small hill top town of Kufr Abil as we passed by during the feast of Eid el Adha. Map 9.

Special equipment and skills. *You're unlikely to find much water en route unless it's very early in the season and the wadies are running. (Wadi Yabis should be flowing but it's not drinking water.) You may get water from the wells at the ruins, but you'll need 7m of rope to reach it. To be sure, carry plenty or ask at any houses you pass, to keep your water topped up, especially if the weather is hot. The only other minor problem is finding the best route through the thickly wooded valleys where there are a choice of shepherd's tracks, but this is part of the fun!*

Moderate trek
36k, descending from 1000m above sea level to 60m below with about 600m of ascent along the way (about 430m on day 1 and 170m on day 2). 10-12hrs or two days of around 5-6hrs.

Approach Drive N from Amman taking the left fork at the roundabout as you enter Jerash, from where it's 24k to Ajlun. (About 60k from Amman.) 1½hrs. Bus services connect Amman, Jerash and Ajlun.

From Ajlun roundabout (Restaurant and Coffee Shop on right - good food and coffee), turn to the left and walk or take a taxi up the road for about 2k to the Castle (alt 1000m). Just before the castle, a small track forks W and descends the hillside beyond. The walk starts here.

The Route After about 0.5k it's nicer to leave the track and follow the ridge to the SW. (At this point there are a couple of big farm buildings down to the right.)

The ridge goes pleasantly through trees and karst boulders crossing the track again at a small saddle

Bitter almond, north Jordan

Mary Hartley

53

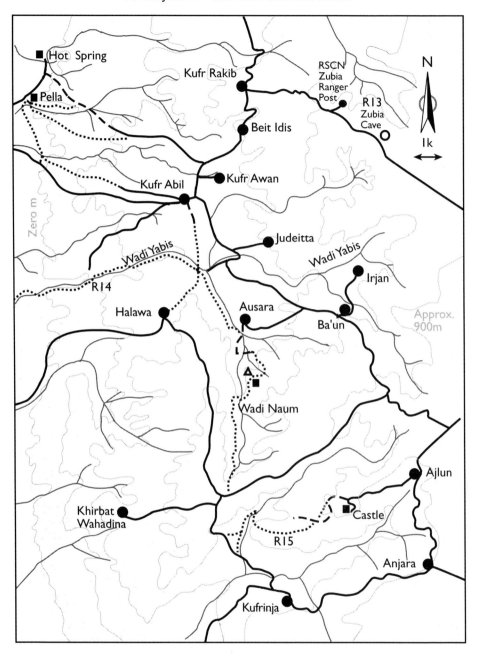

9. Ajlun to Pella

(840m). Continue still generally SW along a path on the ridge past a small farmhouse (where you may be offered tea, goats milk and cheese and superb wafer thin Bedouin bread called 'shrak'). The farm dogs may also give you a noisy welcome! Beyond, the ridge rises slowly up, turning W to a small top at 870m.

It is now necessary to descend into Wadi Muzeirib. Bear right (N) rather than left as there is a 20m high overhanging limestone cliff to the left! (This is Sami's Main Cliff - see R16). Head diagonally down until you pick up a path going N through trees towards a limestone cliff on the opposite side of the valley. Where it meets the wadi, cross to the W bank and follow a path down the valley for about 0.5k until opposite and below the first mentioned cliff (alt 550m). Just beyond, fields will be found above the path. Go up the right side of the fields, through woodland, trending left above the fields and emerging through trees into a wadi. Just above, on its opposite (S) bank an old track will be found which follows the wadi (W) to meet a country road which winds up the hill heading N for 2k to reach first a road on the left then, immediately after, the main road (840m) with a new panorama opening out N down Wadi en Naum. The small hill just SE of the T-junction is Tell Mash-had. 3hrs from the start.

Take the main road right (E) for about 200m, before turning left (N) between fields on the left and a big building on the right.

Scramble down into the wooded valley, and follow Wadi en Naum for a short way on small paths, until the valley floor becomes choked with trees. At this point a path rises out left. Follow it, rising gently across the wooded hillside and heading N above the wadi bed on a series of sheep and cow tracks through clearings in the trees. After about 3k a side wadi enters from the left (W) and a path should be found heading down the shoulder to the main wadi. A ruin is visible to the NE on the opposite side of the valley; this is the objective. Cross the wadi (450m) and rise diagonally NNE up its true right bank to reach the ruin which is probably 17-18C. Ottoman in a superb position facing N with excellent views down the valley beyond (550m). There are two old wells carved out of solid limestone on the N side of the building, both about 6m deep. (You will need rope to lower your water container in - both had water in April '98.) There is also a beautiful campsite just beyond the walls.

Day 2 Contour round onto the next shoulder to the N and descend it keeping to the left of a wall and fields, then continuing down and right until a track is met which winds down to meet a small road in olive groves, back in Wadi en Naum (360m). Turn right on the road which goes across the side wadi, over a bridge. (The road then goes up hill steeply to the small hill-top town of Ausara whose tall minaret is visible from the campsite.)

Leave the road immediately after the bridge and take a track NW through ancient 'Roman' olive groves until that too starts to rise up hill after about 0.5k. Instead go left on a path to meet Wadi en Naum again, and follow the beautiful valley NNW for about 3k. If there is water in the stream, it could involve wet feet as the wadi bed has to be crossed frequently as it descends the narrow valley. It eventually emerges near ruins (on the left bank) at the confluence with Wadi Yabis which was, in April '98, a fast stream flowing between orchards from the NE then turning NW to flow down into the Jordan Valley some 12k to the W. This is about 2hrs from the campsite, 6k (alt 260m). (It is possible to continue down the delightful valley of Yabis from here (R14), arriving in the Jordan Valley 8k S of Pella.)

Cross the stream about 50m E of the bend where Wadi en Naum joins it. At this point, it was about 4m wide and knee deep in April. Just right of the crossing, a path should be found going though orchards and rising directly N then NW across fields to the hill-top town of Kufr Abil (420m). (About 3k from the stream.) A road then runs along the SW side of Kufr Abil, towards the mosque. There are also a few small grocery shops here if you need some food and drink. A number of options now present themselves:

a. The road past the left side of the small turquoise domed mosque leads W out of town for 4k to a point between two small hills -Tell ez Zeitoun on the left and Khirbat Miryamin on the right. Here the view opens out towards the Jordan Valley and the road trends NW down hill for 2k, to where it passes a small cluster of traditional houses on the left. It is now possible to continue on the road, for 2k to Wadi en Nuheir, where a track goes N to reach Pella, 2k.

b. To escape this final stretch of road, leave it at the cluster of old houses and scramble N across and down a hillside to cross Wadi en Nuheir higher up, in a small gorge (40m below sea level) before scrambling up to meet a track. (We were told there is a Roman Bridge near here, but didn't see it.) Follow the track NNW for 2k, descending a valley then continuing NE to emerge suddenly in the ruins of Pella (60m below sea level). The Rest House will be seen above.

c. It may be possible to eliminate the whole 6k of roadwork by taking what may be a parallel track just to the N (probably from the right of the mosque), leading NNW to the small hilltop of Khirbet Miryamin, then on down the hillside still parallel to the road, meeting the above route where it crosses the wadi just N of the old houses. (Not checked by the authors.)

d. Another option is also possible: instead of going left into Kufr Abil, go right and right again for 1k to reach the signed right turn to Kufr Awan (0.5k). Don't go up to Kufr Awan, but continue along the main road as it dips and rises across the small valley of Wadi Salih. 0.5k ahead, a track goes left onto the small hill with trees and houses. Follow this track first NW for 2k then W, downhill for 1k, with the Jordan Valley opening out below.

Two more options now present themselves: perhaps the nicest is to leave the track where it veers NW and continue due W down the sparsely wooded hillside and up to the obvious rounded hilltop of Khirbet Sartaba (309m), 2k from the track, with its 1st. C. Hellenistic fortress. (See R5). It is then possible to continue NW down the hillside keeping left of Wadi el Jirm, for another 2k to Tell Hism, the small hill just S of Pella. A track goes down to the site of Pella from here.

The other choices of route are either to continue down the track for another 4k to reach the road between Pella and the Natural Bridge, 1k from either (Pella being to the SW), or, after 2k to take paths down Wadi el Jirm directly to Pella (2k) or, just beyond, to take the

Poppies, north Jordan   *Mary Hartley*

shoulder of the hill immediately N of Wadi el Jirm and follow it W for 2k over Tell Abu Khass to reach the Rest House above the ruins where a cool drink is likely to be appreciated!

The above options were visually checked by the authors using 4 w.d., after walking option b.

Up in the idyllic oak forested limestone hills of Ajlun again there are also recently discovered opportunities for rock climbing:

16. Sami's cliffs, Ajlun

These three cliffs which were found by Sami Sabat offer excellent sport on superb 'Mediterranean-style' limestone - solid rock, sharp holds, steep or overhanging walls and easier cracked buttresses of around 10 - 20m in height with excellent belays on top. Prior to their discovery in 1998 there was no recognised rock climbing in Jordan outside of Wadi Rum. There's also plenty of wild-life in the area. We've twice seen eagles above this valley, as well as numerous other birds, tortoises and a viper sneaking into a hole at the bottom of the Main Cliff! Map 10.

Special equipment and skills *Ropes, harnesses, rock shoes and a rack of climbing protection equipment will be required. A good place to learn abseiling and climbing on easy routes, or polish your skills on the hard ones!*

Approach The cliffs are located 2 - 4k W and SW of the Castle of Ajlun in beautiful wooded country at an altitude of around 700m. From Amman, drive N to Jerash, taking the Ajlun road at the roundabout on the S side of town. 20k further on, the road reaches Anjara where the Ajlun road forks right. Instead, go straight on for about 6k to Kufrinja which has a strange little four columned monument in the town centre. About 1k from there, take the second turn down right

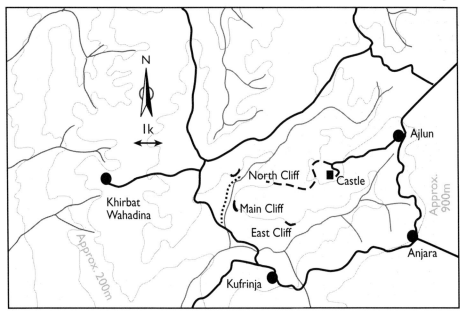

10. Sami's Cliffs, Ajlun

(N) towards a narrow wadi and old olive groves. Just over 1k along this over a bridge, take the right fork, and 1k further on the small road passes a spring emerging from rocks on the right. This is fed along a channel, across the road and over a small wadi via an aqueduct. Just beyond, a wadi (dry in May 1998) goes right (N) into a wooded valley. The S end of the W facing Main Cliff is just visible on the skyline to the right. Half-way between is a white house on a small cliff. Walk up left of the house, and left of a field on small paths until level with the cliff, then contour left to reach it. (About ½hr from the road.)

The main cliff
Starting at the right end of the crag, there are two easy climbs with big sharp holds, perfect for beginners:
Route 1. 10m Grade 2. Start behind and left of a tree and climb the left edge of the buttress.

3m to its left is:
Route 2. 10m Grade 2. Climb the tower starting at cracked blocks.

3m left again is a corner with a steep left wall and an undercut prow:
The Infidel. 12m Grade 5+. A star route. Climb diagonally left from the corner onto the nose, move left and up the steep cracked wall above.

7m further left past a steep wall with a very tempting crack-line in its centre, is a superb arête up the left edge of the wall:
Saladin's Nose. 15m Grade 6a. A three star route! Start behind a tree, left of the nose and move diagonally across the wall to gain the impending arête above the undercut lower wall. Follow it steeply on small, sharp holds. Superb.

Above the starting point of the previous route is a narrow buttress with deep cracks on either side, which should offer a pleasant climb up its centre. Starting at the foot of the left crack, is:
Baldric. 15m Grade 5. Move up a broken crack and then left below an overhang, to reach the next clean crack. Ascend this steeply to a ledge then the corner above to the top. (Or, from the ledge pull out left onto the exposed upper wall to finish.).

Left of here, the crag eventually becomes blood red, offering two steep provocative crack lines. The right hand one starts high up the crag. The left one finishes in a hole just under the top and provides:
The Red Lion. 20m Grade 6b. A star route. Ascend the lower crack then move delicately and steeply right to reach its continuation. Up this on good holds to the cave which is left with difficulty up the overhanging groove.

Immediately left again is an impeccable grey wall undercut by a huge overhanging prow after which the crag continues for about 30m with a selection of steep grey walls, cracks and corners: plenty to go at!

The above routes were climbed by various people on the first two visits to the crag in spring and autumn '98 - Sami Sabat, Charles Heatly, Hanna Jahshan, Tony Howard, Claude Zoumot, Tamara Seikaly, Mick Shaw and Di Taylor. The hardest routes were top-roped as there is little or no protection on them.

We would suggest that until the emerging group of Jordanian climbers are experienced enough to decide for themselves whether or not to bolt certain routes or cliffs, these crags should be kept 'clean' and unprotectable routes should be done with top-ropes or climbed bold and clean, leaving the crag unblemished.

The north cliff
From the Main Cliff this is visible across the valley about 1k to the NW. Although quite extensive there is less good quality rock than the Main Cliff.

Approach Instead of going up the steep forested hillside to the Main Cliff, follow the track alongside the wadi for15mins or so until the crag is visible above to the left.

The cliff faces SE. Its right side is quite high but broken and yellow and contains some caves where we found some old pottery. A smaller cliff of good steep grey rock extends to the left and gives numerous short climbing problems. None recorded.

The east cliff
As you drive W from Anjara this crag is visible across the wadi to the N almost opposite Kufrinja. There are some fields above it, and Ajlun Castle is higher up to the NE. Between here and the Main Cliff there are other, smaller crags, along the hillside. They would no doubt all repay a visit.

The other good looking limestone climbing cliffs we saw in N Jordan were in Wadi Yabis which is 10k N of here, below Kufr Abil. They have 'Roman Caves' in them and should be worth a visit. (See R14.) Other crags of around 10m in height have also been reported by Charles Heatly but we have not yet had time to visit them.

With our rock shoes reluctantly off and our tourist hats on, moving S, we arrive at:

Jerash
This excellently preserved Roman city is one of Jordan's best known antiquity sites, 24k SE of Ajlun and 1hr N of Amman. If you get the urge to head for the hills after half a day seeing the sights, try:

Dibbin Park
This is a pretty, forested hill-top area with a Rest House and accommodation 12k SSW of Jerash by road and 7k N of King Talal Dam.

17. Dibbin Forest Walk
There are opportunities for walks in the forest where there are supposed to be some caves. Also the views over the surrounding area are excellent once you've got beyond the disgusting amount of picnic litter along the road side.

THE NORTH EASTERN DESERT
This region of flat basalt desert known as The Badia extends N and E to the borders of Syria, Iraq and Saudi Arabia. Here are the desert castles and ancient caravanserais of Um el Jimal, Jawa, Qasr Burqu and Azraq, the latter two now being the location of RSCN Nature Reserves:

The RSCN Azraq Wetland Nature Reserve

Azraq is a unique wetland oasis located in the heart of the arid North Eastern desert. It contains several pools, a seasonally flooded marshland, and a large mud flat known as Qa' al Azraq. A variety of birds flock to the reserve each year, stopping for a short rest along their migration routes, staying within the protected areas of the wetland. At the Ramsar Convention of 1977 the Azraq Oasis was declared to be an internationally important wetland. A small wetland reserve (12 sq.k) was established in the southern areas of the oasis. At that time the wetland contained large areas of permanent marshland and several deep spring-fed pools. Unfortunately, many of these areas have dried up because of massive extraction of ground water.

The best time to visit Azraq is in the winter or early spring. Winter rains often create pools and marshes over the reserve, which continue to attract many seasonal species of birds. The success of a bird-watching visit depends largely on the amount of water that has accumulated in the reserve.

Entrance Fee

For non-Jordanians, 3JD, for Jordanians, 1JD.

Camping / Accommodation

Camping is not permitted inside the Azraq Wetland Reserve, however, a small campsite located at the nearby Shaumari Reserve and the RSCN lodge near South Azraq can be used. For details, contact the RSCN. There is also accommodation in the nearby town. A short walking trail is currently being developed around the marshes of Azraq. (Details from RSCN):

18. Azraq Marsh Trail
Easy walk, 1.5k, 1hr for the round trip.

The RSCN Shaumari Reserve

Shaumari Reserve was created in 1975 as a breeding centre for endangered or locally extinct wildlife. It is home to some of the most rare species of animals in the Middle East. In this small 22sq.k reserve, you can find the Arabian Oryx, Ostriches, Gazelles and Onagers. These animals are rebuilding their populations in a

Azraq castle   *Peter Hall*

60

safe haven, protected from the hunting and habitat destruction that nearly wiped them out.

Shaumari represents one of the greatest success stories in the international fight against wildlife extinction. Many different countries have shown their support by donating wildlife species, conducting breeding programmes, and helping to establish Shaumari as a suitable new home for their animals. Visitors to Shaumari have an opportunity to see the living results of this global co-operation.

The Oryx can be seen roaming freely in the desert grassland, and the Ostriches, Gazelles, and Onagers can be observed in their enclosures. Shaumari's breeding enclosures provide a small "zoo" for visitors, making the Reserve a popular spot for children and school outings.

Entrance Fee
For non-Jordanians, 3JD, for Jordanians, 1JD.

Visitors' Centre
Shaumari's Visitors' Centre is currently being renovated, and will contain a small museum, with a variety of interactive materials, slide shows and videos on the history and wildlife of the Reserve. Outside, there is a playground and picnic area.

Accommodation
Camping is permitted near the Visitors' Centre, where you will also find drinking water and toilets. The campsite will contain 7 large tents and can host a maximum of 30 visitors per night. Camping permits are required for all overnight camping in the Reserve. Permits and rental tents can be obtained at RSCN headquarters in Amman or on site at Shaumari.

There is an RSCN lodge located near South Azraq. The lodge contains a cosy common room with a fireplace, and five private two room bungalows that can host a maximum of 20 visitors per night. Bookings for the bungalows can be made at RSCN headquarters in Amman or on site at the RSCN lodge.

Camping fee, 5 - 6JD. Lodge accommodation, 7 - 10JD/person, singles/doubles.

The observation tower is a good place to try and spot the Oryx, particularly in the early morning, whilst Safari Tours through the Oryx enclosure are available aboard the RSCN Shuttle Bus.

Beyond Azraq and Shaumari the road continues NE across the interminable basalt stone desert for another 200k to Iraq. About 40k along this road and 8k before Safawi down a signed gravel track to the S is the lone Begaaweyeh Tree where the Prophet Mohammed is reputed to have rested in the shade. Nowadays, visitors and local Bedouin tie bits of clothing to the branches for luck.

There is a newly made pool nearby where water fowl can sometimes be seen (we also saw an owl and an eagle - the latter no doubt on the look-out for one of the local pigeons!).

About 120k along this road from Azraq (80k after Safawi) is a sign to the ruins of the 'Palace of Burqu', which are in:

The lakeside ruins of the 'Palace of Burqu'   *Peter Hall*

The RSCN Qasr Burqu Reserve
'Think, in this battered caravenserai
Whose portals are alternate Night and Day,
How Sultan after Sultan with his Pomp
Abode his destined Hour, and went his way.'
The Rubaijat of Omar Khayyam. E. Fitzgerald. 1859.

The ruins of the caravanserai of Burqu about which the above lines could well have been written are 18k into the desert NNW of Muqat at the side of a 2k long Roman reservoir only accessible by 4 w.d.

19. Burqu Lakeside Walk
After 250k of driving past inhospitable rock strewn basalt desert from Amman, it's a refreshing place for a walk by the waterside! Obviously birds think so too, as this is the only large expanse of water in the area, so you can expect to see ducks, waders and raptors.

THE CAPITAL AREA
The capital of Jordan is the rapidly growing city of Amman on the site of ancient Philadelphia. There are numerous important historical sites within the city which is built on rolling limestone hills giving pleasant walks within easy reach of town. The Dead Sea and the great canyons that split the Mountains of Moab are only 1hr away to the SW whilst the hills surrounding the Roman city of Jerash and the Zerqa river are only 1hr to the N.

King Talal Dam Area

"The next day we travelled to 'Ain Roman, a most delightful ride over beautiful country of hills and dales strewn with scarlet anemones. 'Ain Roman is a spring which trickles down a gorge and joins the River Zerka - the Old Testament Jabbok - an important tributary of Jordan. Near this place is a settlement of Turcomans. In the evening we walked down the gorge, through which the stream runs. Oleanders fringed its banks, big rocks were strewn about on each side, it is a very picturesque place, and reminded us of a Dartmoor glen. Here were many of the large blue pigeons of Gilead, and other birds."

With the Bedouin. Grey Hill. 1890.

Only about 40k or little more than half an hour from Amman, the Zerqa River was once the boundary between the Land of Og, a fierce giant and the king of Bashan, and Sihon, king of the Amorites. It is a beautiful area of rolling hills and forests, with small villages, orchards and olive groves set above the lake formed by the King Talal Dam. The area is popular with bird-watchers and is ideal for a half day or more in a hire-car, with many possibilities for short walks on the hill-tops or in the wadies. Below are some possibilities:

Approach Head out of town following Jerash signs through Suweileh. 9k further on the road passes right of some telecommunication dishes. Turn left (signed Rumeimin and Jalad) almost level with the dishes and then immediately right to pass right of them. Another 9k on, along a winding country lane, the road reaches the village of Rumeimin.

20. Rumeimin Waterfall

Turn right and descend a narrow lane to a small cafe. Park here and walk for 5mins up the side of the wadi to a pool below a waterfall, spouting 10m over on overhanging limestone escarpment into a pool. If it isn't full of local children, you may like to have a swim! (Women should remain clothed.)

21. Walks in The Sumiya Hills

Approach Back on the road, continue for 2k from Rumeimin then right at the junction and keep right on the main road for about 6k. Here take the left fork. (There are many small roads, villages and wadies, so it could be easy to get on the wrong track.) Basically, from Rumeimin,

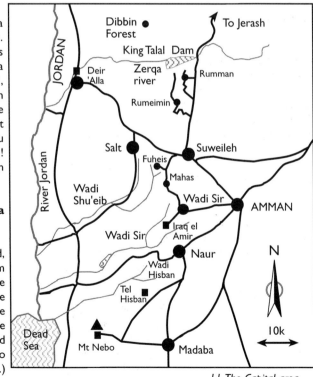

11. The Capital area

head generally NW for 4k, then N.) From the left fork the road deteriorates and eventually becomes a rough track going N for 6k along the ridge of Sumiya to a hilltop at 348m overlooking the dam about 170m below.

The hills and wadies around offer shorts walks in beautiful scenery with forests and the lake below to the N and E. The Jordan Valley can be seen in the haze to the W with numerous antiquity sites near the confluence of the rivers such as Tulul edh Dhahab, Tell Hammeh, Tell Damieh and Tell Deir 'Alla. Whether or not there is a path or way down alongside the Zerqa River (the Biblical Jabbok) to reach the Jordan Valley, we don't know, but the lower river is supposed to be "a nice picnic-site".

Other alternatives Instead of turning off the Jerash road at the telecom. dishes, continue N another 2k and take the old Jerash road to Er Rumman 7k to the N. (Or continue on the main Jerash road for 8k from the dishes and turn left for 2k to Rumman.)

2k N of Er Rumman the old road enters a Forestry Reserve at which point the vehicle can be left and permission obtained to walk down to the lake where the road disappears into the flooded valley of Zerqa. The walk can be continued through oleanders and woodland near the shoreline to the Zerqa bridge on the Jerash road. (Info. Sami Sabat. Not checked by the authors.)

There are also possibilities for short walks outside the Reserve and on the hilltops of Jebel esh Shubeil S of Er Rumman and between the old and new Jerash roads.

Moving S again into the suburbs of Amman, there are still some very nice places for short walks, for example:

Wadi es Sir

"The ride from Ain Mahis to Arak el Amir was more beautiful than anything we had yet seen in Gilead, though from the first, the scenery of the country had so far surpassed our expectations that we ceased to be surprised at anything. Except where now and then a gorge commenced, where the combination of rock and wood was most picturesque, and where the ground was

Lion-head, Iraq el Amir   Peter Hall

North Jordan/Mountains of Moab

Above: R21 The King Talal Dam. Jerash and Dibbin Forest (R17) are on the hills beyond.

Below: The Dead Sea.

Mountains of Moab

Top: View down Wadi Libb and Wadi Zerqa Main towards the Dead Sea. R27

Centre: The Canyon of Zerqa Main. The route crosses the upper canyon mouth (left centre) before traversing the plateau and eventually descending into the main canyon. R27 (& 29)

Right: The Upper Hidan Gorge. R39

Mountains of Moab

Top: The Lower Mujib Gorge. R43

Centre: Abseil into The Falls, the Mujib Siq. R44

Right: Swimming out from The Falls, the Mujib
Siq. R44

Mountains of Moab/Dana Area

Descending into the lower Canyon of Wadi ibn Hammad. R48

The steps to the hilltop Bronze Age ruins of Selah. R54

Below: Exploring ancient cave dwellings near the Dana RSCN Rummana campsite. R61

carpeted with anemones, cyclamens, asphodels, iris and many flowering shrubs, we rode knee-deep through the long, rich, sweet grass, abundantly stubbed with oak and terebinth trees."
Land of the Gilead. Laurence Oliphant. c1887.

7k W of Amman is the suburb of Wadi es Sir. To its SW are the caves and antiquity site of Iraq el Amir which can be reached by taxi from Amman. It is possible to walk along the hillside past the caves before continuing on and down to the ruins. There is a Queen Noor Foundation Centre here producing craftwork, also a cafe. Despite being so close to town the whole area is particularly beautiful with small farms, olive groves and orchards which are particularly pretty when the almond trees are in bloom. The many valleys can be walked or sometimes driven through with 4 w.d.

22. Walks in Wadi es Sir
This valley runs down to the S for about 7k from Iraq el Amir. Tracks can be taken from there up to the road coming up from the Jordan Valley to Naur and Amman. It is also reputedly possible to carry on down the wadi on foot to the Jordan Valley. Neither way checked by the authors.

7k NW of Wadi es Sir suburb is the small hillside town of Mahas (Mahis), 3k N of which is:

Old Fuheis
This is an old Christian village which seems to have escaped some of the travel guidebooks despite its proximity to Amman, just 10k W of Suweileh in N Amman.

Approach To reach it from the modern suburb of Fuheis (green signs to Old Fuheis), head down the hill to the N, then W. It is nicely situated to the E of Wadi Shu'eib (R24) in pleasant rural surroundings, with two old churches and a shrine to St George. There are some craft shops in the old buildings selling pottery, embroidery, weaving, metalwork and the like, and two very pleasant restaurants (at European prices), The Zuwwadeh and the Al Hosh. The shops are open from around 3.00 p.m. until about 9.00 p.m. and the restaurants from 10.00 a.m. until midnight.

23. Walks near Old Fuheis
If you follow the small road down past the lower church, it becomes a narrow lane descending into the wadi. The wadi itself has rocky sides, and a path in the bottom can be reached by following the road down for 1k. The path can then be taken back up to the NE side of Old Fuheis (2k), or it would be possible to scramble up the rocky limestone slopes on its W side to reach the top of Jebel el Khandaq (720m), just 100m or so above, from where there are views down the small Wadi Azraq to Wadi Shu'eib and the Jordan Valley.

Directly across the deep valley to the NW is Salt, another old suburb of Amman, which is also easily accessible from Amman via Suweileh. Close by are:

The Jal'al and Zai Hills
These forested hill 'Parks' overlooking the Jordan Valley are a favourite escape for citizens of Amman which is less then an hour's drive away. Access is via Salt from the scenic road which descends Wadi Shu'eib for 30k to S Shunah in the Jordan Valley, beyond which the King Hussein Bridge spans the river to the West Bank.

24. Walks in Wadi Shu'eib

Numerous short walks can be done either in the valley by the river, near orchards and gardens, or on the hillside above on the opposite side to the road. The valley is also accessible by tracks down from Mahas and Fuheis. (See R23.) There are a couple of picnic spots with soft drink shops towards the lower end of the valley, the last being on the edge of a dam just before S Shunah. This area is particularly busy on Fridays!

25. Walks near Tell Hisban

The huge mound of Tell Hisban dates back to around 1000B.C. and was described in the Book of Numbers as the city of Sihon, King of the Amorites, capital of the country he had captured from Moab. It is close to the old Moabite, Nabataean, Roman road about 25k to the SW of Amman.

Approach From Amman, go first along the airport road from the seventh circle, then the Dead Sea road towards the suburb of Naur, then SE along a road signed to Madaba. A few k along here are signs to Tell Hisban.

The surrounding area is very rural despite its proximity to town with pretty little valleys winding down towards the Jordan Valley and the N end of the Dead Sea, giving both a pleasant drive and nice short walks. Wadi Hisban passes 2k to the N of the Tell and has an intriguing cave in the cliffs of its S side just below its start at Um el Qanatid 6k N of Hisban.

Just to the S, about 30k from Amman so still easily accessible from there for day trips is the bustling town of Madaba on The King's Highway, with its churches, mosaics, Queen Noor Foundation craft centre and restaurant and the Bani Hamida weaving centre. Starting at Madaba are The Mountains of Moab described in the next section.

Horned poppies, north Jordan

Mary Hartley

THE MOUNTAINS OF MOAB

"Moab howleth over Nebo and Madaba."
Book of Isaiah.

The Biblical land of Moab extends from the hills immediately N of the Mujib Gorge and above the N end of the Dead Sea all the way S to the next great natural barrier which is Wadi Hasa at the S end of the Dead Sea.

Accommodation and transport

The N of Moab is easily accessible from Amman, though there is also a small hotel at Madaba costing about 10JD. In the Mujib Gorge there are proposed RSCN campsites whilst Kerak is conveniently placed in the S and has hotel rooms costing between 3 and 30JD mostly near the castle gates. Down at the Dead Sea there is a lot of development going on at the N end with rooms starting from around 35JD. It would be possible to camp in or near some of the gorges, but stay above the high-water mark!

Public transport anywhere in this area should not cost more than 1JD, but ideally you're going to need a hire car or private transport to reach many of the walks. Hiring a guide solves this problem!

Guides

Most of the Mujib area is within the Mujib Reserve and you will consequently need permission and guides from the RSCN to enter it. Otherwise there are many tour and adventure travel

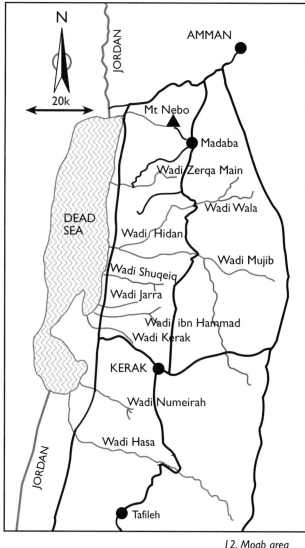

12. *Moab area*

operators in Amman and S Jordan who are familiar with at least some of these routes. See addresses in the N and S Jordan sections of this book. There is one company specialising in trips in the Madaba area: if you fancy joining a 'camel caravan' leaving Mt Nebo in the early morning and travelling along 'century old tracks' for 3hrs to the Dead Sea, contact: Ziad Odeh, P.O. Box 27, 17117 Madaba, Jordan Tel: 08 545526. For a guided visit to the wadies near Kerak, in particular Wadi ibn Hammad, ask any Jordanian travel co. or try Hassan Shamaileh tel: 353789, fax: 354293 at the Karak Ram Hotel but give at least two weeks' notice.

Maps
The following 1:50,000 topographical maps of the K 737 series (from the 1960s), cover the area of this section of the guide. Permission is unlikely to be given, but enquire at the Jordanian Royal Geographical Centre. (See notes on 'Maps' in intro. chapter.)

3153-IV:		Mt Nebo
3153-III	3153-II:	Wadi Zerqa Main & Madaba / Hidan area
3152-IV	3152-I:	Wadies Mujib, Hidan & ibn Hammad
3152-III	3152-II:	Kerak / Numeira area
3151-IV	3151-I:	Wadi Hasa

MADABA AREA
Travelling S from Amman on The King's Highway, the first town you reach is Madaba. Just beyond, is the hill top high above the N end of the Dead Sea where Moses is reputed to have died, having seen 'the promised land':

26. Walks near Mount Nebo
"From the summit of Mount Nebo you can see the whole of Palestine. You see the mountains above Hebron to the south, the highlands of Judea and Samaria, and the Jordan Valley to Hermon. It is one of the finest views in the world and there is no sound on Mount Nebo but the eerie sough of the west wind coming up over the edge of the mountain."
In the Steps of The Master. H.V. Morton. 1934.

Approach To reach Mt Nebo (known in Arabic as Jebel Siyagha), drive 30k S from Amman to Madaba and take the signed road to Mt. Nebo 10k beyond. About 1k before reaching the site there are a few shops selling carpets and souvenirs near the Siagha Restaurant. Just beyond, a track goes left into rolling hills.

This area offers nice walking country with superb views of the Dead Sea and Jordan Valley and is undisturbed by the tourists attracted to Mt. Nebo. Sunsets can be memorable. (It should be possible to walk S for 10k along these hilltops above the Dead Sea, to Main and then on down a 4 w.d. track for 10k to join the Libb - Hammamat Zerqa Main walk, R27.) There are also short walks on Mt. Nebo itself including one down to The Springs of Moses (Ain Musa).

Zerqa Main is the next big valley S and the first of the gorges which cleave their way through the rugged mountains of Moab to the Dead Sea:

Wadi Zerqa Main
"In the time of the Maccabees [Madaba] was a strong fortress. A Roman road leads hence to Ma'in, another spot full of ruins covering the hillsides. Towards the Southwest is the Wady Zerqa Ma'in - a

magnificent gorge; but there are only tombs to be seen in it. Thence a steep and difficult path leads to the hot springs of Callirhoe.

The top of the cliffs in this valley is two thousand five hundred feet above the Dead Sea, and the sides are precipitous. The scenery is extremely picturesque. The south cliff is of black basalt and brown limestone, whilst the north cliff is broken into precipices of red, pink, purple, and yellow sandstone, contrasting with gleaming chalk above and the rich green of palm groves below. Wady Zerka Ma'in is supposed to be the "Valley of God" Nahaliel mentioned in the Bible as a camping place of the tribes; and by others it is thought to be 'the valley in the land of Moab over against Beth-Peor', where Moses was buried; for the ridge of Minyeh (identified with Beth Peor) is just north of the gorge. The springs are said to be for rheumatism.

The bottom of the ravine is full of canes, and palms rise in tufts on the hillside. It was at these springs that Herod the Great sought the health and life he would never possess again. Major Conder tells us that the Arabs have a legend that a demon slave of Solomon found this spring."

Palestine Past and Present. L. Valentine. c1919.

The Wadi runs from Main 50k S of Amman all the way to the Dead Sea, passing by the famous Hot Springs and Spa Resort of Hammamat Main, its therapeutic waters having been used since Herod's time. Its descent is described in two sections as below, each being of a totally different nature:

27. Libb to Hammamat Zerqa Main

Yet another gravitational luxury with hardly an up-hill step following donkey-tracks now abandoned by all but Bedouin and shepherds down from the Madaba - Mukawir road into the hanging valley of upper Zerqa Main, then continuing by a mixture of 4 w.d. tracks and almost lost Roman roads down to the Hot Springs in the dramatic lower gorge.

Easily accessible from Amman, easy walking and route finding in peaceful, sometimes beautiful and sometimes wild surroundings; as always, particularly pretty in the spring-time when wild black irises bloom along the Mukawir road. Numerous Beni Hamada Bedouin camps may be seen en-route, offering possible opportunities to meet local people at their invitation. Map 13.

Moderate trek, but easy for its grade. 14k, descending 940m to finish 200m below sea level. 3½ - 4hrs.

Approach From Madaba, take the King's Highway S passing through the traffic lights by the Apostle's Church on the E side of town. From there, its 13k to the village of Libb,

The Black Iris, Jordan's national flower.

Mary Hartley

previously Roman Libona. Just beyond, signs will be seen pointing right to the Beni Hamida weaving co-operative, Mukawir and 'John the Bap'! (Mukawir is where John the Baptist reputedly lost his head at the request of Salome.)

Take this road W and after about 5k the road rises over a small shoulder between two small rounded hills to arrive abruptly high on the edge of the S side of Wadi Libb at 740m. (It's about another 15k from here to Mukawir.) If you walk a short way down the slopes of the wadi there is an excellent view all the way to the black basalt rocks of the gorge that hides the Hot Springs. This is the walk.

(If you don't have transport there are buses from Amman to Madaba and Madaba to Mukawir.)

The Route Leave the road and head W diagonally down the side of the wadi, picking up the trail almost immediately just below some rocks and following it past some small areas of ploughed land for 20 - 25mins. It then drops more steeply, zig-zagging down to ploughed land just above the wadi bed and opposite some cave shelters on the true right bank, used by Bedouin (½hr from start). Here, the track becomes more obvious again, crossing a small side wadi and following the true left bank of the main wadi about 20m above its bed (dry in April '98). There is a parallel path on the right bank from the lower of the cave shelters (alt 450m).

Continue along easily until the wadi bed ahead is seen to narrow into a small gorge about 1hr from the start. Here, there are two options - either cross the wadi to join the path on its right bank (this could be difficult if the river is running), or continue along paths on the left bank, rising up slightly over a shoulder. If the right bank is followed, the path goes over a rocky shoulder above the gorge and descends right to join a 4 w.d. track entering from the N down the winding valley of Wadi Zerqa Main (coming from Main 10k away). There is likely to be running water in the wadi which irrigates some farmland and small orchards at the junction of the two valleys, about 4k from the start (alt 300m).

Follow the track, first along the right (N) side of the valley then over the wadi to its S side where the path coming from the left bank of Wadi Libb joins it without having crossed any rivers. Continue along the left bank to where the track forks just before the wadi drops into a basalt ravine. (About 2k from the confluence of the Libb and Zerqa Main Wadies.) Here again, there are two choices: continue by the track on the left or, as previously, with more interest and water levels permitting, take the way to the right.

Cross the wadi where the old Roman road used to cross and follow the track along its right shoulder on fairly flat land (possibly many Bedouin camps and offers of tea), keeping left at any major forks in the track, more or less parallel to the wadi, and heading towards a black basalt hill. The track then passes through some agricultural land (more potential offers of tea from the farm workers!).

Eventually the track veers left passing between the basalt ravine and the black hill. Ignore the track visible in the bottom of the ravine and continue along above the cliffs and across flat stony ground. The track deteriorates to a donkey track and eventually descends by zig-zags into the ravine (where there was a pool of clear running water , April '98). You are now just over 2k from the previous river crossing and about 1hr from the junction with the Zerqa Main Wadi (alt 160m).

70

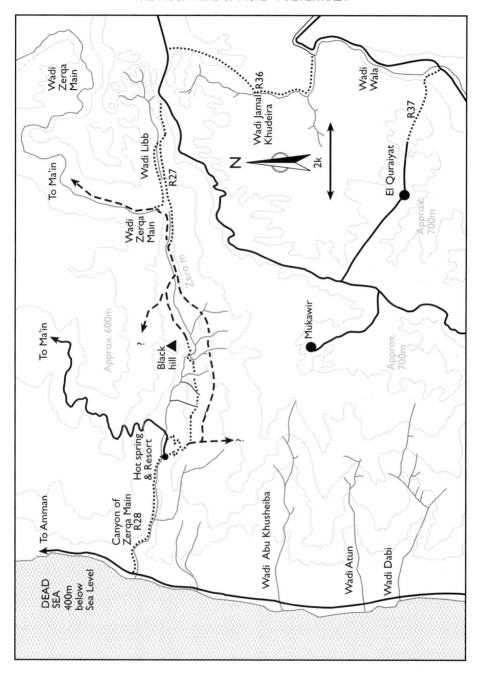

13. Wadi Zerqa Main and Wadi Wala

A 4 w.d. track enters the wadi from its true left (S) side. Go up it but about 100m or so after the first hairpin bend, close inspection reveals the donkey path going diagonally up out of the wadi up the rocky hillside and heading W. Follow it onto the shoulder of flat land above the cliffs (alt 220m) where you will get your first views out across the still concealed lower ravine to the Dead Sea.

From here follow the old track S along the stony plateau, possibly passing more Bedouin encampments. (Further back and going in the same direction, a 4 w.d. track can be seen which is the one you would be on if you had stayed on the left bank earlier.) Follow the ill-defined paths W for about 3k across two or three small wadies until it meets an old S - N road coming from the 4 w.d. track directly to the edge of the Zerqa Main Canyon on your right. (The spectacular new road which winds down into the canyon on its N side is easily seen directly opposite.)

Follow the road down into the canyon of Zerqa Main. It rapidly deteriorates before it reaches the first hairpin. About 200m beyond it, the old donkey-track will be found again if you look closely. Follow it W across a flat area and down the steepening hillside, the waterfalls of the Hot Springs coming into view in the bottom of the canyon, on the opposite side. Eventually, the track narrows to a small path and zig-zags ever more steeply down to arrive directly at the Ashtar Hotel (200m below sea level).

Hammamat Zerqa Main
"The hot streams of Callirhoe flow from the northern slopes; they are ten in number, and their temperature varies from 110° to 140° F; they are strong of sulphur. There is a main stream which forms occasionally pools covered with underwood, in which are numbers of fish; this stream flows from springs higher up the valley, and is of cold water."
Palestine Past and Present. L. Valentine. c 1919.

The Hot Springs are now a Resort where, as well as the Ashtar Spa Hotel with its modern health facilities (rooms about 60JD/double), there are a number of natural pools. It is possible to bathe under the falls of the Hot Springs but don't go at holiday times or on Fridays!

Return There are taxis 20k back up to Main, and Madaba and a late afternoon JETT bus to Amman.

Or, you can continue down to the Dead Sea by:

28. The Canyon of Zerqa Main
You can't get lower than this! Not checked by the authors, but this canyon is said to provide good sport and to pass through some beautiful and contrasting verdant and rocky surrounds. Map 13.

Special equipment and skills *Although there is plenty of water, no special equipment is needed, but swimming would be useful! Trainers are preferable to boots.*

Moderate canyon
4k. Allow 4hrs to descend from 200m below sea level to 400m below.

The Route Follow the road under the Ashtar Hotel bridge to its end 100m beyond and take the walk-way and steps on down the gorge to a natural sulphur spa-bath and a 'sauna' cave (normally men only). The canyon starts here, but we have no further details other than it involves quite a lot of walking, scrambling and swimming and is popular with the more 'sporty' young Jordanians despite rumours that the water is dangerously polluted by the resort - this seems unlikely as we are informed the water is highly sulphurous and radio-active (!) hence its therapeutic properties.

The return There is limited public transport along the Dead Sea Highway so ideally you need to arrange to be met or you will have to hitch out. It's about 20k from the N end of the Dead Sea and 1hr back to Amman.

The Canyon can also be ascended from the Dead Sea gaining entry where it goes under the road near an old military post 11k S of The Dead Sea Spa Hotel.

29. The Roman road from the Jordan Valley to Wadi Mujib
The remains of this long stretch of Roman Road can still be found starting from the ruins of Tuleilat Ghasul 5k N of the N end of the Dead Sea. It goes SE then SW across a plateau at an altitude of around 350m (750m above the Dead Sea), before turning E above the chasm of Zerqa Main to a high point of around 680m (1,080m above the Dead Sea) at Rijm al Mureijib. It then descends into the upper valley of Zerqa Main at a point above the falls at the head of the canyon. This is a distance of around 30k and was considered as a day's march.

From there, the road climbs again to the S to the ruins of Boz al Mushelle, previously a Bronze Age Moabite stronghold. It then goes SE to cross Wadi Wala (see R36) and on to Dhiban and so to the Mujib Gorge about 2k E of the present crossing point of the King's Highway. This is another 30k and another day's march - not checked by the authors.

THE RSCN MUJIB NATURE RESERVE
"One looks down into horrible precipices and deep, khaki-coloured chasms where the foot of man has never reached. Below is the Dead Sea."
In the Steps of the Master. H.V. Morton. 1934.

This Reserve centres on Wadi Mujib, a deep and magnificent canyon which cuts through rugged highlands and drains into the Dead Sea. Most of the Reserve consists of rocky ravines and cliffs with sparse, desert vegetation. Seasonal streams flow through many of the wadis, supporting luxurious aquatic plants in the river beds. The Reserve was created in 1987 and is the second largest reserve in Jordan, extending over 212 sq.k. It contains a large enclosure which is being used to breed the Nubian Ibex for reintroduction into the wild. (A group of twenty Ibex were released in October 1998.)

The Reserve was created to protect the great variety of flora and fauna that inhabit the region around the Lower Mujib Gorge and other permanent rivers which plunge through great canyons to the Dead Sea. It commences about 18k downstream of The King's Highway and extends for about another 18k to the shores of the Dead Sea. Its N boundary lies along the edge of Wadi Zerqa Main including the region around Herod's hill-top fortress of Mukawir and the Dead Sea hot springs of Zara (ancient Callirhoe), whilst to the S the Reserve extends across wild hills to the edge of the canyon of Wadi Shuqeiq W of Faqua.

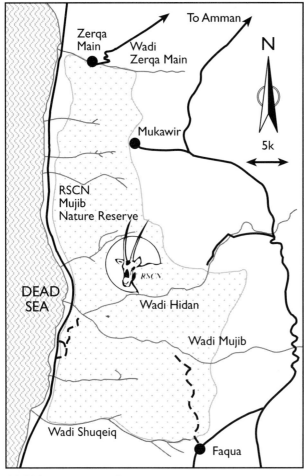

To enter the Reserve permission is needed from the RSCN in Amman. There are two proposed campsites, one where the river enters the Reserve, which is reached from Faqua about 20k S of the point where the King's Highway crests the S top of the gorge, and the other near the ibex breeding station 2k E of the Dead Sea and 3k S of the awe-inspiring final chasm of The Mujib Siq.

Entrance Fee
For non-Jordanians, 3JD, for Jordanians, 1JD.

Camping
There are two designated wilderness camping sites in Mujib. Both are situated in prime scenic areas of the Reserve in close proximity to hiking trails and points of interest. These two sites are designed for primitive wilderness camping, and contain no visitor facilities. Each campsite will contain 7 large tents and can host a maximum of 30 visitors per night. Water and toilets are available from the nearby Faqua or Radas Stations.

14. RSCN Mujib Nature Reserve

Camping fees	4JD	Non-Jordanian
	3JD	Jordanian
Tent hire	5JD	

Wadi Mujib Campsite
This campsite lies on a flat mountain ridge overlooking Wadi Mujib and located in Faqua Ranger Station.

Radas Campsite
The campsite is located temporarily in Radas Ranger Station above the lower end of the Mujib. Visitors staying at this campsite can enjoy a dip in the Dead Sea, a walk up to an old castle and

seeing the Ibex in the enclosure. They may also visit the pools in the Lower Hidan and Mujib Gorges, above the entance to the Mujib Siq.

Camping is not permitted outside these two campsites. Camping permits are required for all overnight camping in the Reserve. Permits and rental tents can be obtained from RSCN headquarters in Amman. If you are trekking into the Mujib Reserve from the King's Highway, you must make previous arrangements with the RSCN.

The trek down the Mujib avoiding the final Siq or the actual descent of The Siq itself can both be done without the need to camp. Either can be done in a day using RSCN vehicles to access the Reserve.

Guides' fees
6JD for short trails, or 30JD for a full day.

Walks, treks and canyons of the Mujib
Three guided trails have been designated in the reserve. Details are available from the RSCN.

30. Qaser Riyash Trail *Easy walk 4k, 2hrs for round trip*

31. Mujib Circuit Trail *Easy walk 8k, 4 - 5hrs for round trip*

32. Wadi Mujib Trail *Moderate canyon 18k, 7 - 9hrs (The Lower Mujib Gorge R43)*

The other route in the Mujib Reserve which requires special equipment and skills as well as RSCN approval is the splendid canyon trip of:

33. The Mujib Siq *Serious canyon 1.5k, 2 - 3hrs (R44)*
        Other than the RSCN we know of only one Jordanian Adventure
        Tour agent who has done this canyon to date, namely Hanna
        Jahshan of Outdoors Unlimited.

The RSCN advise visitors that the Mujib Gorge can be extremely hot in the summer months though that would no doubt be a safe time to experience the excitements of the final chasm. During the winter and to a lesser degree in spring and autumn there is risk of high-water and floods. Check the situation out first with the RSCN.

Contact the RSCN for full information and book your trip early - visitor numbers are very limited.

Before describing the trek and canyon trips of The Mujib Gorge it is first of all necessary to mention other routes and potential routes in the N of the Reserve:

34. A short walk to Mukawir
"Machaerus or El Mashnaka 'the hanging place' as the Arabs call it, lies on the top of one of the wildest mountains of Moab on the eastern side of the Dead Sea. No roads lead to it and the hills are full of armed nomads."

In the Steps of The Master. H.V. Morton. 1934.

Approach Machaerus or Mukawir is 16k S of Libb by road then 4k W. The ancient citadel of Herod is in a splendid location on a small isolated hill at 700m, surrounded on all sides by wadies which descend to the Dead Sea 1100m below. It was here that John the Baptist was beheaded by order of Herod at the request of Salome the dancing girl.

It is a pleasant stroll up the hill to the site from where ancient routes connect to:

Zara Hot Springs
There are at least 38 separate thermal springs at Zara ranging in temperature from 45 - 64°, and rich in mineral salts. The ruins are 200 metres east of the Dead Sea Highway and about 1.5k south of Zerqa Main Gorge. The old port of Zara is 200 metres to the south of here, 35 metres above the present water line.

It is believed these are the 'hot baths of Callhirhoe' referred to by Pliny and Josephus in the 1st C. AD. If this is the case, the springs at Zerqa Main are those called Baris by Josephus, and indeed, a Roman road linked the two, and continues south to Machaerus (Mukawir), the site of Herod's hill-top fort.

Source, Antiquities of The Jordan Rift Valley. Rami G. Khouri. 1988.

35. The Roman Road from Mukawir to the Hot Springs of Zerqa Main and Zara
This road descends 10k from the old hill-top fortress of Mukawir to the hot springs of Zara on the Dead Sea. It starts just N of the fortress and follows the ridge down generally WSW meeting another Roman Road connecting Zara to Hammamat Zerqa Main en route.

We have no further details of these routes though that from Mukawir to Zara was a popular walk but now passes through the Mujib Reserve so permission is needed from the RSCN who have not yet given it 'designated trail' status.

Next, stepping briefly and marginally out of the Reserve on our journey S, we arrive at the beautiful valleys of:

Wadi Wala and Wadi Hidan
"I think the richest and greenest region we had come upon since we left Egypt was the Wadi Waleh ... the stream cascaded clear and cold through thickets of reed and oleander, laurel and willow herb. The smell of it was English."

In the steps of Moses the Conqueror. Louis Golding. 1938.

The Wadies of Wala and Hidan form a green and fertile valley whose perennial river passes through minor but nevertheless impressive canyons for about 20k before disappearing into the jaws of the ominous black basalt canyon of the Upper Hidan Gorge where the RSCN Mujib Reserve commences. This winds tortuously down to reach the awe-inspiring Hidan Falls beyond which the river continues through the chasm of the Lower Hidan Gorge and Hidan Siq to meet the Mujib Gorge just above the Mujib Siq. The whole of the Lower Hidan Gorge and Siq are in a totally protected wild-life zone with no access permitted.

Wadi Wala which is easily reached from Amman is well worth a visit, having beautiful scenery. It is a popular area for weekend 'picnickers' from Amman though people have drowned swimming in the pools of Wala in springtime.

A number of short walks are possible in Wala both E and W of the King's Highway, and are self-evident. Also, some tracks are marked on our 30 year old maps along the approximate routes of old Roman Roads, for example:

36. Wadi Wala to Wadi Libb and Zerqa Main
" ... [the Israelites] marched to Mattanah which is the Wadi Waleh, where there is a brook and rude stone heaps. From [thence] they went to Nahaliel (the valley of God), where are the hot and cold springs of Callirhoe. This valley, called the valley of Zerqa, is one of the most lovely and picturesque places in the Holy Land."
Palestine Past and Present. L. Valentine. c1918.

A track is marked on the map but has not been checked by the authors. Map 13.

Approach Go S on The King's Highway from Amman to Madaba (30k) and continue for about 26k until about 8k N of Dhiban a signed road goes W down the left bank of Wadi el Wala. After 6k Wadi Kirdah enters from the W and the two wadies continue S as Wadi Hidan. 4k down the road from the King's Highway, the road splits and meets again 1k further on by the side of the river. Opposite, on the W side is Wadi Jamal Khudeira.

The Route It would appear possible to walk this wadi for 5k, following a track which reaches the road from Libb to Mukawir just 2k E of the track which goes down into Wadi Zerqa Main (R27). 7k in total.

37. Wadi Wala to Mukawir
Another old Roman road. Most of this route may now be on modern roads. Not checked by the authors. Maps 13 and 15.

Approach About 5k downstream from the above (10k from The King's Highway), the road down Wadi Wala crosses a bridge onto its W bank.

The route A track is marked on the map going W from here up the side of the valley for 4k to El Quraiyat village then NW for 4k to meet the road from Libb. 1k S of there a road forks right and goes for 4k to Mukawir. 13k in total.

Wadi Hidan
Continuing down the valley for another 6 - 7k from the bridge (16k from the King's Highway), the wadi, which is now next to the road, plunges over some small falls into pools then into a narrow gorge with black cliffs of basalt columns. On the hillside about 0.5k to the NW is a huge cave entrance:

38. The Cave of Maghrar el Wadid
More of a hole than a cave! Map 15.

Easy cave, moderate scramble!
Less than 2k to the cave and back. Allow 1hr.

Approach A dirt track approaches close to it, just to its NE.

The route A short walk leads to the foot of the cave. Scramble up from its left side across the cliff (Grade 2) into the cave. Despite its huge gaping mouth which is about 10m high and wide, it is little more than 10m deep, so hardly worth the effort though plenty of pigeons and falcons can be seen.

There are similar caves in the same escarpment just to the W sometimes occupied by Bedouin. Whether or not they go further underground is anybody's guess!

2k further on the track makes a hairpin bend and winds up the hill to the N away from the gorge. If you have a 4 w.d. it can be followed up to the Mukawir road.

The upper section of the Hidan which is now immediately below to the S is not yet a 'designated' RSCN Trail, whilst after the Hidan Falls the river passes through a totally protected zone of the Mujib Reserve with no access allowed. The Upper Hidan Gorge as far as The Falls is nevertheless a superb trip in unique and spectacular scenery and it may be that permission could be obtained from RSCN for this part of the canyon. Don't go without asking!

39. The Upper Hidan Gorge

Mega! This is a superb canyon, much of the route being actually in the river which winds between frequently inescapable vertical black basalt cliffs for 5k to the upper edge of the impressive Hidan Falls over which the river plunges into The Lower Hidan Gorge. From that point on, the river and surrounding hills are in a totally protected Wild-life Reserve which is part of the Mujib Reserve. Access beyond this point is consequently forbidden so a return journey must be made back up-river for 1k then across the N slopes of The Upper Hidan back to the starting point.

There are reputedly ibex and other large mammals in the area though all we saw were eagles, kestrels and other raptors, small fish, some amazingly noisy frogs, and a lot of extremely large oleander hawk moth caterpillars. You can't miss them - they are green, blue and orange with light coloured dotted striations and large eye-spots. They are 7 -10cm long and about 2cm thick and seem to like the warmth of sleeping bags, so don't be too surprised if you sleep near any Oleanders only to wake up in the night with these rather large creatures exploring your body! They home in on the groin like heat-seeking missiles which is hardly surprising since the Hawk Moth can fly at up to 50kph! You may see the moths at night as they are also large, up to 12cm in wingspan!

Special equipment and skills Although the river was never more than chest deep when we went down (March '98), it would be useful to be able to swim in emergency! Otherwise we recommend a buoyancy jacket. Ropes and abseil gear would be needed to descend the 10m falls but they can be bypassed which saves carrying extra kit. A waterproof bag would be useful for camera gear though we managed without. Map 15.

If permission is given, an RSCN guide may be compulsory

Moderate canyon
9k (6k in the canyon), descending 200m to 100m below sea level before returning to the start. Allow 5 - 6hrs.

Approach Turn off the King's Highway at Wadi Wala, as above. (There should be little or no water in the river bed at this point if the Gorge is to be passable.)

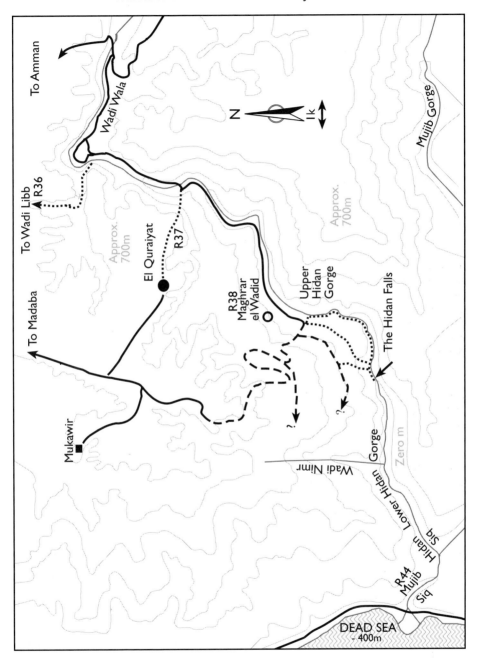

15. Wadi Wala and the Hidan Gorge

Drive down for about 18k passing the point where the black basalt canyon starts, to where the road makes a hairpin bend and starts to rise away from the river. There is a small pool and orchard just beyond the bend with a white painted cairn visible to the E on the headland and a small wadi a few metres away to the S (alt 100m).

The route Descend the line of the small side wadi to where it drops over a cliff. Pass the cliff on its right (S) and scramble down to reach the basalt gorge just below a small waterfall and large pool.

Follow the gorge down through a series of impressive basalt and sandstone canyons, frequently walking waist deep in the river. After about 3k a waterfall drops about 10m into a pool. With equipment, it would be possible to rappel and swim or, it can be by-passed by scrambling out up the true right bank (Grade 2) and back down the gully beyond.

Continue downstream alternating between rocky beaches and dramatic gorges for a further 2k to the upper edge of the overhanging Hidan Falls plunging around 80m over the projecting igneous rock into a deep pool in a huge sandstone bowl. Here the river enters the Lower Hidan Gorge and Wild-life Reserve where entry is forbidden. It then continues through an extremely narrow canyon with flooded sections between overhanging walls festooned with 'jungle' foliage for about 9k, passing numerous hot springs before reaching the Mujib Gorge via the extremely narrow 1k chasm of the Hidan Siq, just upstream of the Mujib Siq.

Unfortunately as this dramatic section of the canyon is off-limits it is necessary to return from here: back-track up the canyon for about 1k to an open area where escape is possible on either side of the river. (In actual fact there are Bedouin shepherds' paths if you search carefully, the one on the S side being the most obvious.) Take the one to the N, zig-zagging up the right (E) side of a side wadi, then follow the path right through a small pass to the next wadi. Go up this for 1k to reach a 4 w.d. track. Follow this E (2k) to meet the original track just above the hairpin bend where the track commenced.

Alternatively go easily upstream a short way to the next narrowing of the canyon. Scramble out N here up the line of a gully onto the hillside above the cliffs. The starting point is now about 3k away to the NNE. To reach it, continue to rise slightly up the hill first generally NE then contouring more N following the approximate line of the river but about 0.5k above it to its W, to reach the road again.

Back on The King's Highway and travelling S again for 8k the road passes through Dhiban which was once the Moabite capital and the site of the famous stone on which Mesha, King of Moab had engraved "I built Aroer, and made the highway by the Arnon." The Arnon is the ancient name for the Mujib Gorge and Aroer is an Iron Age settlement on its N rim 4k E of the King's Highway which reaches the canyon rim 3k S of Dhiban. Close by Aroer is another ancient site:

40. Lahoun
A short stroll around and across an Iron Age site with dramatic views of the Mujib Gorge.

Easy Walk
1 - 1½k. Allow 1hr to enjoy the views and see the excavations.

Approach Lahoun is about 10k by road to the ESE of Dhiban, on the N rim of Wadi Mujib. It is reached by driving on narrow roads until the mound of the old ruined settlement is seen to the S with a sign indicating 'Belgian Excavations'. It can be reached directly from the road which is about 200 - 300m away. Or, more enjoyably, from the E side of Wadi Lahoun, which is immediately E of the ruins. Park by the 'Dig-House' - a new building destined to become a museum.

The Route Walk W descending to the dry limestone bed of Wadi Lahoun. From the lip of the waterfall, continue W just below the upper edge of the Mujib Gorge with fine views, rising up on a small path to a better path under huge overhangs just below the plateau. Here there are old sheep and goat pens. Follow the overhangs round until the path rises up to the ruins above.

Return directly, crossing the head of the wadi just below the road, and back up to the 'Dig House' .

Heading S again, the King's Highway begins its long and tortuous descent into Jordan's 'Grand Canyon':

The Mujib Gorge
"The view which the Mojib presents is very striking; from the bottom, where the river runs through a narrow strip of verdant level about forty yards across, the steep barren banks rise to a great height, covered with immense blocks of stone, which have rolled down from the upper strata, so that when viewed from above, the valley looks like a deep chasm formed by some tremendous convulsion of the earth, into which there seems no possibility of descending to the bottom."
Travels in Syria. Burckhardt. c1812.

The Mujib Gorge, which extends for over 50k from the desert uplands 800m above sea level to the Dead Sea 400m below sea level, is one of Jordan's most spectacular features and is often referred to as 'The Grand Canyon of Jordan'. In Biblical times it was known as the Arnon and The King's Highway or 'Royal Road' referred to in the Book of Numbers passes through its upper reaches. The modern King's Highway crosses the gorge at much the same point winding a tortuous 18k to descend and ascend the canyon which at this point is over 600m deep and 5k wide.

There are Iron Age ruins along its crest at places like the above mentioned Aroer and Lahoun (See R40), and though the Mujib formed an obvious natural boundary between the Kingdoms of Moab to the S and Ammon to the N the Moabites actually held the N side as far as Madaba for a considerable time: a line of old beacons can still be seen which served the purposes of the Moabites and later the Nabataeans and Romans. After the Romans modernised the old Highway, creating the Via Nova Traiana, Eusebius described the Mujib as *"a very treacherous place with ravines ... in which the garrisons of soldiers keep guard everywhere due to the terrifying nature of the region."*

When Louis Golding looked down on the gorge from Aroer in the 1930s, he described it perfectly, capturing the spring-time essence of this wild and majestic valley: *"Far down twinkles interruptedly the silver thread of the torrent, the 'sounding' torrent (as the Hebrew word announces) so soundless here, eased over with the dark green of laurel and arbutus and the paler green of oleander. Along the less steep slopes hurry currents of springtime flowers, the yellow daisies, marigolds and purple irises, and the guttering red anemones. But for the most part the slopes are too grim for flowers, with cliffs of limestone, sharp swirls of gravel and loam."*

Water Levels in Wadi Wala, the Hidan and Mujib Gorges, and the Mujib Siq

Due to the not infrequent floods that can inundate these valleys, the river bed and pools can and do change so situations can alter year to year. In 1993 for example, it was necessary to swim to enter the final Mujib Siq whereas in spring '98 you could walk in as the water had fallen to less than waist deep. In October '98 it was even shallower.

The lower reaches of the Hidan and Mujib, namely the Hidan Siq and the Mujib Siq are, geologically speaking, comparatively new features. To the S of both these awesome earthquake-cracks in the earth's surface and over 200m above the present water level are the alluvial remains of the old river beds. These rise in ghostly pale mounds of dried mud and silt left behind when the rivers gushed into the great cracks that now offer such splendid canyons. (You drive in through the old Mujib river bed when you come up from the Dead Sea to reach the start of The Siq.)

The point is, don't be surprised if you find the situation to be other than that described here!

41. The Mujib Gorge Trek

A magnificent two day trek starting from The King's Highway, and going through continuously interesting, beautiful and varied country, always close to the sound of water and sometimes in it! There is an abundance of wild-life: we saw porcupine, mongoose, snakes, fish, crabs, frogs of various colours and croaking abilities and, of course, lots of birds including kingfishers, peregrines, eagles and vultures as well as small reptiles and numerous flies with a nasty bite! There are also said to be hyenas as well as wolves and Egyptian Cobras in the Mujib area, whilst Ibex can be seen in the RSCN breeding station and also inhabit the surrounding hills.

The last section of the gorge goes through The Mujib Siq which requires abseil equipment. It cannot be done with heavy sacks as there are long sections of swimming. The Mujib Siq is therefore described separately, the trek ending by an 'escape' route to the S of The Siq.

If it is intended to walk the whole gorge, the RSCN must be notified well in advance. At the end of day one you should either camp just before entering The Reserve or make arrangements to camp at the Reserve Campsite. Map 16.

*Anemones,
north & central Jordan*

Mary Hartley

RSCN guide required after the first day.

Moderate Trek and Canyon.

36k, 2 days, descending from 150m above sea level to 400m below, with some ascent on both days to bypass obstacles.

The first day of the trek goes through:

42. The Upper Mujib Gorge (This area is outside the Reserve)

The route passes through some agricultural areas as well as wild country in an increasingly spectacular gorge. You are likely to meet Bedouin shepherds as well as farmers.

Some route finding skill is needed to pick the easiest way. The possibility of flooding should be borne in mind. With regard to drinking water, we used water from the river though it is considered by some to be polluted with chemicals used in agriculture, or from the villages above. Watch out for small springs of good water along the way. Map 16.

Moderate trek
18k, 8 - 10hrs, descending from 150m above sea level to 200m below with 150m of ascent over 3k to reach the Faqua track before descending again to the river. (An extra 3hrs is needed if you finish by walking out to Faqua instead of camping by the river, rising 800m over 10k and making a very long and arduous day. Not recommended!)

Approach From Amman drive The King's Highway S to the dramatic gash of The Mujib Gorge. After a tortuous descent the river crossing is reached about 1hr from Amman. Start by the tracks just left (S) of the river.

The Route Follow the track down to a field and cross over the river, crossing back soon to a track on the S side again. Leave this for paths running parallel to and 50m or so above the river and follow these until after 2hrs a huge horizontal strata of rock forms a large overhang with a little (dry) stream bed below.

Continue, on paths below cliffs, just inside the lower river gorge until eventually another track is met and followed down a short way before continuing under cliffs to yet another track leading down to a field with palms and a water pump. Continue along, close to the river and round a bend eventually rising up a little to meet another track parallel to the river. Follow this down to another pump.

Now it is necessary to follow the river itself, most often by paths on its right (N) side until some huge limestone boulders are reached, where we camped, having started late (about 5hrs including stops). You are now on the zero (sea-level) contour, though it's difficult to believe!

Continue down the true right (N) bank of the river, often in lush vegetation - oleander and fragmites reed beds - to fields and a track in Wadi Aiyanat which rises NE up the steep side of the gorge for 3k to the village of El Mathlutha.

Follow the track briefly down river with big cliffs on the right with hanging gardens and waterfalls, until it crosses the river just after two bends to the S and back W again. Leave the track and follow paths rising up above the river gorge (or it may be better to follow the gorge?) until an area of fields is reached. Pass below these (little path through boulders) rising up from the last field to another track which goes over a shoulder to finish at a Bedouin camp (which may or may not be there!). On a path again, contour along and into a steep side ravine, to reach a field on the other side. The village of Khirbet es Sahila can be seen approx. 6k away, on the N rim of the gorge, just E of N.

From here, rise up to pick up a track which goes up out of the gorge, to Faqua - a 3hr walk. (There is an RSCN Ranger Post at Faqua.)

To continue the trek, go down the track which descends quite steeply to the river, reaching it at a deep pool on a bend about 5k lower down from the earlier crossing point and just downstream of an impressive canyon. Possible campsite before entering The Reserve or pre-arrange to use the RSCN facilities.

The second day of the trek, or the first if starting from the RSCN Post at Faqua, is:

43. The Lower Mujib Gorge - The Mujib Trail
You can't get much lower than this! Now within the Nature Reserve, the route follows the canyon continuously until an escape is forced over low hills above the Dead Sea, to avoid the Mujib Siq. The scenery is ever more spectacular as the river rushes through a narrowing gorge between cliffs and boulders. Much of the walking is in the river itself, sometimes knee deep, so beware of flash floods as the canyon is frequently inescapable. Vegetation is sometimes abundant in areas of hot springs, whilst dry, inhospitable mountains loom above. A great day out! Map 16.

RSCN guide required

Moderate canyon
18k, 7 - 9hrs from the campsite, descending from 200m below sea level to 400m below sea level with a short ascent of about 150m over 1k to bypass the Mujib Siq before the final descent to the Dead Sea.

Approach Either by R41/42 or from Faqua with the RSCN (R32).

The Route Follow the river, through thickets of vegetation and steep walled canyons, passing a valley and waterfall entering from the left on a bend (Wadi Juheira).

If you are still trying to keep your feet dry by 'boulder hopping', you may as well soon abandon the idea, as river crossings become more and more frequent and it soon becomes necessary to actually walk in the river itself for increasing distances between the cliffs of the canyon. After about 5k the river gets even narrower, passing through a siq, where the water can be quite deep, but not much above the knees (spring '93).

Continue walking down (and usually in) the river through more impressive and winding canyons, reaching the river of Wadi Hidan where it comes in from the right through the narrow canyon of the Hidan Siq past large boulders and deep pools. 1k further downstream the combined waters of the two wadies plunge into a dark high walled ravine, via a deep pool where it is sometimes necessary to swim. This is the Mujib Siq. To continue down the river, ropes and a knowledge of abseiling and canyoning techniques are required. **The next 1.5k is for experts only and should not be attempted by those without the proper equipment and knowledge (see R44).**

Instead: on the S side of the river and just at the side of the barrier of cliffs, a bush filled sandy and stony wadi descends to the pebble beach. It looks most unpromising but scramble up its left side and within 100m you will find the remains of an old track. Follow this up for 1k through a wilderness of rubble sided sandy hills (once the ancient bed of the Mujib before it broke through the chasm of The Siq), reaching a pass and a view of the Dead Sea after ½hr.

Follow the track along, turning right at a T-junction but then ignore the next two right turns both of which lead down towards the Dead Sea but are totally unusable, ending at the top of loose cliffs! The third right turn leaves the main 4 w.d. track which continues to the Ibex breeding station run by the RSCN. Follow this down to the Dead Sea Highway and walk 2k back N up the Highway to reach the Mujib Bridge with its dramatic view of the exit from the Siq which is just 100m upstream.

Return If you made arrangements you can be met here by car and be back in Amman in 1hr, otherwise there are occasional buses or you could hitch!

44. The Mujib Siq
Welcome to the lowest adventure on earth! The final ominous chasm of the Mujib is

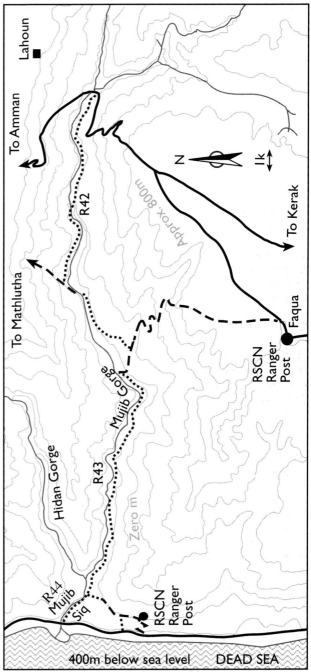

16. The Mujib Gorge

one of the best, most exciting and most memorable adventure trips in Jordan! It is a serious and challenging undertaking following the combined rivers of Mujib and Hidan as they force their way through a great crack in the earth's crust to emerge 400m below sea level at the Dead Sea - the lowest point on earth. The chasm is rarely more than 5 or 6m wide and its 100m high walls are so steep or overhanging that at times they appear to meet, causing the rushing waters to reverberate continually in its dark depths. About half way through there is a 20m waterfall - The Falls - which have to be abseiled, making return impossible. These are followed by The Cascades, a series of small falls, boulders and pools, the last of which have to be swum before emerging from The Siq.

Special equipment and skills Anyone descending the Mujib Siq should be able to swim and should also wear a buoyancy jacket. Abseiling competence and equipment is also needed. Although the main abseil is only 20m, or two at 10m, two 45m ropes should be carried in case of emergency as well as a prusik system, also about 15m of spare cord in case the in-situ gear is missing or damaged. At least one fully waterproof sack will be needed for photographic equipment and a small first-aid kit: beware of twisting an ankle on the boulders or getting sucked under a powerful waterfall! Map 16.

Guide required for inexperienced groups, and RSCN approval for access. *(Outdoors Unlimited of Amman are the only Jordanian travel co. to have currently been through The Siq.)*

Serious canyon
1.5k, descending from 350m below sea level to 400m below! Allow 2 - 3hrs which includes time for photography.

Approach Whilst it would be possible to include the descent of The Siq after walking down the Mujib Gorge, it is usual to come up from the Dead Sea. Arrangements should be made to meet a member of the RSCN at the Mujib Bridge on the Dead Sea Highway (about 90k from Amman - 1hr).

You can then be driven up a rough 4 w.d. track into the mountains through a barren area of dried mud-hills about 200m above the Dead Sea which are the remains of the ancient bed of the Mujib before it carved its way through the chasm of The Siq. The track passes the Nubian Ibex breeding station and the proposed Lower Mujib 'Radas' Campsite. On the E side of these hills the track becomes so bad it is necessary to walk the last 5mins down to reach the gorge where it enters The Siq (alt 350m below sea level). Allow ½hr for the journey, 2 if you have to walk it!

The Route The dark chasm beckons ahead, but even though harnesses will not be needed until about half-way, it is best to put them on now, before plunging into the river. When we went through the first week of May '98, the water in the first section of the canyon was never more than waist deep (on a previous visit on April 2 1993 not only were we carrying camping gear having walked down from the King's Highway but the water was so deep it would have been necessary to swim - whether this would have made The Falls impossible to negotiate, we don't know, as we had to take the alternative walk out - certainly you don't want to be carrying anything other than the minimum essential gear down the canyon!)

As you continue down the chasm the walls close imperceptibly in and the noise of the river increases warning of obstacles to come. Eventually The Falls are reached where two or three abseil options are possible. Perhaps the safest is from a point above and left of the main fall. If the gear is in, this gives a 20m abseil into the deep pool below. Swim out with care keeping to the left edge and avoiding the crashing volume of water cascading into the pool immediately to your right.

It should also be possible to abseil from a rope loop high between two boulders just right of the main left-hand fall, directly into the pool (20m). Or there is a third entertaining option from a rope loop round a small boulder embedded in the river and half hidden underwater between these two previous options. A 10m abseil goes through a hole, passing directly through a small waterfall to enter a cave under the giant boulder. A second abseil from a rope loop at the back of the cave (about 10m of rope required to make the loop) then goes over an overhang to descend into the pool on the inside of the two big falls that block out the view beyond. Ahead and to the right, the river is a mass of white foam - swim close to the left side to reach a shingle beach about 20m beyond - take care with the ropes in The Falls.

Once down the falls, the crux of the descent is over but there are still more adventures ahead as the canyon gets even narrower, the walls above appearing to touch so that the river descends into the gloom down the next section - The Cascades. This series of short falls down boulders commences with a 5m drop for which the rope is again advisable, looped over a boulder low on the right. Beyond, a series of leaps into pools, or slides down water-worn boulders or through the chicanes of water chutes takes you on down the river. A palm tree jammed between the walls of the canyon 20m above indicates the high-water flood-mark and gives you some cause to wonder at the depth and power of the river in flood!

The Cascades finish in the lower reaches of the chasm, much of which is totally flooded from wall to wall, so that swimming is frequently necessary before emerging into the sunlight almost at the Mujib Bridge.

There may be one more obstacle to pass in the form of the RSCN fence that crosses the canyon barring entry to it from the road (following some deaths in the river by inexperienced people). Make sure you have arranged for the RSCN to unlock the gate for you!

If you find this trip and the whole of the Mujib Gorge as magnificent as we did, contact the RSCN and support their efforts to stop the Mujib, Wala and Hidan rivers being dammed and their request for prior studies to be made concerning the use / abuse of existing water supplies before this unique environment is destroyed forever.

Moving S, the next big wadi which forms the S edge of the Reserve almost reaches up to Faqua which is signposted (in Arabic) off the King's Highway 2k S of the S edge of the Mujib Gorge:

45. Wadi Shuqeiq
This wadi flows almost 20k down from Faqua (alt 900m) to the Dead Sea at 400m below sea level. It passes through some wild and desolate scenery and seems to be dry throughout its length. There are a couple of siqs where there may be small dried up waterfalls requiring ropes. The valley ends about 10k S of the Mujib Gorge - visually checked from the air by the authors.

Now out of the Mujib Reserve, we come to:

THE KERAK AREA

Another 10k S the next valley down to the Dead Sea can also be reached by taking the Faqua turning, but continuing through Faqua and Imra for 23k from the King's Highway to reach the village. Here there are excellent views from the old ruins of Sirfa down into Wadi ibn Hammad, whilst to the W is:

46. Wadi el Jarra

This wadi **almost** provides an easy descent by 4 w.d. from the cliff top village of Sirfa which is about 85k S of Madaba and 5k S of Faqua. It is possible to descend the wadi on a rapidly deteriorating road for about 17k with the Dead Sea visible ahead. Unfortunately, just 2k from the Dead Sea the now poor track has been completely washed out by floods. (Though of course it would be easy to continue on foot!)

S again, ending at the Ghor which extends W into the Dead Sea, almost bisecting it, the next wadi has formed a particularly wild and beautiful valley, the head of which reaches SE for 25k almost to Kerak with its great Crusader Fortress dominating the hilltop and surrounding country.

47. Wadi ibn Hammad

This is a spectacular wadi from almost any viewpoint. Its N cliff top with its excellent views can be reached by the route described above. The 'Hammamat' or Hot Springs are 800m below and 3k away but not accessible by vehicle from this side due to the cliffs guarding the lower canyon. The road to the Hot Springs starts from the villages at the E end of the wadi. Map 17.

Approach Head for El Qasr on the King's Highway about 15k S of the upper S edge of the Mujib Gorge. From there, take the small road W for just over 1k past the pretty valley of Wadi Zuquuba with Iron Age sites on its rim. The road then veers SSW for another 1k or so, then turns down the left side of Wadi Yarut with its small limestone escarpments and caves. Eventually it crosses the wadi by a bridge in the valley bottom (which is filled with pink flowering oleanders in May) and continues W and SW along its N side to cross back through the river.

Oleander, central & southern Jordan

Mary Hartley

It then goes up over a shoulder towards an area of orchards, before branching right over the side stream of Wadi Manasih, to follow the S side of Wadi ibn Hammad above a canyon filled with large fallen blocks. Another 3 or 4k further on (about 20k from El Qasr) the road, now a narrow badly deteriorating track, descends into the canyon, crosses the river and ends abruptly at Hammamat ibn Hammad in an area of fragmites, palms, oleanders and other vegetation. The hot bath which was clean and warm when we visited it is just across the river in the shade of some trees. It is rumoured a cafe is going to be built here.

Beyond, the stream disappears into a sub-tropical ravine festooned with ferns, palms and other foliage with stalactites hanging from the cliffs formed from minerals in the dripping water. If you don't have the time to descend the 12k of the canyon to the Dead Sea, it's very easy to scramble down for 15mins or so either in the canyon or above on its right bank to where a rocky scramble on the right side of the gorge just before it becomes even narrower, permits escape or entry. (Or, of course, you can return by the same route.)

48. The Canyon of Wadi ibn Hammad

Indiana Jones or what! The route starts at a hot spring and goes downhill all the way through a stunningly beautiful sub-tropical siq leading to a wild ravine in the heart of the barren inhospitable lower mountains, yet the walk is always in or alongside a rushing, sparkling river. A superb day out. (Watch out for the climbing fishes and beware of the Pterodactyl!!)

In the villages S of the end of the wadi, in springtime, the incredibly beautiful Poiensiana (Delonix-Regia) trees are in full bloom, their blood red flowers contrasting vividly with the blue skies, the turquoise Dead Sea and the otherwise arid surroundings. Map 17.

Easy canyon
10k, 4hrs. (Or 12k if you have to walk out to the Dead Sea Highway) descending from about 150m above sea level to 360m below.

Approach As above to the hot springs or, via the Desert Highway turning W just before the Kerak junction to Er Rabba on the King's Highway then NW into Wadi ibn Hammad to join the small road from El Qasr.

If starting from Kerak it may be possible to arrange transport at The Kerak Ram Hotel (see the beginning of this section. With your own transport, take the King's Highway, E then N towards Amman, turning left after 11k towards Bafir, then fork right and right again 2k further on, then right again after another 3k to reach Bafir. There, go left towards Wadi ibn Hammad meeting the small road from El Qasr (R46) after 8k and turning left (W) along the S side of the gorge, finally descending a deteriorating road to reach the hot spring after another 9k (34k from Kerak). It is rumoured a cafe is going to be built here.

The Route Just across the river is the pool of the Hot Spring - have a hot bath if you like, to put you in the mood before entering the palm and fern festooned chasm beyond. Walking in the river, descend the siq for ½hr or so, the walls coming ever closer until you pass through a subterranean passage, its roof dripping with stalactites and water.

About ¾hr from the start a pretty side wadi enters from the left via a waterfall between pink flowering oleanders, fragmites and palms. The wadi then opens out for a while before closing in again through a boulder filled ravine leading to a waterfall which is by-passed by crossing water polished limestone slabs on its left.

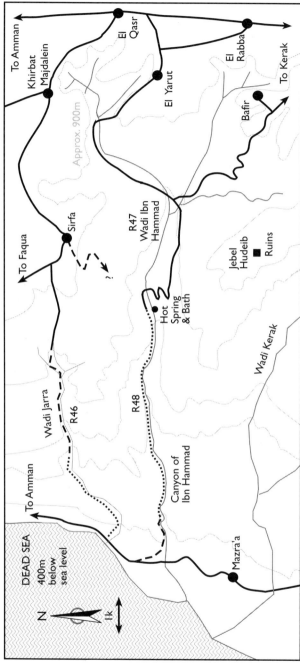

17. Wadi ibn Hammad

The scenery then changes again as the river enters a limestone canyon about 1½hrs from the start. In places, marine fossils can be seen in the riverside boulders. ½hr downstream the rushing waters enter new terrain as steep cliffs of solidified sand and mud rise up above, opening out briefly then closing in again until 3k from the start the cliffs drop away and a water pumping site is reached.

Beyond, the cliffs close in again almost immediately and soon a huge nest of branches can be seen high on the cliffs on the N side, below an overhang. It looks to be at least 2m wide and 1m high! Just beyond, the cliffs close in further and the river plunges 5m into a siq. Fortunately, a track goes right here on a wide ledge across the cliffs, to descend steeply down rock and scree (take care!) back into the river bed where we saw small fishes struggling up vertical water covered rocks in the stream bed. 10mins downstream from here is a deep pool and a water pump.

If you have arranged to be met by 4 w.d., the car can get up to this point by driving up the wadi, otherwise its a further 2k out to the road.

To reach the meeting point with 4 w.d. From the junction of the Kerak Road with the Dead Sea Highway, drive 6k N past El Mazraa to cross the bridge over Wadi ibn Hammad. Continue N until it is possible to go right onto a parallel track, then follow this track back S and onto the gravel river bed of the wadi. Drive up the wadi for about 1.5k to a pool and water pump. (Don't drive through the pool - it's deep - ask our driver!)

It is just over 100k from Wadi ibn Hammad back to Amman via the Dead Sea Highway, or about 38k up to the hilltop Crusader Castle and town of Kerak. There are buses from Mazraa to Kerak. Immediately below the N side of the Kerak road is:

49. Wadi Kerak

This great chasm descends about 20k NW from the Castle of Kerak to the isthmus of Ghor Mazraa by the Dead Sea. The Kerak road skirts along the top of its S edge, but we have no details of any routes in the rocky gorge below other than that it is "very dangerous and people have died there."

Kerak

The imposing Crusader Castle and modern town of Kerak is 130k S of Amman and accommodation will be found here as a base for exploring the surrounding area. The cluster of hotels near the castle have rooms from 5JD upwards as well as pleasant street cafes.

10k S of Kerak down the King's Highway is the small town of Mouta. A pleasant side trip from here is to turn right (signposted El Iraq). Drive down to the village of Kathraba (10k, good views of the Dead Sea), or turn left after 5k and go down to El Iraq (9k) for more excellent views of the Dead Sea down Wadi Numeira as well as extensive orchards which look beautiful when covered in their springtime pink blossom. From El Iraq, continue round the head of the wadi to Taibah (10k) then turn left and drive along a ridge with panoramic views over Wadi Hasa to the S, and down to Wadi Araba in the W. Continue along the ridge top road past Majra to rejoin the King's Highway 16k from Taibah, and 7k S of Mouta.

The next route which starts from these villages is particularly beautiful finishing with a siq and collapsed natural arch. It is possibly the location of 'The Waters of Nimrin' referred to in the Bible, and starts from a fan of smaller tributaries below the pretty villages and orchards of Iraq and Taibah (see above). It emerges in Wadi Araba about 15k S of the junction of the Kerak road with the Dead Sea Highway. Its lower end is adjacent to the Early Bronze Age ruins of Numeira on a flat hill top dating from around 2,500 BC. It was abandoned following an earthquake about 2,350 BC. which caused the wadi bed to move, leaving alluvial remains high among the rocks to its N similar to those on the S side of the exits of the Hidan and Mujib gorges.

The only sad note is that a bromide production plant is to be built on the edge of the Dead Sea just below the exit from the siq, which is likely to severely threaten its wilderness aspect, though people already enter the lower siq from the highway and have left a lot of picnic litter there.

50. Wadi Numeira.

Another downhill delight! A great trip, no difficulties or route finding problems, and a stunning exit. Get down and do it!

Easy canyon 13k, 5-6hrs, from the end of the 4w.d. track at 800m or 18k 6-8hrs from El Iraq at 900m, descending to the Dead Sea highway at Ghor Numeira, at 320m below sea level.

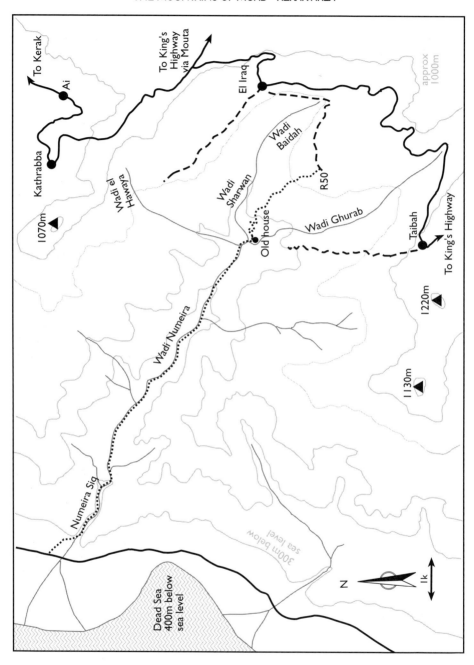

18. Wadi Numeira

Approach From Kerak, either appoach via Mouta as described above, or take the narrow road behind (S of) the Castle which twists down through Shehabieh and Ai (3k and 5k) to Kathrabba (9k) and so to El Iraq (29k). This is slightly longer than the Mouta route but more scenic.

In El Iraq take a narrow road right (W) down through the village (about 200m before the school). Fork left a short way down this road and bear left through orchards to reach a dirt track (visible from the village) which contours S then W above an escarpment, round the head of Wadi Baida to reach the nose of a peninsula of land between Wadi Baida and Wadi Ghurab. (5k from El Iraq).

The route Descend the increasingly steep nose of the hillside, eventually following a well-cairned zig-zag path down to the junction of the wadies where there is a small old house with an ancient millstone near a stream and trees (alt.100m). This area is Seil Jadeira, 2k from the track, 1hr. (A hyena was killed here a couple of years ago.)

The direct approaches to Seil Jadeira down Wadi Baidah (which becomes Wadi Sharwan) or Wadi Ghurab are, we were variously informed, "very, very, very difficult - you will need ropes and a full day" or, conversely "not a problem." Which of these statements is correct, we couldn't say, probably the former!

From Seil Jadeira, follow the stream of sparkling clear water down Wadi Numeira for about 8k (approx 2hrs), with wild, barren mountains on all sides, but greenery in the valley bottom. A couple of 'dripping-springs' on the right bank provide opportunities for delightful cooling showers.

Some small, water-polished canyons hint at more dramatic things to come and eventually, the sides of the valley close in to form the extremely impressive gash of the Numeira Siq. Its100m cliffs are so steep and close it is almost a cave for much of the next 2k! At one point there is a 2m drop best passed on the right down 'bedouin-steps' (Grade 1).

Just before the end of the canyon, a few shallow pools and cascades offer opporturnities for a relaxing bath before emerging from the siq under a huge arch formed by a fallen rock. (Expect some litter here as it is easily accessible from the road). Round the corner is a view of the Dead Sea. The highway is ½k further on.

Back on top, on the King's Highway, Wadi Hasa is reached 21k S of Kerak where the road reaches the edge of the plateau at 1,220m and starts its long descent via Wadi Falqa to enter the main ravine after 4k, before continuing down SE to the river bed at 400m. From there the river descends for about 40k to emerge at the S end of the Dead Sea.

Across the river is the ancient land of Edom.

SOUTH JORDAN

"O thou that dwellest in the clefts of the rock, thou that holdest the heights of the hill: though thou shouldst make thy nest as high as the eagle, I will bring thee down from thence, said the Lord. Also Edom shall be a desolation: everyone that goeth by it shall be astonished and shall hiss at all the plagues thereof ... no man shall abide there, neither shall a son of man dwell in it."

Jeremiah. Old Testament, speaking of the Land of Edom, now southern Jordan.

Well, he certainly got it right about being astonished! Edom is full of surprises - beautiful canyons with perennial streams and hidden oases, the forests, valleys and mountains of the Dana Nature Reserve, magnificent Petra (where it must be admitted nobody dwells) and, way down south, the unique and colourful deserts and mountains of Rum.

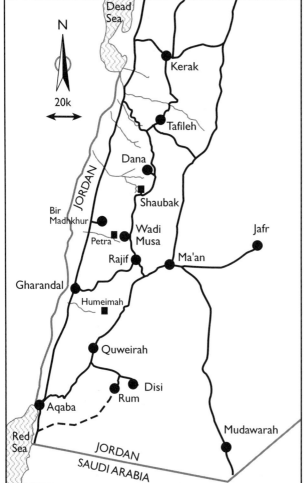

19. South Jordan

Accommodation and transport

The northern Tafileh Area is easily reached from Kerak. Tafileh has nothing much in the way of accommodation, but at Dana there are the hotel and campsite of the RSCN (which should be booked in advance) as well as a small hotel in the village run by the local people. Costs vary from 5 - 35JD.

Down in Wadi Musa there seems to be a hotel on every corner to service the needs of Petra and you can pay anything from 2 or 3JD to sleep on a roof at the top of town in places like The Musa Spring, to 100JD or more for the real up-market places. In between are places like the Sunset Hotel not far from the Petra gate at 18JD breakfast included. Further along The King's Highway there are more new hotels springing up, the most remote but best of which is the converted village of Taybet Zamman where prices are top-end.

Further S there is a campsite at

Wadi Rum costing IJD, or you can camp or sleep in the desert. Finally, Aqaba has, of course, numerous hotels, varying from around 5JD for the popular cheapies like The Petra, The Jerusalem and The Jordan Flower near the market through mid-range hotels like the friendly Alcazar with its private pool and a long history of catering for the needs of Adventure Tourism (tel. 03 2014131, fax. 03 2014133) to new five star beach hotels.

The S of this area is well served by local and express transport services, none of which cost more than a couple of JD, including a daily bus service between Petra and Rum. There are also Service Taxis and ordinary taxis but public transport around Tafileh is not so fast or frequent! In Wadi Rum you can hire 4 w.d. vehicles with a Bedouin driver or camels to get out into the desert - details are in that section. Horses and camels can also be hired in Wadi Musa for journeys into the surrounding area or all the way from Petra to Rum, or vice versa.

Guides
In addition to travel companies operating from Amman, we are familiar with the following companies which specialise in trekking and adventure tourism:

La Bedouina Tours, PO Box 60, Wadi Mousa, Petra - Jordan
Tel: 03 2157099   Fax: 03 2156931, e-mail: Bedouina1@go.com.jo

Nyazi Tours, PO Box 1136, Aqaba, Jordan
Tel: 00962 3 2022801   Fax: 00962 3 2019461, e-mail nyazi:@index.com.jo

Petra Moon Tourism Services, PO Box 129, Wadi Mousa, Petra - Jordan
Tel: 03 2156665/2157665   Fax: 03 2156666, e-mail petram@ go.com.jo

Petra Caravan Tours PO Box 119, Wadi Mousa, Petra - Jordan
Tel: 03 215 6925 Fax: 03 215 7750, e-mail petravan@go.com.jo

The Desert Guides (Horse Safari), Alcazar Hotel, PO Box 392, Aqaba, Jordan
Tel: 03 2014131 (2,4) Fax: 03 2014133, e-mail: alcsea@alcazar.com.jo

The person to contact in the Selah area is Fahad Shabatat, the Ministry of Tourism representative at Ain Al Beidah, Tel: 03 366333

Maps
The following 1:50,000 topographical maps of the K 737 series (from the 1960s) cover this section of the guide. Permission is unlikely to be given, but enquire at the Jordanian Royal Geographical Centre. (See notes on 'Maps' in intro. chapter.)

3151-IV	3151-I:			Wadi Hasa & Selah area
3051-II	3151-III:			Buseira, Dana, Feinan, Shaubak area
3050-I	3050-II	3049-I:		Petra, Sabra, Humeimah area
3049-II	3149-III	3048-I	3148-IV:	Wadi Rum area
3050-II	3049-IV	3049-III	3048-IV:	Wadi Araba

THE TAFILEH AREA
This commences at Wadi Hasa, referred to in Biblical times as Wadi Zered, the old natural border between Edom on its south and Moab to the north:

51. Wadi Hasa

"Wadi Hesa, the gorge of great width and depth and difficulty which cut off Kerak from Tafileh, Moab from Edom."

Seven Pillars of Wisdom. T. E. Lawrence. 1926.

Wadi Hasa is almost as impressive a gorge as Wadi Mujib. It is about 45k S of Kerak and descends from the desert plateau over 50k to the E at about 1000m down to the S end of the Dead Sea at 400m below sea level. It is around 4k across from rim to rim and is 600m deep where the King's Highway crosses it. Barren at its E end it is quite verdant in its middle reaches where there are a couple of hot springs before it descends again through its lower gorge. The section from the King's Highway to the zero altitude level has good tracks down it and is used as farmland. It was described by Louis Golding in 1938: *"There are many oleanders whence perhaps the ancient name of Zered, the willows. There are hedges of prickly-pear and even a thicket of bananas. On sheltered slopes are shelves of wheat and barley, hanging orchards of silver-grey olives, fig trees just sprouting, almond and pear in thick bloom ... Along the valley bottom a stream twinkles under its curtaining of tamarisk and bamboo and laurel into a narrow gorge, then appears again, making for swift asphyxiation in the sulphurous pan of the Dead Sea."*

Looking at the map, the lower end is indeed a tortuous river in a deep canyon. Not checked by the authors, though tracks are visible leading down to it when viewed from:

52. Jebel Tannur

This is the small pyramidal hill with the Nabataean temple of Khirbet Tannur on its summit. There are the remains of a stone floor, pillars and ruined walls. The isolated hill rises from the S side of Wadi Hasa almost opposite a black basalt hill known to the local Bedouin as "the mountain of evil." Its ascent is a pleasant walk and gives good views of the huge gorge of Wadi Hasa as well as an opportunity to visit a quiet antiquity site.

Oporanthus, central and southern Jordan

Mary Hartley

Easy scramble
4k up and down, 1-1½hrs for the round trip ascending and descending 160m.

Approach 4k S of the point where the King's Highway crosses Wadi Hasa, the road goes through a small pass (alt 540m) marked by a stone plinth. 2k to the right is Jebel Tannur (704m). A dirt track goes off towards it for 0.5k. Park here.

The route Follow the path to the top gaining height easily up the ridge of the hill.

Down below, 4k WNW of Khirbet Tannur in Wadi Hasa, are:

Dana Area   *Top:* In the gardens of Dana on the Village Trail. R63
Above: The domes of Jebel Barra at the start of the trek down Wadi Hamra to Feinan. R66

Dana Area

Right: The final black canyon of Wadi Adethni and Wadi Ghuweir. R66 & R67

Below Left:
View down Wadi Adethni to the hidden oasis of Hammam Adethni. Wadi Araba can be seen in the distance. R66

Below Right:
Looking out to Wadi Araba from the pass above the Roman mines of Umm el Amad. R69

Dana & Petra Areas

Above Left:
Nabataean tomb.
Wadi Hamra. R66

Above Right:
The world famous
Petra Siq. R71

Right:
Nabataean trail to
'The Monastery',
Petra. R73

Petra Area

Top: Nabataean steps to Jebel Harun summit. R90   *Above:* The Tibn Siq. R98

53. The Hot Springs of Hammamat Borbita and Hammamat Afra

They are signed 2k S of Jebel Tannur, where the road crosses Wadi La'ban. Take this turn then fork right after 7k for Borbita or continue down the poor track for another 6k to a stream. Walk a short way down to reach a little valley the sides of which are stained by minerals. The sulphurous Hot Baths of Afra are situated here (two baths, segregated for the sexes).

Back on the road, it's another 27k S to:

Tafileh

The hillside town of Tafileh nestles dramatically in a great bowl of hills at an altitude of 1,000m, above the upper canyons of Wadi Tubl el Humur which plunges 20k NW to the S end of the Dead Sea. There are a few small restaurants here and one basic hotel.

Tafileh was the site of a famous battle mentioned in Lawrence's Seven Pillars of Wisdom, though it was obviously a less pleasant place than today; he writes *"We were penned in verminous houses of cold stone; lacking fuel, lacking food; storm-bound in streets like sewers, amid blizzards of sleet and an icy wind: while there in the valley was sunshine among spring grass, deep with flowers, upon flocks in milk and air so warm that men went uncloaked"*.

There is a new road which goes through a particularly beautiful and wild mountain area along the S edge of these impressive deep valleys:

The Tafileh - Wadi Araba road

Continuing through Tafileh on the King's Highway for 4k SW of the main Tafila Mosque (and about 7k N of Selah, see below), a new road forks right (W) heading along the hillside for 4k to Sinifha at 1,020m. It then zig-zags down to reach Fifa in Wadi Araba, S of the Dead Sea at 300m below sea level. There is a superb viewpoint 9k down the road: just go up onto the small hill on the right for an unbeatable panorama of the Tafileh Canyon of Wadi Tubl el Humur to the N. Just beyond, there are more good views of Wadi Ikhnaisser (see R55 and R56) to the S. At the Wadi Araba junction there is a road sign to Aqaba, 173k and Amman 157k.

Going S again on the King's Highway, the next excursion goes to:

54. Selah

" ... a most strange mountain on the further side of a vast and profound ravine, a great flat-topped rock rising from the centre of it like a round tower ... the cliffs of it nearly vertical lapped round by a stillness and secrecy ... after some time the eye made out that men had the handling of the mountain ... squared windows and doorways cut out of solid rock and carved stairways dizzily ascending ... the holders of the heights ... had made their nest truly as high as an eagle. But it had not been high enough. I will bring thee down from thence saith the Lord. And the carved square windows of its houses stare like the eye-sockets of a skull."

In the Steps of Moses the Conqueror. L. Golding. 1938.

The impressive natural fortress of Selah was a hill-top refuge occupied from the early Bronze Age, through to Mediaeval times. It is possibly the site where the Judaean King Amaziah threw 10,000 prisoners to their deaths over the cliffs but for those more upwardly mobile it provides a great little walk in very impressive mountain scenery. Map 20.

Guide recommended. It is the responsibility of Fahad Shahabat at Ain el Beidah (on the King's Highway above Es Sil) to be aware of and assist tourists going into these hills or visiting the site of Selah. You should consequently contact him first, tel: 00962 3 366333. If he cannot accompany you himself, he will arrange a guide for you.

Easy scramble
3k. If you drive down, allow 1hr each way from and to Es Sil and 1hr to look around Selah. 3hrs in total. Add another 1hr if you walk from Es Sil and back, descending from 1100m to 700m before climbing up to the summit of Selah at 840m, making 540m of ascent and descent.

Approach 9k beyond Tafileh, towards Petra is the village of Ein el Beida, on the crest of a hill. Turn right here to the small village of Es Sil on the lip of a deep wadi. A nice site with picturesque old stone flat-roofed houses reminiscent of Dana. If you have 4 w.d., continue down through the village, round a hairpin bend descending steeply to the N until the track curves S and stops in a hollow.

The Route 100m back from the end of the track is a cave on the right, and small pool (Bir K'sair) on the left. Just beyond here, a path goes right (W) over rocks through a defile, fairly well defined with some cut steps to a little valley (Khenduk).

From Khenduk, the trail continues in the same W direction into the next obvious defile in the mountain wall, winding up to meet a hewn staircase on the right side of the ravine and eventually turning left 100m before the top, to reach the summit area (20mins from Bir K'sair). There are walls to the left and what are probably observation posts at strategic points along the perimeter, with magnificent views in all directions. Beware of falling into the many water cisterns cut in the summit plateau, with small entrances but large chambers below!

Return the same way.

Below Selah and snaking a tortuous way NW through rugged mountains is The Mother of all Siqs! The canyon system of Wadi Jamal extends at least 13k and, for all we know may continue as far again down the lower reaches of Wadi Jamal, through Wadi Khnaisser, to Wadi Araba. It also, apparently, extends upstream for 6k through Wadi Buseira and Wadi Labun to Buseira (see R56). It's a long way - over 30k in all - and a long story!

55. The Canyon of Wadi Jamal, from Selah to Jamaileh
A long, and uncompleted trek into the heart of lonely mountains. So far, only partially explored, with a big blank on the map beyond ... the route starts on map 20.

Guide recommended, especially if you want to continue to Wadi Araba, see R54 for contact.

Serious trek, Easy canyon
17k so far. Allow 6hrs each way. If you plan to explore further, allow at least 2 days and make sure someone knows your intentions.

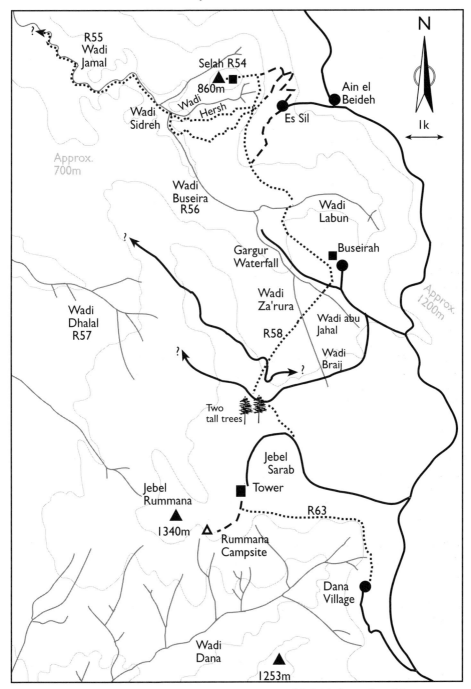

20. Selah, Buseirah and Dana area

Approach As R54 to Es Sil.

The route There are various routes down from the hilltop village of Es Sil (see R58), into Wadi Jamal and its eastern tributary, Wadi Buseira (see R56). To find either of the two ways in from the olive groves below and N of Es Sil you should really take a local guide until further details are available.

The two routes from the olive groves go down almost due W through white sandstone domes and are difficult to locate (hence the advisability of a guide). One is a 'hunter's route' taking a direct line and requiring some agility, the other is a 'shepherd's route' following a winding donkey-track. Either way will bring you in 2hrs to the junction of Wadi Hersh (S of Selah) with Wadi Jamal. This place is Al Faqarah and there was a small, almost stagnant, pool here in mid October 1998, with an attendant shepherd and a herd of goats. The young guide who took us down to this point - Redwan Al Qararah - said that "in springtime it is too beautiful to describe; sometimes there is water three metres deep in Wadi Jamal." (Wadi Jamal is here known as Wadi Sidreh due to the large Sidreh tree with its edible sweet orange-brown berries which is just down stream.)

In October the main wadi was dry but after walking down through impressive canyon for ½hr or so we reached the Waters of Mushrada, with a few fragmites clusters and oleanders. The siq then closes in again dramatically and it is sometimes necessary to jump down small waterfalls and across pools before emerging at a cave-like 'dripping spring' or Nuwatif on the left. (There is also an old copper mine on its left, at least 10m deep, maybe more, it's history not known to us.)

Continuing down the siq, the waters disappear again and it is necessary to walk between canyon walls often only 2 or 3m apart, and once through a 'cave' about 50m long under large fallen boulders. Occasional logs jammed across the siq indicate floods of 2m depth or more but driftwood can be seen considerably higher than that, so winter and springtime explorers should beware!

About 2-2½ hrs from the Waters of Mushrada, the Waters of Jameilha 'the beautiful place' commence. Here, there were many signs of Bedouin shepherds, also 'hides' for hunters of birds and other wild-life. Downstream of Jameilha the siq becomes completely choked with tall fragmites reeds and progress becomes virtually impossible. It's better to take to the hillside, where careful seaching reveals a cairned shepherds' path on the right about 50-100m above the siq. However, after following this a short way the cairns disappear and the path becomes less and less evident. After 1-1½k it's becoming non-existent. We reluctantly decided to retrace our steps back to Es Sil the following day as we were expected back and couldn't be sure of reaching the other end in time.

Whether or not there is a way on, we don't know, but it's a further 13k out to Wadi Araba through the continuation of the valley which is known as Wadi Khnaisser (Wild Boar Valley). (See notes on Wadi Khnaisser in the Wadi Araba section.) Having originally been told by various locals "there is no problem", it became apparent on our return to Es Sil that no-one seemed to know anything about the route on from Jamailha. We'll try again next year perhaps, or if you go, take care and let us know how it goes!

Buseira

7k on the Petra road from Ain el Beidah, turn right to Buseira (about 2.5k). There are Iron Age ruins mentioned in the Bible as Bozrah both in and just beyond the town to the N with good views down into Wadi Buseira to the NW and on towards Wadi Araba down the aforementioned Wadi Jamal. There are other ways into the system from Buseira:

56. Wadi Labun - Wadi Jamal - Wadi Khnaisser
On the E side of town, in springtime (March) you may well see a big waterfall falling free into Wadi Labun over a 60m cliff - an unusual sight in Jordan! The Wadi continues down from there to meet Wadi Za'rura coming from the W side of Buseira which passes over a waterfall called Gargur. R58 from Selah crosses Wadi Labun where it passes through an impressive siq 1k E of this junction. Downstream of here, the wadi is named Wadi Buseira until, after 4k it meets the two wadies which enclose Selah (see R55); at that point the name changes to Wadi el Jamal - Valley of the Camel - before becoming Wadi Khnaisser - Valley of the Wild Boar. The whole system is reputed to be an ancient way down to Wadi Araba though our experience in Wadi Jamal indicates that this is unlikely. Going through with a local guide may clarify matters! Not yet fully checked by the authors (see above notes).

Serious trek, Easy canyon
30k, descending over 1000m. We were told 12hrs which is just possible but seems unlikely given potential route finding problems. If you try it, allow at least 2 days and make sure someone knows where you have gone.

The Route The only information we have is that the route is very scenic, which is certainly true of the section we crossed on R58 as well as the very impressive route through Wadi Jamal (R55). Apparently the canyon can also be accessed easily down Wadi Za'rura, avoiding Wadi Labun.

Another old trail reputedly goes directly W from Buseira:

57. Wadi Dhalal to Wadi Araba
*This route was used by Lawrence on the 20 February 1918 and described in Seven Pillars of Wisdom.
" ... the cliffs and the hills drew together so that hardly did the stars shine into its pitchy blackness ... We halted a moment while our camels stilled the nervous trembling of their forelegs after the strain of the terrible descent. Then we plashed, fetlock deep, down the swift stream, under a long arch of rustling bamboos, which met so nearly over our heads that fans brushed our faces. The strange echoes of the vaulted passage frightened our camels into a trot."*

Moderate trek
About 30k from Buseira, 6 to 10hrs depending on where you walk from, descending from 1140m to 100m below sea level in Wadi Araba.

The route. Not checked by the authors, but there are tracks heading out from Buseira, crossing the wadi immediately W (see R58), then 8k W along the N edge of Wadi Dhalal headwaters before descending into it. The wadi is exactly on the N boundary of the Dana Nature Reserve. The dirt road down it has been destroyed by rain. Information supplied by Tareq abul Hawa of RSCN Dana. Due to its proximity to the Reserve, an RSCN guide may be required - ask at Dana.

Another series of old trails once led between Selah and Buseira and on to the S:

58. Selah to Buseira and Dana

A considerable amount of descent and ascent links these ancient hill top sites, each in a commanding position above valleys leading down to Wadi Araba. The original way has been considerably altered by 4w.d. tracks to areas of agriculture so that it has lost much of its original character and ambience. It nevertheless passes through a variety of interesting country needing route finding ability and currently forms the first link in a chain of treks which can be extended all the way S to Aqaba. Map 20.

Moderate Trek

16k, 7 - 8hrs, starting at 700m, the route first descends a little then ascends 350m before descending 360m to Wadi Labun, then a long haul up 500m to Buseira before descending a little to rise another 500m again to Jebel Sarab above Dana. From there it's an easy 200m descent to the Rummana campsite at Dana.

Approach As R54. Walk (or preferably drive) the 2k down from Es Sil (1,100m) to the saddle at 700m below the hill of Selah (840m).

The route 2k to the S on a shoulder of the hill just SW of Es Sil village, a small field (green in springtime) can be seen. This is the first objective. To reach it go S across flat land and small fields to a gap between steep rock towers. Pass between them and carefully scramble down a narrow siq, then keep on its left side across the shoulder beyond and descend carefully into the wadi. Now rise diagonally up the hillside, still in the same general line passing through olive groves to reach a good track which contours round past a cave shelter then along the top of the green field on the shoulder, 1000m, about 2k, 1hr. Just beyond is a large cairn and a 4 w.d. track coming down from Es Sil 0.5k above to the NE. (A direct approach from here would be very easy and save 1hr or more.) It is probably the best way to commence the trek as a new 4 w.d. track has been made through the olive groves (Oct '98), bisecting the path described above.

Follow the track down to the SE towards Wadi Labun. After about ½ hr, it curves towards the E passing left of a small hill with two small tops. (To the right there are steps cut in the steep slabs with grooves worn down the sides of them by Bedouin children sliding down them on stones, (these features can also be found in Wadi Rum). From here, pass N of a deep ravine with some cave shelters visible in it below, then continue down the left side of this ravine and go left across a small wadi then descend again to emerge above the 50m cliffs hiding the canyon of Wadi Labun. There is only one way in and finding it is the key to the route.

The entry point should be a little to your left, where a donkey track winds steeply down into the ravine which is otherwise guarded by cliffs, forming an impressive siq. Not so obvious at first, it passes a small juniper tree, becoming more defined as it nears the wadi bed (alt 640m) 2hrs from the start. The impressive Petra style siq extends both E up to the location of the springtime waterfall at Buseira, and W down to Wadi Araba. (See R56.)

Go about 50m down the wadi to find the donkey track going up the left bank onto the hillside above. Cross a small wadi and go up the shoulder of the hill trending right and eventually reaching a track. Continue up this and the path above to emerge on the ridge directly above and about 0.5k from the springs and waterfall of Gargur which is to the SW with a road passing it en route from Wadi Labun up to Buseira. (About ½ - ¾ hr from Wadi Labun.)

Ignore the road and continue up left of a fenced field above Gargur Falls until, just above a concrete water tank, paths are followed towards a distant shoulder passing through some previously concealed fields and up an improving track to the shoulder and the first view of the houses of Buseira beyond. (1hr from Wadi Labun.)

Follow the track which rises easily up to Buseira (1k). The ruins of 2,000 year old Iron Age Bozrah are immediately N of the present village on the end of the promontory between the two wadies but unless you're into archaeology they hardly merit a special visit. If you do go up there it's a bit of a slog directly up the hillside from the track. (Alt 1140m, 3½ - 4hrs from Selah.)

Otherwise, continue along the rising track along the W side of the comparatively new village, passing by some old houses. Just beyond, by a house on the right with a small fruit garden, some steps leave the road. Go down these to the road below and take the track forking right that can be seen winding S down into Wadi abu Jahal.

Just before the track reaches the wadi, leave it and descend directly on paths into the wadi, (900m) across it and up the other side, below then right of a small cliff, to meet another good track. On the far horizon a saddle will be seen between two hills with two large trees on its right side - your next objective. Take the track towards them, eventually following limestone pavements along the left side of Wadi Braij en route, then forking right to cross the wadi. (½ hr from Buseira.)

Immediately beyond, leave the track and head up fields past a small juniper, then up through more fields to a path going round the left side of a hill above the top field. Keep going round and up, heading for the saddle and reaching a road about 20mins above Wadi Braij. Go left on the road for 100m or so to just before a walled field with cairns on the left of the road. (Just beyond, the road crosses the wadi at a hairpin bend.) Here, go right over a small field and past a tree, heading up towards the saddle again.(Now about ½hr from Wadi Braij.)

Ahead you will once again see the saddle and the two large and ancient protected Cypress trees on the N edge of the Dana Reserve. Reach them across fields and over a road. (1300m.) Beyond to the S, the Reserve is protected by a fence on the other side of which is an area of forest in a totally protected zone. To bypass this, it is necessary to head uphill E on the outside of the fence eventually contouring S towards Ain Lahdha at 1454m before heading back W to the RSCN gate-tower at Jebel Sarab, above the RSCN Camp. The campsite is below at 1180m, 3½hrs from Buseira. (Accommodation at the camp must be booked in advance.)

The last section from the big Cypress trees has not been checked by the authors who were permitted through the normally protected area of 'The Forest Trail'.

THE RSCN DANA NATURE RESERVE

11 February 1918 "Rain came on, and soaked me, and then it blew fine and freezing till I crackled in armour of white silk, like a theatre knight: or like a bridal cake hard iced." As the rain turns to snow, Lawrence's camel falls but he continues " ... sounding the path in front with my stick, or digging new passes when the drifts were deep ... looking down across the chess-board houses of Dana village into sunny Arabeh, fresh and green thousands of feet below."
Seven Pillars of Wisdom. T. E. Lawrence. 1926.

The Reserve is a system of wadies and mountains which extends from the upper edge of the Rift Valley down to the desert lowlands of Wadi Araba. Dana is truly a world of natural treasures.

Visitors to Dana can experience the beauty of Rummana Mountain, the mystery of the ancient archaeological ruins of Feinan, the timeless tranquillity of Dana Village, and the grandeur of the red and white sandstone cliffs of Wadi Dana, as well as visiting the wilderness areas in the company of approved local guides.

Dana is home to about 600 plant species, 37 species of mammal and 190 species of birds including 80% of the known world's population of Tristram's Serin. For full information on the fauna and flora, contact the RSCN.

Entrance Fee
For non-Jordanians, 5JD, for Jordanians, 1JD.

Visitors' Centre
The Visitors' Centre is located at the edge of Dana Village. The centre contains displays and information about Dana and the RSCN. The souvenir shop sells organically grown produce from the Village's terraced gardens, and silver jewellery and pottery created by the women of Dana Village. The Dana Visitors' Centre also contains a refreshment stand, meeting room, bathrooms, information centre, and an outdoor terrace with a spectacular view of Wadi Dana.

Reserve Manager, Tariq Abul-Hawa, tel: 03 368477 / 98 / 99

Camping
Camping is possible at the two campsites, Rummana near the village, and Feinan down near Wadi Araba. Meals can be provided or self-cooked. Costs start from around 8JD/night for non-Jordanians (less for Jordanians).

21. The RSCN Dana Nature Reserve

Rummana Campsite
Camping facilities are provided and the campsite is open for overnight visitors from March 1st to October 31st except Tuesdays. Visitors must check into the campsite before 8.00 p.m. and should leave their cars at the Tower entrance. Transportation to and from the campsite will be provided by a shuttle bus at 1hr intervals. The campsite contains 20 large tents, bathrooms, and barbecue grills for visitor use. Each tent comes equipped with mattresses, blankets and pillows. The camp can host a maximum of 60 visitors per night. Drinking water is available, charcoal can be purchased, small gas cookers

can be rented and catering services can be provided for groups of 6 or more. The campsite is in a beautiful area about 3k N of Wadi Dana with a breathtaking panorama over orchards, green hills, sandstone domes and savage valleys out to Wadi Araba.

To reach the campsite, turn off the King's Highway 1k S of Rashadiya (sign Lahtha) and follow the track for 300m, keeping right at a huge major road leading to a quarry. Leave this to the right after 2k, as the road curves towards the NW and N, then fork left as the road goes W then S, descending slightly to the Tower and gate on Jebel Sarab on the upper edge of the Reserve. All vehicles must be left there before going down to the camp in RSCN transport. Superb views across the smaller Jebel Rummana to Wadi Araba, with Wadi Dana deep down on the left (S).

Feinan Campsite
This campsite is simpler and was established in 1996 in the lower area. The campsite has a kitchen, 10 tents and bathrooms. Each tent comes equipped with mattresses, blankets and pillows. The camp can host a maximum of 40 visitors per night. Drinking water is also available.

Dana Village and Guest House
Perched like an eerie on the edge of Wadi Dana, overlooking the spectacular scenery of the Dana Nature Reserve, is a classic example of one of Jordan's few remaining traditional villages. The building interiors are divided by stone arches which support the roofs, large timber beams being unavailable. Alongside, and built in the same harmonious architectural style is the unique Guest House and Visitor Centre run by the RSCN. Prices, inclusive of breakfast, vary from 8 - 35JD/person dependent on season, size of group and other requirements. Bookings should be made well in advance. An overnight stay in the smaller Dana Hotel run by local people in Dana Village costs around 5JD.

Traditional architecture, Dana village   *Peter Hall*

Old doorway, Dana Village   *Peter Hall*

Walks in the Dana Reserve

The best way to experience Dana is on foot. Some areas, such as Dana Village and The Tower picnic area are accessible by car, but many of Dana's treasures remain hidden in wilderness zones of the reserve where vehicles are not permitted. Dana offers a selection of trails to key points of interest for both the casual and adventurous walker. Four of the trails are clearly marked with cairns along the route, and can therefore be hiked independently or with an RSCN guide. Guided hikes offer visitors a unique opportunity to enjoy a stimulating walk and learn about the geology, wildlife, and history of Dana. Guides are available at the Rummana Campsite, Dana Village, and Feinan upon request.

The RSCN have some 'Marked Trails' in the Reserve. (Details from the RSCN):

59. Rummana Trail   *Easy walk*   *4k, 2hrs round trip*
To the top of Jebel Rummana above the campsite with excellent views of the surrounding area.

60. Dana Campsite Trail   *Easy walk*   *2k, 1hr round trip*
To the forested hills around the campsite.

61. Dana Cave Trail   *Easy walk*   *3k, 1½hrs round trip*
To abandoned cave shelters previously used by Bedouin shepherds and earlier inhabitants.

62. Khirbet Sarab Trail   *Easy walk*   *2k, 1hr round trip*

There are also other 'Unmarked (Guided) Trails':

63. Dana Village Trail   *Easy walk*   *5k, 3hrs*
Connects the village and campsite. Maps 20 and 22.

64. Feinan Trail   *Moderate trek*   *15k, 5 - 6hrs*
Connects Dana with Feinan in Wadi Araba. (See R65, map 22.)

Dana Adventure Expeditions

For nature lovers and adventurous visitors special expeditions for 1, 2 and 3 days can be arranged, giving you the chance to explore the hidden secrets of the Dana Reserve and discover more about the reserve and traditional Bedouin life.

65. Wadi Dana to Feinan

"High over a green valley hangs the red mountain. Straight towards the hazy Arabah thrusts the deep valley, flanked by sheer precipices, enriched by woods and waters ... the village of Dana spreads out fanwise on a fan shaped buttress of rock ... it looks so improbable."

In the Steps of Moses the Conqueror. L. Golding. 1938.

A pleasant walk down the long valley which forms the core of the Dana Reserve. The orchards of Dana give way to wild and mountainous then more barren surroundings as the trail descends to ancient Feinan, once the site of notorious copper mines but now the considerably more hospitable location of an RSCN campsite! Maps 22 and 23.

RSCN guide required

Moderate trek
15k, descending from 1200m to 200m, 5 - 6hrs.

Approach The route starts in Dana village. (Transport provided from RSCN campsite.)

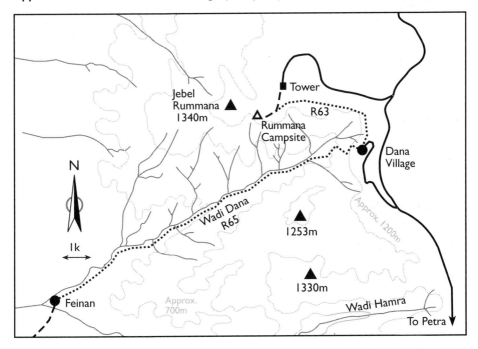

22. Dana to Feinan

The route When we did it in 1985, we simply followed the trail from the village down steep hairpins for 2k to the floor of the canyon. The RSCN guides have their own more interesting variations before continuing down the wadi, passing some of the copper mines and other points of interest to the camp near the site of Feinan.

Feinan

"It had been a city, it had even been a Bishopric, but they had not served Christ here, but copper ... Here died the Christian martyrs condemned by the pagan emperors, Maximinus and Diocletian. Here the Catholics were sent to die by the aryan schismatics. St Sylvanus and thirty three of his companions were beheaded here. The Egyptian Bishops, St. Peleus and St Nile, all of them died, soon and terribly, only copper lived on. And then even that died, and the husks of it only remained, like heaps of blue-green baked rigid for all time in that gross heat."

In the Steps of Moses the Conqueror. L. Golding. 1938.

There is another excellent and varied trek down to Finnan from Dana, along the S edge of the Reserve. To reach it, it is usual to go by vehicle from Dana village or Campsite, or you can walk. No guide is required for the trail between the campsite and village (R63), but an RSCN Guide is compulsory for the walk from the village to the head of Wadi Hamra. This approach has not been checked by the authors.

66. Dana to Feinan via Wadi Hamra

An outstanding trek through ever changing scenery, descending from pretty sandstone domes and springtime flower filled meadows past Nabataean tombs to a long valley with red sandstone cliffs ('hamra' means 'red'). The route leaves this via a pass with good views before descending though juniper trees down to the lush wild oasis of Hammam Adethni beyond which the trek, despite its now barren and rugged surroundings, becomes quite aquatic, walking the rest of the way in or next to water before emerging into the wilderness of Wadi Araba.

There is a great variety of wild-life due to the different eco-systems, including ibex (which we didn't see) and very big fresh water crabs that we did! In addition to other birds, we saw Lesser Kestrel and other raptors and the beautiful Palestinian Sunbird. Map 23.

Guide recommended. An RSCN guide may be necessary.

Moderate Trek
20k, allow 7 - 8hrs, descending 450m before rising 150m to a pass and descending another 900m to the RSCN campsite at Feinan, near the ancient copper mines.

Approach Go by vehicle from Dana Campsite or village to a point on the King's Highway about 4 to 5k S of the Dana Village junction, where a track goes right (W) for 1k to the white domes of Jebel Barra which can be seen from the Highway. The track ends close by the rocks at which point Wadi Hamra (also called Wadi Sharir) is just below to the S but guarded by the domes.

Alternatively, you can walk to Barra from Dana with an RSCN guide - a pleasant 2 - 3hrs along wooded hills with sandstone towers. This walk can be arranged at the Visitor Centre. Or there is yet another alternative start: the RSCN sometimes drive people along the S side of Wadi Hamra, then enter by the donkey-track which descends to its W end down a side valley with natural rock pools (see below), thereby saving 5 or 6k of walking, but missing the nice entry

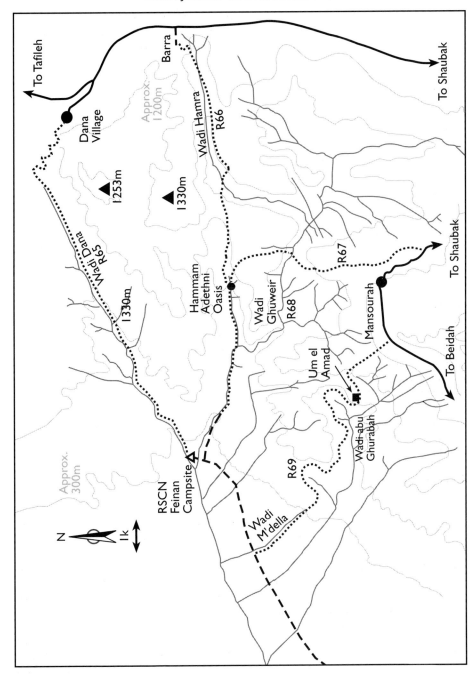

To Tafileh

Barra

To Shaubak

Dana Village

Approx 1200m

Wadi Hamra

R66

1253m

1330m

To Shaubak

Wadi Dana R65

1330m

R67

Hammam Adethni Oasis

Wadi Ghuweir

R68

Mansourah

Um el Amad

To Beidah

Approx. 300m

RSCN Feinan Campsite

Wadi-abu Ghurabah

N

1k

R69

Wadi M'della

23. Dana, Feinan, Shaubak area

down through the domes of Barra.

The route To the left of the Jebel Barra Domes, a little valley will be seen between small white domes, which are themselves left of the higher ones. Descend into it on white rock, and where the valley goes left continue directly W up slabs towards a finger of rock on the skyline. Pass left of the finger and scramble down towards the valley, but then contour left along a rock terrace to emerge at an antiquity site near Nuwatif - the Dripping Spring - and only 20m directly below the starting point. The path then winds down past carved Nabataean caves directly under the traverse ledge. Continue past some more rather 'up market' caves, first on the left then on the right, and on into the valley beyond which defines the S edge of the Reserve (½ hr from start). The valley is full of herbs such as the sweet smelling Artemisis (called 'shia' by the Bedouin and used for upset stomachs). Here we saw Lesser Kestrel and the beautiful Palestinian Sunbird. Eventually the path and valley descend below the white sandstone reaching the red sandstone strata which gives the valley its name.

Eventually the path crosses the wadi to its left (S) side where numerous sheep tracks contour along the steep, sometimes scree-covered hillside 50 -100m above the wadi which narrows into a siq below. The path eventually meets the wadi again beyond the siq after about ¾hr in the valley. (1¼hrs from the start.) A good donkey-track then rises up, still on the left side, zig-zagging steeply then levelling out onto a shoulder and continuing across a small side wadi just below limestone slabs.

Follow the good path descending slightly to reach a major side valley (1¾hrs from the start). The path crosses this below natural rock pools (dry in April) and continues as a good trail along and down the hillside to reach the bed of Wadi Hamra again just after passing between two small tops. (2hrs from the start.) Here is a key stage which must be followed carefully: immediately after the tops, the path crosses a small side valley on the left. Leave it just beyond and walk down the actual bed of Wadi Hamra for about 200m, then leave this for a small side wadi on the right (N). Go up this for 50m then take a good track rising diagonally up the right side of Wadi Hamra. Continue up this over a shoulder on top of the ridge, marked by a few trees on its left. Go through a small rocky pass to see Wadi Silwan and Wadi Hammam Adethni beyond and, in the distance, Wadi Araba. (¾ hr from Wadi Hamra, 2¾hrs from the start, about 7k.)

A good track now descends NW between and over tilted limestone pavements and out onto a shoulder above a valley, then down and across small side wadies (a few cairns and small paths). Continue beyond, descending slightly again through an area of dead junipers (½hr from the pass). After another 10mins descend a rocky shoulder to a large cairn (which marks the edge of the Reserve), above the edge of the deep wadi. From here there are good views out W to the tree-filled wadi of Hammam Adethni. Beyond is a black cone shaped summit, then the arid wastes of Araba (about 1hr from the pass).

Immediately ahead is a small red sandstone top. Descend to its foot and pass it on its left side. The black cone and green wadi are now directly ahead. Follow the crest of the ridge until it ends on a small black top. The palm filled wadi is now directly below. Descend by a gully just back from the top then follow the donkey-track as it zig-zags steeply down the shattered black rock to reach the abrupt edge of the oasis.

Cross the small permanent stream and go though a 'forest' of fragmites reeds on the S bank, just left of a magnificent cluster of date palms. The path then goes W for a short way past oleanders, figs and other trees to reach a clear area and a permanent 'holy spring' revered by local Bedouin. (The actual source is in a small pool just behind the palm tree where the water can be seen rising up in the bottom of the pool). A nice place for lunch! (1¾hrs from the pass, 4¾hrs from the start. About 12k.) Surprisingly there are fresh-water crabs and snails here!

Now, follow the path as it descends back to the wadi through the 'fragmites-jungle', then down the thickly vegetated stream bed for a short way before gaining the right bank. Follow the stream along on a path just above it, through an area of pink granite boulders, then alongside and finally in the stream itself until you reach the junction with the fast flowing Wadi Ghuweir (Wadi Shaubak - see R68 - ¾hr from the spring.) Here, take some time out to walk up Wadi Ghuweir for 10mins or so, to appreciate the magnificent rock scenery of this deep canyon; watch your toes, there are king-size crabs there!

Back at the junction again, continue down the river through a long and beautiful black canyon (a lot of river-hopping - expect wet feet!), for about 1hr, to reach a weir about 7hrs from the start. (If you have made arrangements, you can be met here by 4 w.d.) Otherwise you must continue for another 1k down the river to where the valley opens out, and the river disappears into the stones. 2k further down the stony wadi bed a track will be crossed. Follow it right (N) for 3k to the RSCN campsite - far better to have a vehicle for the last section!

SHAUBAK AREA
The next route leaves the Dana Reserve, returning to the King's Highway via Shaubak Castle, starting up the lower half of the above route. (It would therefore be possible to combine the routes without actually descending the last section to Feinan.)

67. Feinan to Shaubak via Wadi Hammam Adethni
Takes R66 in reverse up the waters of Wadi Adethni to the oasis, or 'hammam', then rises over wild hills to descend S into Wadi Ghuweir (Wadi Shaubak), leaving that almost immediately to climb up to Mansourah, thence by road to Shaubak. Not checked by the authors. (Info. Jalel Bouagga.) Map 23.

Guide recommended

Moderate trek
14k, ascending from 200m to 1,200m with an intermediary ascent and descent of about 300m. Allow 5 - 6hrs.

Approach Best started from the RSCN campsite at Feinan, with 4 w.d. up Wadi Adethni (the reverse of R66), until the first signs of water are met.

The Route At the start the wadi is dry, but soon you enter the gorges and canyons and find oleanders and tamarisk. (4 w.d. can be taken to here.) Several springs appear and the higher you go up the wadi the more abundant the water and the vegetation become.

Continue walking in the wadi (wading through the water) until you find two tributaries, Wadi Shaubak going straight on and (to the left) Wadi Adethni. Go up Wadi Adethni. At the start the path is not visible, and the vegetation becomes very dense as you approach the oasis, with a lot of palm trees, oleanders, tamarisk, fragmites rushes and other vegetation at the sides of the wadi and in the depths of the canyon: a unique forest amidst barren hills. There is a lot of water in the stream and a hidden spring in the oasis (see R66) but no spring visible until you arrive at a small col which dominates the small forest where a tiny spring flows from a little "grotto" under a large tree.

From there the view ahead is clear. R66 comes down the main valley slightly N of E, whilst another a narrow path which is hard to see at first goes E then SE for 1k towards the mountain, reaching a col at about 1000m. Further on, descend to cross Wadi Shaubak where there is an abandoned 4.w.d. track which leads to the village of Al Mansourah (alt 1200m).

Al Mansourah is a small town with terraced fields. The asphalt road appears again and leads to the castle at Shaubak 9k above. There is local transport available.

It is, so we are told, also possible to ascend or descend Wadi Shaubak from the Fortress of Shaubak:

68. Wadi Shaubak to Feinan

"The Lord had announced he would not give [the Israelites] of the Edomite land ... because he had given Mount Seir unto Esau for possession. It may have seemed wise to get down to the plain again, perhaps by the Wadi Shobek to Punon [Feinan] and then march northward again."
In the Steps of Moses the Conqueror. L. Golding. 1938.

Shown on the map as Wadi Ghuweir this impressive wadi system starts in the hills E of Shaubak and descends through an increasingly deep and impressive canyon to meet Wadi Adethni about 5k SSE of the RSCN campsite at Finnan. Not checked by the authors, but the bottom end of the canyon looks good! Map 23.

Guide recommended

Easy canyon (or so we were told!)
16 - 22k, 6 - 8hrs dependent on choice of route, either way descending 1,000m.

Approach Drive down the road from Shaubak towards Mansourah.

The route Tracks leave the road either at Mansourah or 2k before at El Muqar'iiyah, and descend N and NNE respectively reaching Wadi Shaubak after about 4k. The route then descends the wadi which, we are told, is problem free - information supplied by Tareq abul Hawa of RSCN, Dana.

69. Feinan to Mansourah (Shaubak) via Um el Amad

Up-hill all the way but none the less enjoyable for that! The route goes through some wild country with constantly changing scenery and good views out over Wadi Araba. The journey is split at half way by a visit to the Roman copper mines of Um el Amad - Mother of Columns, and finishes on the small road 2k W of Mansourah. Shaubak Castle is another 9k up the road from Mansourah from where a taxi or small bus can be taken. Otherwise, arrange to be met on the Mansourah road by the RSCN or whoever you have organised the walk with. Map 23.

Guide recommended

Moderate trek
16k, rising from 200m to 1360m. 5hrs.

Approach Drive about 4k WSW from the Feinan camp until just past some ruins, where the trek starts (not obvious).

The Route Head SSE up Wadi M'della along its right (true left) bank. At the head of the wadi (½hr) a donkey-track zig-zags up slightly left to a small gap in a rocky col with good views SW to Wadi Araba. Turn left here and go up the rocky ridge over a small shoulder to gain a broader ridge beyond. Follow this up and take an improving track up its right side to the next shoulder (1hr from the start).

Keep on the track, rising across the right flank again and up to the saddle beyond, ¼hr from the last shoulder. An old 4 w.d. track will be seen below. Descend towards it and go left on a path 50m above it on rock ledges, to descend to the track a little further on round the bend (1½hrs from start). Follow the abandoned track as it descends into a wild mountain valley with a canyon below and cliffs above.

The track makes a big swing round the valley and up the opposite side to reach a pass cut through the ridge with more excellent views S. Continue on the track as it curves E and ends at the mines of Um el Amad (2½hrs from start), above the ravine of Wadi abu Ghurabah. Time to take a rest and contemplate the horrors of the copper mine slaves!

There is no architectural finesse here, just an awful austerity carved painfully out by slave labour: the rough columns of rock left standing to support the roof and the small recesses in the walls for oil lamps are simply concessions to necessity. There was no joy at Um el Amad, just an incessant hammering, rock dust, darkness and death. A visit here will leave you glad to be alive and free to escape into the mountains beyond! Louis Golding in his book In the Steps of Moses the Conqueror, 1938, has nightmares about the Feinan mines " ... *even the hardened criminals who are condemned to the mines of Phaenon, do not survive there many more than a few days ... the wretches passing from an outer to an inner hell, from the airless oven of the Arabah in high mid-summer, to the furnace heats of the mine galleries. I saw the yellow faces, and the leathery lips and green copper-dust in the sunken hollows of their eyes. It was a mercy after all, was it not, they did not survive here more than a few days.*"

Back outside, and high above to the left of the wadi (right of Um el Amad looking up), a narrow rocky pass will be seen above a gully with many juniper trees. Scramble up into it, to find a donkey-track which zig-zags up it into a spectacular and beautiful area of white sandstone domes, and continue up to the pass (40mins from Um el Amad) from where the distant flat topped hills of Shaubak can be seen to the SE.

Go left up the rocky ridge for 100m or so then right on small paths (a few cairns), descending and ascending here and there, but basically contouring along above the upper valley of Wadi abu Ghurabah, and level with a plateau of small domes on its opposite side. Continue on the donkey-track gaining the shoulder up to the left towards the next top, well-worn between domes, to reach a summit. (Just over 1hr from the mines, 3¼hrs from the start.) From the little top (good views) head directly SE across flat white sandstone forming the divide between two wadi systems to the NE and SW and heading for the high flat summit to the SE. Continue in the same line up a convenient slope and up again to pass the right end of a long limestone encampment (1hr from the domes). At this point the good track goes right a short way before regaining its original SE line which is followed up to meet a good 4 w.d. track. (1½hrs from the domes.) Mansourah is 2k to the left.

Mansourah

17k S of Dana there is a junction of the King's Highway with a major road leading to the Desert Highway. 4k S of this is a sign to Mansourah on the right. Follow this down for 9k to the end of the road. There are fine views down the wadies towards the ancient site of Feinan at the junction of Wadi Dana and Wadi Shaubak, also out towards Wadi Araba.

The road also passes through Abu Makhlub 3k from the highway, where there are many old cave dwellings still in use. Just past here, coming back up to the highway, it is possible to turn right and wind up a narrow steep wadi directly to Shaubak Castle, this unusual angle of approach giving a true appreciation of its commanding situation.

Shaubak Castle

"... suddenly the earth fell before us into a great arena where diverse wadis met and swept together ... to a breast-like hill commanding all that country. And on top of that hill was a circuit of stout stone walls, embayed, enkeepened and battlemented, and that was Shobek of the Crusaders, of Christian swashbucklers that had captured Jerusalem stretching forth a mailed first southward towards the unconquered and unconquerable spices of Arabia."
In the Steps of Moses the Conqueror. L. Golding. 1938.

The classical hill-top Crusader Fortress of Shaubak does indeed stand in a commanding position above the complex network of wadies that descend W and NW to Feinan from the edge of the King's Highway. There also used to be a big forest around Shaubak which Doughty commented on in Arabia Deserta in 1888 *"This limestone moorland, of so great altitude resembles Europe, and there are hollows, park-like with evergreen oak timber."* Sadly, it was mostly used as fuel for the trains on the Hejaz Railway during the 1st World War but there are still remnants of these old forests on the rolling hills between Shaubak and Petra which provide pleasant walking country high above the wilderness of Wadi Araba though they are now criss-crossed by small roads.

70. Shaubak to Beidah

" ... suddenly there burst into view a thousand or fifteen hundred feet lower down and not more than three or four miles away, a wonderful mass of castellated peaks, domes, pinnacles and other fantastic shapes, with indescribable colouring, from snow-white at the base, to purple and yellow and crimson higher up, bathed and transformed in the brilliant sunshine till it seemed like an enchanted fairy tale."
The Jordan Valley and Petra. Libbey and Hoskins. 1905.

This route is sometimes walked by groups but has not been checked by the authors. It is mostly roadwork. (Info. Jalel Bouagga.)

Easy walk
22k, approx. 5hrs.

The route From Shaubak go towards the village at the side of the King's Highway and continue along this for 2k to a sign left to Zaytouna village. (Radar station behind.) Here, take a narrow track right for 3 - 4k. This track becomes a narrow path which leads directly towards a hill. Pass through the village of Huorala then over a small col before arriving in a forest of green oak trees. A narrow road now goes down to Beidah and as far as Siq Al Barrid with excellent views towards Petra. It is possible to camp near Beidah (otherwise known as 'Little Petra'). Drinking water can be found at the nearby Bedouin village.

There is also supposed to be a very scenic route passing Roman and other sites of antiquity in the valleys below the Mansourah - Beidah road, reaching Beidah via Wadi Hudeith, Wadi Thugra and Siq um el Hiran. (See section on Petra, the Northern Approaches.) Not checked by the authors but it looks like very nice country from above.

THE PETRA AREA

"Strange and horrible as a pit, in an inhuman deadness of nature, is this site of the Nabataean's metropolis; the eye recoils from that mountainous close of iron cliffs, in which the ghastly waste monuments of a sumptuous barbaric art are from the first glance an eyesore."

Travels in Arabia Deserta. Charles M. Doughty. 1888.

Despite Doughty's apparent abhorrence of Petra, it cannot be denied that Petra is truly magnificent and a visit is imperative for anyone in Jordan. Hidden in the heart of the Shara mountains, it has to be one of the most fascinating sites of antiquity in the Middle East. Unfortunately this means it is extremely busy with tourists. However, you're in luck! Most visitors don't have the time to get beyond the old city in the Petra Basin, probably including a visit to The High Place and a pilgrimage to Ed Deir, The Monastery ... but there's much more to Petra than that!

Tombs in the main Petra Basin   *Peter Hall*

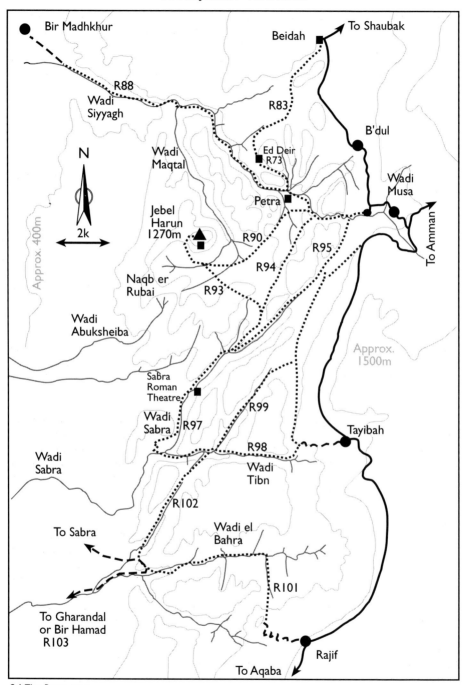

24. The Petra area

Make an early start, stay late, or get off the beaten track and you soon lose the crowds. You could spend weeks in Petra and not see it all. If you go beyond the old city on the Nabataean and Roman trails, you can walk for days in unique scenery passing remnants of civilisations dating back over 10,000 years without seeing anyone! You can link into mountain treks from the hill top Nabataean eerie of Selah, N of Dana, or walk all the way S on ancient caravan routes over mountains and deserts to Wadi Rum, even to Aqaba.

As a visitor to Petra the best entry for a first visit is undoubtedly via the famous Siq, the narrow canyon which emerges into Petra at The Treasury. There are however numerous other trails into and around Petra and regardless of the route you take you will need a Permit for the requisite number of days from the Visitor Centre. Basically, the whole of the area between Beidah and Sabra, W of the Petra Entrance Gates and including the mountains to the W down to the edge of Wadi Araba lies within the Petra area.

Petra - entrance fees and permits

1 day	Non-Jordanian	20JD
2 days	Non-Jordanian	25JD
3 days	Non-Jordanian	30JD

Beyond that there is no increase but your Permit should still state the number of days required. The cost for Jordanians is 1JD/day; children have a 50% discount.

The Petra Tourist Police

The Tourist Police will be seen at or near most sites of antiquity in Petra. They are there to protect the site and for your safety, and will even be found in the more remote places such as Jebel Harun. Naturally, some speak only Arabic and the more zealous ones may try to stop you going "off the beaten track" without a guide.

Though guides are usually good company and obviously enhance safety, many experienced trekkers will prefer to go alone and to be responsible for their own safety. In this case it would probably be useful to have a note in Arabic explaining that you are experienced and capable of trekking without a guide using this book which was written with the knowledge and approval of The Petra Authority and that you have left details of your route and expected time of return at your hotel or with a responsible person.

Guides

If you have sufficient experience you can go without a guide, but you may wish to go by camel or horse or simply to enjoy the company of a guide who knows the area well. There are some very good local Bedouin guides in Wadi Musa and B'dul and some good adventure travel companies operating from Amman, Wadi Musa and Aqaba, so finding a suitable trek and guide will be the first move for many. For information, call at the Visitor Centre near the entrance to Petra in lower Wadi Musa, or contact any of the companies listed at the start of this section on South Jordan, two of whose offices are just up the road past the new Mövenpick Hotel.

Maps

Apart from the maps listed at the start of this section, which are difficult to get, there are a number of quite good maps of the Petra Basin in the various Jordan travel guides and in guide books specific to Petra. The Royal Geographical Centre (see intro.) also does a good map available from hotels and book shops. None of them, however, go much beyond the old city which is where the real adventures are!

Walks in and around Petra

"The green slopes end suddenly and the gnome-like mountains begin, so split and cut by millions of crevices that the whole mass is always filled with small patches and pockets of shadow. In the heart of these grotesque mountains is the mysterious city of Petra.

...I have noticed that some mountains, although fantastic from a distance, are apt to become quite ordinary when you approach them. But that is not true of Petra. In fact the grotesque eruption becomes even more grotesque as you draw nearer to it. The Valley of the Dead at Luxor is a cheerful place in comparison with these mountains, which are like the blue, devil-haunted landscapes which early Italian painters have put behind their saints. They are so weird and ominous I was grateful for the sound of the horses stumbling among the stones."

In the Steps of The Master. H.V. Morton. 1934.

So it wasn't only the formidable Doughty that found Petra a foreboding place! But these "gnome-like" mountains are marvellous! We'll start as we must, by walking into Petra through its world famous Siq - that dramatic chasm splitting the mountains which provides what must be the most remarkable entrance to any city: a unique and unforgettable experience. Once you have become familiar with the main sights of the old city and the view from the High Place, you may wish to spend more days in this beautiful part of Jordan, and look a little further into the quieter, less frequented parts of Petra.

If you have not yet been up to Ed Deir 'The Monastery', situated high above Wadi es Siyyagh and the distant Wadi Araba, this can be combined with a walk into one of Petra's three northern valleys, or to Beidah, the 9,000 year old Pleistocene settlement and nearby 'Little Petra' - Siq el Barrid.

Jebel Harun, the legendary burial place of Aaron, brother of Moses, is a sacred mountain well worth visiting. Go there, if you can, in the spring when the area around the white summit tomb is rich in flowers, in stark contrast to the barren mountains and canyons leading to the desert of Wadi Araba far below. The trek to Jebel Harun can be combined with a journey to the remote Roman Theatre in Wadi Sabra, a green oasis to the S either on foot or by camel, from where Nabataean and Roman camel routes lead W to Wadi Araba or S, to Wadi Rum and Aqaba. Other Bedouin trails go from Sabra up to Tayibah and Rajif high on the escarpment on the King's Highway.

Yet another old route from Petra descends a canyon close to Jebel Harun down to the windswept village of Bir Madhkhur in Wadi Araba. This same village can also be reached by 4 w.d. through the wild and beautiful valley of Wadi um Elda which is N of Wadi Musa. Once there, you can return on foot up the verdant canyon of Wadi es Siyyagh, past waterfalls and pools back into Petra - a long but incredible journey.

These are some of the walks and scrambles; there are other shorter ones in Petra itself which are seldom followed by tourists such as the Nabataean ways to the mountains of Al Khubtha and Umm el Biyyara, or to Petra's last aqueduct near the hidden Siq el Ma'jan. There are even guides tours at night under the stars. The routes are endless - here are a selection:

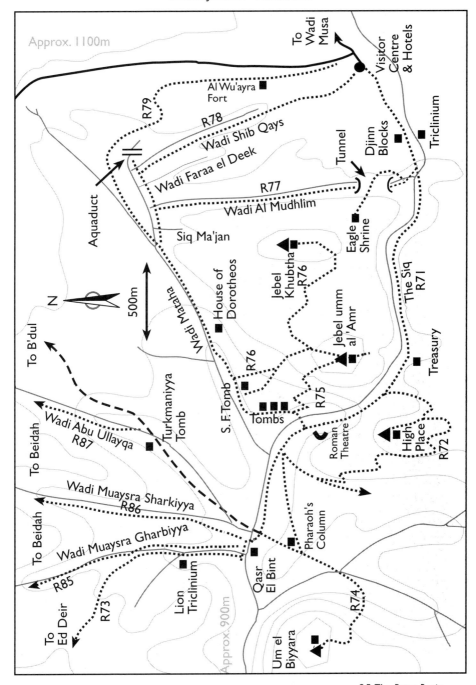

25. The Petra Basin

71. The Petra Siq

By far the most well travelled walk in the book! And why not - it is truly amazing, combining historical interest with majestic surroundings and a breath-taking entrance to Petra at The Treasury. It's unbeatable and unforgettable! Get there in the early morning before the day gets busy to catch the sun on the facade and to avoid the multitudes. Then spend the rest of the day enjoying Petra and perhaps including some of the other walks. Map 25.

Easy walk
3k, only 2hrs there and back but you will want to spend a full day seeing the sights!

The Route Really no description needed. Follow the track down from the Visitor Centre past the Petra Gate, (ticket, please), and on down the side of the wadi (taking a horse if you wish, but

only as far as the Siq entrance). Almost immediately the walk passes various monuments all well documented in the various guides to Petra, the most striking being the Djinn Blocks, The Obelisk Tomb and The Triclinium.

In about 0.5k you arrive at Bab es Siq - the entrance to The Siq. (The tunnel carved out of solid rock by the Nabataeans in AD50 to take any flood water away from The Siq is to the right - R77.) Once in The Siq you pass immediately beneath the remains of a Monumental Arch painted by David Roberts in 1839 - you will no doubt have seen it on postcards! Then on you go down The Siq marvelling at its proportions and torn between hurrying to see what lies round the next bend and wanting to linger and appreciate where you are. Along the way there are the remains of Nabataean water channels, sections of Roman road and various niches and shrines but what really impresses most apart from The Siq itself is the first view of The Treasury.

The Treasury   *Peter Hall*

After The Treasury, the walk continues down The Outer Siq, probably at a more leisurely pace as you feel you are now 'in' Petra and have time to look around, explore and enjoy the sights. As you emerge from this section of canyon about 0.5k further on, the steps leading to The High Place are on your left, the Roman Theatre is just beyond with the impressive Palace Tomb and Urn Tomb etc. up to the right. The Lower Petra Basin is 1k further on down the Roman road, finishing near Qasr el Bint beyond which are some small cafes and a restaurant. At this point the wadi slips mysteriously and temptingly into the canyon of Wadi Siyyagh through which it passes to Wadi Araba (R88) "... *beyond the Roman colonnades, the walls of the canyon close again and the well-worn paths of tourists end. The shadows of high mountains with tombs and castles on their tops draw closer as the dry bed of the wadi leaves the city and its ghosts to pass through pink flowered oleander bushes. Beyond, it finally disappears into the gloomy unseen recesses of the final canyon.*" Petra's Secret Canyon. Howard. 1985.

It is also in this area that the trails to Ed Deir (R73) and Beidah (R83 - 87) begin or end whilst the ways S to Jebel Harun, Wadi Sabra and beyond also start from this general area. The next five routes all start in the Petra Basin:

72. The High Place or Attuf Ridge
The way hardly needs description - it must be the second most popular route in this book being taken by most visitors to Petra: best to go very early or late to avoid the crowds! The panoramic view of Petra from the top couldn't be better! Map 25.

Easy walk with a bit of scrambling dependent on exact route.
2k up and down, allow 1-1½hrs to enjoy it, rising from 930m in The Outer Siq to 1070m on the top.

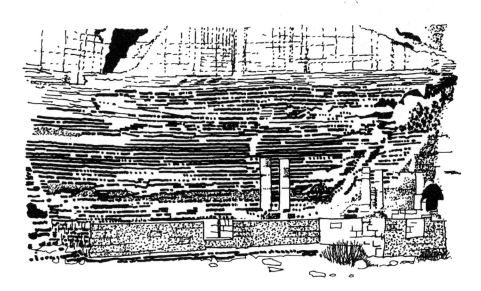

The Roman Theatre, Petra   *Peter Hall*

The Route The way is obvious, starting near the exit from the Outer Siq at a sign on the left. Follow Nabataean steps up the big ravine for 15mins then go right and up below a quarried wall with Crusader ruins above. From the col go right to reach the High Place with views around the Petra Basin and out towards Jebel Harun and Wadi Sabra. ½hr from the Outer Siq.

Descent Return down to the col (Bedu cafe). On the left are two stone 'Dushara' obelisks. Do not go left back down the ascent path but continue directly ahead to the S for about 150m before turning right (W) through cut passages and down steps and along a sandy path back below the High Place, on the W side of the mountain. Continue by steps over and round domes eventually descending left again through great mountain scenery and down past the Lion Fountain. Continue down cut stairways in colourful rock to reach the Garden Triclinium and the Roman Soldier Tomb. ½hr from the High Place. A further 10mins along the base of the mountain leads one to the top end of the Colonnade street, or, go down the obvious wadi to the Crusader Fort of El Habis and the cafes at the lower end of Petra. The Nabataean Restaurant in the Bedouin tent near Qasr El Bint is particularly popular and is run by local B'dul Bedouin whose families were born in Petra.

73. Ed Deir (The Monastery)

"We came out suddenly into unconfined air. Brown Eagles were slowly circling under our feet. Below these unquivering wings, red sandstone peaks and grey limestone flanks tumbled down into the sweltering trough of Arabah, here wider than we had hitherto seen it. Rivers of heat slid sluggishly along its devious channels. Far off, beyond the gulf, the blunt tops of Et Tih extended in phalanx. Only southward the view was checked, where Jebel Harun was blocked against the intense sky, holding up for all Islam to see, the white tomb which houses the bones of the Sheikh Harun."

In the Steps of Moses the Conqueror. L. Golding. 1938.

The way to Ed Deir is probably the third most frequented walk in this book combining great mountain atmosphere with a walk to a truly majestic antiquity site over 2,000 years old, with excellent views of Petra along the way as well as awe-inspiring views of Wadi Siyyagh and Wadi Araba just a few mins away to the W. Map 25.

Easy walk but in mountainous surroundings
2k for the round trip from and back to Qasr el Bint in the Petra Basin
Allow ½hr to enjoy the ascent rising over 200m to 1060m and the same for descent.

The Route From the cafes at the lower end of Petra, cross the bridge past the Forum Restaurant and go N up the stony wadi with oleanders, and up steps, in a little side valley on the left leading to the Lion Triclinium. Continue up the carved stairway, curving left and zig-zagging up to the NW. Eventually a cave will be seen in a cliff over to the left. This is 'the Hermitage' and can be reached by an easy scramble.

Back on the main stairway, it eventually becomes a cut passage on the edge of a ravine with spectacular views back down into Petra. After rising through a little pass, the track arrives unexpectedly on a plateau with the amazing 'Monastery' revealing itself impressively on the right and a welcome Bedouin tea shop in a cave on the left, run by the Daqlalah family. (They were actually living here in 1984 when we first visited Petra, but in 1985 the B'dul Bedouin were all moved out of their homes in the tombs and caves of Petra into what was then the new B'dul village.)

Ed Deir 'the Monastery'   *Peter Hall*

It was possible until recently, following a fatal accident, to climb steps on the left of 'Ed Deir' to reach its top. To see someone up there is to truly appreciate its size but it is unfortunately no longer permitted and the steps have been blocked by a rather unsightly new wall.

Whilst at the Monastery, it is worth making the 5min walk out W rising slightly up the plateau away from Ed Deir to reach the lip of the huge canyon of Wadi es Siyyagh and views of wild mountain and desert scenery; a good place for the sunset if you have made the necessary arrangements to stay the night in this inspiring place.

Descent is by the same route. Allow a similar time or, you can take the route to Beidah (R83). A much less travelled and rather more difficult route to a Petra mountain top is that to:

74. Umm el Biyyara

The imposing mountain whose sheer cliffs dominate Petra to the W.The route to it and up it is not always obvious and once found is quite steep and exciting in places! There is an excavated Edomite village on the top, with cisterns and inscriptions in Greek and Nabataean, also, of course, excellent views of Petra and the surrounding mountains.

Don't attempt this route without a guide unless you are confident on rock and have a head for heights. At the very least, take the advice of the sign at Pharaoh's Column "Attention - venturing from the regular route on your own is not advisable. It is highly recommended that should you wish to do so beyond this point we strongly advise either a local guide or at least one companion." Map 25.

Guide recommended.
Easy scramble, but quite exposed in places.
2k from the Roman Theatre, I - 2hrs to the top, climbing almost 300m to 1160m at the summit. Allow the same time for the descent.

The Route Follow the broad track W from just beyond the Roman Theatre to Pharaoh's Column and descend into the wadi ahead. 100m after crossing the wadi, go right towards a stony gully 50m left of some tombs. Pass through a rocky defile into a little basin surrounded by caves then out through the other side and up diagonally left past more small caves and a juniper then zig-zag left and right to enter the gully at a new wall.

Go up the ravine which presents two majestic incut ramps in corridors to the left or right. Continue up the ravine above the ramps (cairns) and up a defile, moving right into a parallel

The carved Nabataean way to Umm el Biyyara   Peter Hall

124

corridor. Above, steps zig-zag up right to a stepped corridor followed by more steps left from a large dead juniper and along a cut edge to 'Bedouin steps' (Grade 1, exposed). Above, more ledges and steps zig-zag up the mountain then left along a cut path into a gully, then right to a terrace. Go immediately left again onto the SW shoulder and up a gully (Bedouin steps) to the top, where the end is marked by a cairn so you can re-locate it for the descent!

Take some time to wander round the remains of an Edomite settlement, also Nabataean sites and cisterns (particularly on the E side overlooking Petra). To the NW there are some caves and, after a little scramble (Grade 1), good views down Wadi es Siyyagh towards Wadi Araba. There is almost no wood, so don't damage the trees to make a fire.

A shorter and easier scramble takes you to the top of:

75. Jebel umm al 'Amr
A seldom visited Petra mountain but nevertheless interesting with excellent views from the top. Map 25.

Easy scramble
Less than 1k, ¾hour for the ascent from 900m in the valley below the Urn Tomb to the top at 1070m; slightly less for the descent to the Florentinus Tomb.

The Route Start below the Urn tomb, taking the staircase on the right as you approach from Lower Petra. It's then a 30min climb. There are four 'high-places' on top and a large walled cistern. To the right it is only a short way up domes and steps to fine views over Petra, particularly of The Roman Theatre positioned perfectly below, and The High Place, opposite. There is also a scramble down to an unusual view of The Treasury:

The Treasury Viewpoint From the cistern, instead of back down the gully to the Florentinus tomb, go left (S) down a little valley for 5mins to reach a platform above the inner entrance to The Siq and opposite The Khazneh. Return the same way. **(The loose gully which continues directly down to reach the Outer Siq just opposite The Khazneh is dangerous and should not be descended.)**

Descent Go NW through the steep valley of Wadi Zarnuq with a spectacular section cut through vertical rock on the left side. Follow the gorge (the way over boulders is sometimes rather difficult in places - see R76) until it ends near the Sextius Florentinus Tomb.

76. Jebel Khubtha via Jebel umm al 'Amr
A more difficult way up going all the way to the two summits for those wanting to test their rock scrambling and route finding skills! Map 25.

Moderate scramble
1k, 1hr for the ascent, climbing from 930m to 1130m; similar for the descent.

The Route 10m right of the Sextius Florentinus Tomb, large steps lead to an in-cut corridor gained by a huge step! It is left with greater difficulty (Grade 2) up the right wall to regain the steps. Follow these up to the upper reaches of Wadi Zarnuq. (Wadi Zarnuq can be followed all the way up from the left side of the Florentinus Tomb by scrambling between boulders and bushes (see R75); easier, but not as enjoyable or interesting as the above way.) The gully ends

The Petra Basin   *Peter Hall*

at a wall and above are the remains of a cistern, 20mins from the Tomb. To the right it is only a short way up domes and steps to Jebel umm al 'Amr and fine views over Petra, particularly of The Roman Theatre and The High Place opposite.

To the left is the way to the summit of Jebel Khubtha - the big flat-topped mountain behind the Forum Hotel. Go E across the little plateau and left to pass domes, in a cut corridor. Follow steps into and out of a wadi and left round the next domes. Now, trend right between domes (some steps) to a little grassy plateau. Here, go left up a stony slope towards the flat-topped summit then right between domes again. (Remember the way, it is a real maze up here!)

At the base of the big summit dome, go right to the skyline arete where steps can be seen. Follow these up (quite exposed), to reach the top and fine views all round. 30mins from the cistern.

Descent is by the same route.

Having spent some time in Petra and entered through The Siq you may well want to enter or return from Petra by alternative routes:

77. Petra via Wadi al Mudhlim
To appreciate the ingenuity and hard work put in by the Nabataeans, in AD50, this 'side entrance' into Petra is worth taking as a variation. **Do not enter after rain, or if rain may be imminent here, or in the hills to the east.** *Map 25.*

Easy canyon
4k, just over an hour to the Petra Basin. Difficulty dependent on the amount of water in

the siq - it could be more than waist deep, or maybe none at all!

The Route Walk down to just before The Bab es Siq (the start of the Siq) then go right and follow the wadi bed N through a tunnel cut by the Nabataeans to divert flood water from the siq. (A detour can be made before entering the tunnel, by going over its roof then right as far as the second valley on the left up which are several niches carved in the rock including the beautiful Eagle Shrine.)

Once through the tunnel, the stony river bed continues for 1k, with many oleander bushes, eventually narrowing to a ravine only 1m wide with smooth twisting walls and pools. Towards the end, near the deepest pool are small shrines, after which it meets the equally narrow Siq Al Ma'jan at a T-junction. Downstream to the W is joined by Siq al Ujul before emerging into Wadi Mataha, with tombs on the left and, across the valley, the caves of Mughur an Nasra. 1k further downstream, the Sextius Florentinus Tomb will be found on the left, as the whole Petra Basin opens out before you.

Exiting at the same place is:

78. Petra via Wadi Shib Qays
Another route to or from Petra with a rather off-putting start by the waste overflow from the Petra Forum Hotel. Don't worry - it definitely gets better! Map 25.

Easy scramble with possible pools at the exit.
5k, 1¼hrs to the Petra Basin (longer with detours).

The Route From the right side of the Hotel follow the wadi down easily, passing the start of an incut Nabataean irrigation channel in the right wall which continues down the wadi. Keeping left, continue through bushes and caves and on down the wadi to a T-junction 1k from the start. (Go right to find Petra's last remaining aqueduct which doesn't look like it will last much longer!)

Go left at the T-junction down Wadi al Ma'jan which is a

Petra's last aqueduct   *Peter Hall*

beautiful narrow siq polished by water (dangerous if rain is possible, and necessary to wade through pools if it has rained recently). There are some awkward steps down jammed boulders (Grade 2). After passing Wadi Faraa el Deek, another narrow siq enters from the left (Wadi Mudhlim, R77). A jammed log 10m above is all the evidence one needs of the strength and depth of the flood waters!

Continue down the polished and winding siq passing a cluster of votive niches to emerge 50m beyond into Wadi al Mataha where a wall has been built to divert the water away from the left side of the valley. It is now 10mins walk past the House of Dorotheos to the Sextius Florentinus Tomb with the Petra Basin beyond.

79. Wadi al Mataha and Al Wu'ayra fort from Petra
This alternative route out of Petra passes by the Sextius Florentinus tomb and the Crusader fortress of Al Wu'ayra to Wadi Musa. The walk is easy and interesting but route finding is a little complex. Map 25.

Easy scramble
5k. About 1½hrs from Qasr el Bint.

The Route Walk up the colonnaded Roman road to the Sextius Florentinus tomb and continue NE up the right side of the valley past many rainbow coloured rocks and caves until the mountain side meets the wadi. Descend a wall into the river-bed. (The narrow siq on the right is the exit of Wadi al Mudhlim - the stream which the Nabataeans diverted from The Siq, down through a tunnel - see R77.)

Do not enter this, but keep in the main valley and take the next prominent right fork. This rises up a little, then continues in the same direction above the other tributary. Eventually an obvious wadi goes right at 90°. Follow this up into a little flat green valley seemingly surrounded by cliffs. (A cairn on the fort can be seen ahead, on the cliff top and if you continue slightly right and up a ravine you will pass below the fortress bridge but there is no easy way on.)

Instead, go back left up a side entrance and then take an obvious easy ramp of white rock or scree up right until it levels off on rock terraces 100m below the Wadi Musa - B'dul road. Follow the road S keeping below it, passing the entrance of the fort after 5mins. Petra Visitor Centre is 15mins further on.

The northern approaches to Petra
"The Arabs of Petra [were sent] up their hills into the forest towards Shobek. It was an uncaring march in the hoar mist, that of these frozen footed peasants in their sheepskins, up and down sharp valleys and dangerous hill-sides, out of whose snow-drifts, the heavy trunks of junipers, grudging in leaves, jutted like castings in grey iron."
Seven Pillars of Wisdom. T. E. Lawrence. 1929.

Coming in from the N you can connect with treks from Shaubak and Dana or even as far away as Selah and Buseirah making a five day trip to reach Petra. See the relevant sections in this book. The adventure travel companies mentioned at the start of the South Jordan section of this book all have their own favourite variations on this theme. Contact them for details.

The northern outposts of Petra are:

Petra Area

Above: Cleaning the water hole, the Waters of Tibn. R97 (98, 99)

Above Right: 'Bedouin bridge' for pack animals, Tibn Siq. R98

Above: Scrambling out from the ravine to reach Wadi Saada, en route from the Waters of Bahra to the Waters of Tibn. R102

Left: At the Waters of Bahra. R101

Wadi Rum

Top: Wadi Rum village and Jebel Nassrani seen from rocky towers above the village

Centre: Camel riders dwarfed by the immense towers of Jebel Nassrani, Wadi Rum

The people of Rum

Right: Ever-ready hospitality at a Bedouin camp in Wadi Rum

Rum Area

Right: Crossing the exposed canyon wall of the 2,000 year old Thamudic Way up Jebel Rum. R106

Centre: View out across the desert from the ledge above the canyon of the Thamudic Way up Jebel Rum. R106

Below: Small figures scrambling across 'the pink slabs' to enter the maze of Rakabat Canyons, seen from a rock climb on the cliffs above. R109

4-wheel drive - Moab, Rum and Araba

Left: Driving down into Wadi ibn Hammad. R47

Centre: Driving through the Sand Canyon of Wadi Salaada in the south of Rum. R114

Bottom: Driving into the final Siq of Wadi Heimar from Wadi Araba. R118

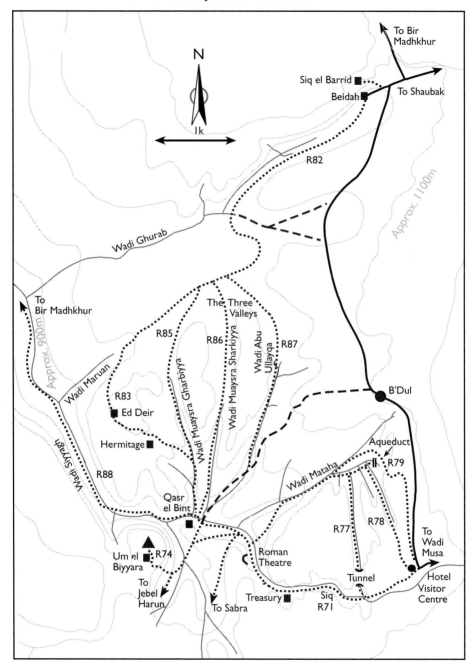

Beidah and Siq el Barrid (Little Petra)

Beidah is a Natufian site (late Pleistocene) dating back around 10,000 years and used regularly by hunter gatherers of that period, with many flint and chert tools and artefacts discovered in the excavations. It is 8k N of Petra at 1050m, dominated by the steep faces of sandstone from which Petra is carved. The excavated site of Beidah is 10mins walk on a good (driveable) track to the left of the car park. It is drained by the seasonal Wadi el Ghurab 'Valley of the Raven' which originates on Jebel Shara, named after a Nabataean god, to the NE and meets Wadi Slehsil, 'The place of steep cliffs' 1k further on before falling steeply into Wadi el Siyyagh and Wadi Araba.

Nabataean tomb, Siq el Barrid   *Peter Hall*

Close by to the NE, just 0.5k away is Siq el Barrid, the Northern Caravanserai for Nabataean Petra, often referred to as 'Little Petra'. It is visible in a ravine just beyond the car park, and well worth a visit for its own unique carvings.

Approach Walk or drive from the Shaubak area (R70) or, more likely, from Wadi Musa - drive down to the lower end of town and follow the road as it turns right just before the Visitor Centre. Continue past the village of B'dul through increasingly pleasant scenery with sandstone domes exhibiting Nabataean steps and caves to arrive after 8k at Siq el Barrid. There is a huge Nabataean water cistern cut into the rock near the car park.

The Beidah - Wadi Araba Road

About 2k N of Beidah the small Wadi Araba - Bir Madhkhur road which soon becomes a 4 w.d. track, forks left (NW) from the main road and goes through a very nice area of domes near Siq um el Hiran at 1k and on to the pretty Siq um el Alda at 6k where it starts the descent to Wadi Araba, reaching Bir Madhkhur after about 25k, or forking right at 20k to head NW across another 20k of wild 'African' desert country through scattered Acacia trees to reach the Feinan road.

80. Jebel Baaga and Wadi Thugra

Follow the above road for 4k from the main road to where the valley of Wadi Jabu can be followed up E for 2k into Baaga Siq. The small summit of Baaga (1110m) is directly above with a Nabataean trail, cistern and gardens. Not checked by the authors, but said to be worthwhile.

81. Beidah to Shaubak or Feinan

Just beyond Wadi Jabu and before Siq um el Alda is a possible trail up the reputedly scenic and historic valley of Wadi Thugra into Wadi Hudeib and all the way N for almost 20k to meet tracks from Shaubak or Feinan. It is believed to offer excellent trekking opportunities with some Roman and Ottoman antiquities. Not checked by the authors but worth exploring. Info. provided by Petra Moon Travel. They and possibly some of the other local Adventure Travel Companies can help - please keep us informed!

82. Beidah (Little Petra) to 'the three valleys'

To do any of the walks between Beidah and Petra, it is first of all necessary to understand this part of the region which crosses the valley of Beidah known as Wadi el Ghurab. This is not so much a walk in itself as the key to the walks between Beidah and Petra. Nevertheless it is a nice quiet valley "far from the madding crowds" of Petra so even a short walk down here is a pleasant experience. Map 26.

Easy walk
3 - 4k, 1 - 1½hrs. Allow 2 - 3hrs if you're just going for a stroll and returning perhaps by the track which leads back out towards B'dul.

The Route From Beidah, follow Wadi Ghurab down pleasantly in idyllic surroundings, the wide track becoming a footpath where it crosses the river bed about 20mins from the car park, near some dunes. A little further on, the cliffs close in to the river and, just after, the landscape opens out as the river bends right.

Take a wide track up left from here (small tomb cut into the nose of the mountain, just above). Continue on the good track, passing right of an isolated rock lump. (About ½hr from the start.)

There is now extensive ploughed land to the right and, not very obvious, a fan of small but deep sandy wadies. To avoid this area, continue about 100m past the rock buttress to where a small track goes right (S) at right angles to the main track, between the fields. It meets another major track a little further on, just at the head of the sandy incut wadies. (Both these main tracks are driveable and meet the Wadi Musa - Beidah road about 3k S of Beidah on the way to B'dul.)

At this point, turn right and follow the good track past the heads of several more of the little sandy wadies to a fork. Keep right (small white rocky dome ahead), between fields. The track splits again; this time go straight on, ignoring the right fork and after 100m there is an area of white flat rocks on the left. You are now above the first of 'the three valleys':

Wadi Abu Ullayqa (See R87) Has fields at its mouth and is identified by a view of B'dul village beyond if you descend into it. Also, if you look closely in the small white domes between this valley and the next to the W you will see a few incut steps leading to two small shrines.

The second of the three valleys is:

Wadi Muaysra as Sharkiyya (See R86) This is distinguished by a long straight and high dark coloured cliff on its right (W) side. To reach it, continue from above the first valley on an indistinct path, left across the head of the wadi towards the low point on the far W skyline. Cross a small tributary which descends into the main wadi, go over a small rise and enter the main wadi by an obvious little stream bed. (About 5 - 10mins from the first valley.)

The third valley is:

Wadi Muaysra al Gharbiyya (See R85) Continue for another 5 - 10mins over the next rise (the mountain on the left between the middle and last valleys is split by a big vertical chimney) and down into the left side of the valley entrance on white rock. (Two little towers on the crest of the rock wall opposite identify the valley.)

The way to Ed Dier also uses the same route to this point (about 1¼hrs from the car park). Instead of going down into these valleys, continue in the same direction, generally W and descend into a wadi (Wadi Maruan) which descends gently W towards the escarpment edge, reaching the last little ploughed field just a few m wide above the edge of the cliffs in about 10mins. (1½hrs from car park.)

If travelling in the opposite direction (Petra to Beidah), the way to Beidah from the heads of these valleys, up Wadi al Ghurab is hidden behind the dark red mountain to the NE. **Do not take the direct way across the fields, but follow the tracks as described above, in reverse. (Circuitous but easy and no damage to the agricultural land.)**

83. Ed Deir to Beidah
From Ed Deir (The Monastery), the walk goes through rugged mountain scenery to the pastoral land above the three valleys, and so to Beidah. The way involves some scrambling on rock down a small cliff. When it is included (as it must be), with the walk to Ed Deir from Petra it makes an excellent round trip though you will either need to get a lift back from Beidah which should not be difficult, or walk back through one of the three valleys. Map 26.

Easy scramble, but route finding not always obvious
6k. 2½hrs from Ed Deir.

Approach From Petra Rest House, it's about 1½hrs up to 'The Monastery' of Ed Deir - R73 - with Bedouin tea and soft drinks available in a nearby cave. (From the Monastery, it is first of all worth making a little detour out W for 5mins to the lip of the huge ravine of Wadi es Siyyagh, an excellent viewpoint - particularly if you've already been down there or are thinking of coming up it!)

The Route From the Monastery follow the wide rock plateau N keeping close to the cliffs. After 200m there is a recess on the right entered by a rising rock ledge. At the back of the bay will be found a cave with carvings of camels and men right of its entrance.

Back on the main rock plateau, a little wadi soon descends through a gap in the rocks, then widens to a small open area, and narrows again. **At this point, do not go down it further (it soon drops steeply over a cliff).** Instead go easily up a rock terrace to the right, just below the main cliff and only about 5mins from Ed Deir. Very soon, the view down into Wadi es Siyyagh opens out, and its junction with Wadi Maruan coming SW from the area of Beidah is seen.

Now, do not go further along the terrace but descend by zig-zagging down ledges and chimneys in the cliff (Grade 1) to scree slopes below. (15mins from Ed Deir.)

At this point take a poorly defined path NE along the very base of the cliff, contouring round with some scrambling over boulders to reach a long sandy terrace below overhangs. Follow this easily, in wild scenery, passing a little side wadi (about 10mins from the cliff descent) until, just after the point where the tomb on the summit of Jebel Harun is visible behind, it is necessary to go up ledges for about 50m into the mouth of the next side wadi. (There is a small man-made wall here, behind a Juniper.) Go up again, past the stump of a felled tree to the next rock terrace. Follow this past Bedouin cave shelters in a small ravine and continue at the same level as the terrace rapidly opens out passing another side wadi. Continue on again, on rock terraces which wind round above Wadi Maruan, eventually meeting it at a little walled field in its bed (about 1¼hrs from Ed Deir).

From here, go up the wadi (marked by a small red-black rock tower), past more little walls and fields, then up easy white slabs to emerge above ploughed fields close to the entrances to the three valleys. The dark red mountain concealing the valley of Beidah is visible to the NE. Follow R82 back or continue on:

84. Wadi Musa, Ed Deir, Wadi Ghurab, round trip
If you're feeling fit, instead of walking the last 2k back to Beidah, why not take one of the three valleys back down into Petra. A superb round trip! Maps 25 and 26.

Moderate trek
14k, 6 - 7hrs with about 300m of ascent and descent.

The Route follow R73 and 83 to Wadi Ghurab then take any of the three valleys back to Petra, and so to Wadi Musa perhaps combining R86 and R79 for example.

The Three Valleys:

85. Beidah to Petra via Wadi Muaysra al Gharbiyya
A pleasant walk in verdant surroundings to the Petra Basin. Map 26.

Easy walk
7k. About 2½hrs

The Route Follow R82 to the head of the wadi. Descend into the valley entrance down white slabs, cross a little side wadi at its head near a large juniper and continue down to enter the main valley of Gharbiyya on its left. Continue on the left through small white rock domes and bits of ploughed land to the lip of the wadi and the first view of Petra.

Descend into it through a defile in the rocks and follow it down until a tomb is seen on the left. Continue down on quite well defined paths. Eventually the track passes a huge split boulder and goes along carved ledges and down purple slabs (some cut steps) to regain the wadi bed.

Continue through oleander bushes which are soon escaped by a rock terrace on the right leading to an area of well carved tombs on the left. Soon, Qasr el Bint comes into sight and after more oleanders, the stream bed drops into a rocky ravine at a bend in an area of many tombs. The path to Ed Deir is visible below. **Do not go down here, there is a vertical drop of 5m!** Instead follow a path left and out into the Petra Basin.

86. Beidah to Petra via Wadi Muaysra as Sharkiyya

The central of the three valleys. A beautiful and constantly interesting valley descending into Petra. Map 26.

Easy walk
7k. About 2½hrs

The Route Follow R82 to the head of the valley. A meandering little stream bed then goes down into the right side of the valley amongst beautiful scenery, until it meets the big cliff face on the right. Here, the wadi bed drops into a tree-filled cleft but the path, which is carved into the rock, continues along the foot of the cliff with the wadi on its left (some pools in spring time), to a junction with a side valley from the right. (Well carved tomb here.) About ½hr from the valley head.

From here, the way down follows the wadi bed, sometimes changing sides (more pools here in spring), emerging eventually in an area of tombs on both sides of the valley. Just beyond here, cross to the left side and continue down past more tombs, going easily down rocks into Wadi Abu Ullayqa, just before Qasr el Bint in the bottom of the Petra Basin.

87. Petra to Beidah via Wadi Abu Ullayqa

The first and most easterly of the three valleys. A road from the B'dul Bedouin village enters Petra down the lower third of this valley, so it makes a fairly quick way back out if you have done one of the other walks and left a car at Beidah. The last two thirds of the valley are nevertheless interesting and may involve wading through one or more pools in spring-time. Map 26.

Easy scramble, perhaps with pools to pass.
7k, 2hrs rising 150m, to 1050m.

The Route From the Nabataean Cafe by Qasr el Bint, follow the road to B'dul up the wadi of Abu Ullayqa passing a new dam and the Turkmaniyya Tomb, at which point the road leaves the wadi to wind up hairpins to the village (about 20mins from Petra).

Now, carry on up the right side of the wadi, on footpaths to where the cliffs close in. Continue in the stony wadi bed through a small gorge almost blocked by a large boulder, to a junction of wadies marked by a huge old tree.

Avoid the narrow siq to the right and keep straight on. It splits again after 50m, and here the way goes left avoiding the oleander choked bed by a goat track on the rocks 10m above it. Continue in the same line, crossing the next right junction then descending into the ravine and passing under another huge boulder (possible pool here may need wading through). Continue up the wadi, scrambling up boulders until it levels out into a beautiful secluded upper valley (about 1hr from Petra).

Follow this up until it forks with a Juniper in the left fork. Take this (the right side is blocked) and rejoin it again after 50m. Carry straight on, along the right side of a rock tower which divides the wadi ahead, to reach a small ploughed plot of land. Fork left here and continue on white rock between small domes to emerge on the Beidah plateau. B'dul village is still visible behind and there are a couple of little incut shrines up some steps on the left. Reverse R82 back from here, to Beidah and Siq el Barrid.

Now we come to something rather more serious - a great way into Petra from Wadi Araba:

The western approaches to Petra
The western caravanserais for Nabataean Petra were at the foot of the mountains where the last sources of water are before the windswept sands of Wadi Araba. One was at Gharandal, to the SW en route from Sinai and Egypt, another was at Khirbat Tayibeh 15k S of Bir Madhkhur, at the mouth of Wadi Tayibeh from the ruins of which an old track goes to Petra. The third was at Bir Madhkhur immediately W of Petra through which routes from the Negev passed on their way to the ancient city.

Nabataean tomb at the caravanserai of Siq el Barrid

Peter Hall

From Bir Madhkhur, one route then took a detour to the N of the barrier of mountains which form the formidable western wall of the old city, going up through Wadi Namada and Siq um el Alda to reach Petra via Siq el Barrid. This is now a driveable track. Another took a more direct but steeper way commencing in the lower end of Wadi Siyyagh. This is the continuation of the Wadi Musa stream which passes through the Petra Basin before disappearing into a chasm in the heart of these rugged mountains. It then avoided the increasingly difficult canyon by taking a side valley reaching the outskirts of Petra on a plateau between Petra and Jebel Harun. (See R89.) The third follows the impressive canyon directly:

88. Wadi es Siyyagh to Petra
"It was good, at last, to be off on our own, walking up the early morning canyon, hills striped with dark coloured intrusions of basalt slowly closing in around us and then suddenly, hungrily, swallowing us into the deep recesses of a cool ravine, to be greeted by that most beautiful of desert sounds, running water. Only a hundred metres back down the wadi we had been in bare dust brown hills and now as we rounded the bend, a waterfall cascaded into a pool surrounded by a jungle of tall green fragmites. As we parted the dense undergrowth, startled birds chattered in alarm and a dark green frog plopped into the pool."

Petra's Secret Canyon. Howard. 1985.

A great day out, packed full of surprises! Starting from a dry wadi bed near Bir Madhkhur, and heading into what appear to be barren and inhospitable mountains, it is not long before you arrive at water in a lush green canyon. The way on is continually interesting, first passing Nabataean irrigation systems then scrambling over rocks and round pools. At one stage the route is forced out of the canyon bed by an impassable waterfall in a narrow ravine; higher some Grade 3 climbing is necessary to pass another waterfall which plunges into a very tempting pool - a great place for a swim which, a few hours earlier, you would have said was an impossibility! More scrambling is needed beyond before emerging into hidden verdant gardens just below the Petra Basin. Map 24.

Guide recommended and a rope for those without climbing experience.

Moderate canyon
16k. 7-10hrs, rising from 800m to 1030m at the Visitor Centre

Approach Coming from Wadi Araba, leave the highway at the signposted desert track about 100k N of Aqaba and drive to the Police Post and village at Bir Madhkhur, a distance of about 8k. Or, drive down to Bir Madhkhur from Beidah. If you have a 4 w.d. vehicle it is then best to drive by desert tracks S then SE to enter Seil Wadi Musa, and up this to a point where driving becomes increasingly difficult (10k from Bir Madhkhur), just past an area of high vertical wadi walls above which is a ruin and, a little further on, a concealed burial ground. Just beyond here is a pleasant camping area, from where the trek begins.

The Route Go easily E up the wadi bed for 1k passing the wadi which goes up SE to below Jebel Harun (R89). (The tomb of Aaron, brother of Moses, is visible as a small white building on the summit.) Here, the going becomes ever more difficult through almost jungle terrain between the canyon walls, with a stream of running water, waterfalls, pools and even frogs and crabs and of course many birds. Some scrambling on granite cliffs (Grade 2) past incut Nabataean irrigation channels is necessary to pass the deeper pools. After 1k of this terrain, the wadi turns abruptly S below a 200m granite and basalt wall, and opens out for a while with a good track high on the E side of the valley, below the cliffs, finally narrowing again after 3k and turning SE. The going is still fairy easy, in amazing, spectacular scenery following the main wadi, past other wadies which enter first on the left, then on the right. (There is a way up E from here to Wadi Ghurab and Beidah.) Eventually the wadi becomes impossible to follow, entering a vertical walled canyon (Wadi es Siq). Here, the water is waist deep and the way is blocked first by a giant boulder then an 8m waterfall!

We wrote about it as 'Petra's Secret Canyon' in 1985 *"There, in the gloomy recesses, the vertical sides of the canyon plunged directly into a murky pool beyond which the way on was blocked by a giant boulder wedged across the gap, its lower end leaving only a chink of light above the water. Wilfried, the French member of our team, otherwise known affectionately as 'Le Frog' was obviously better suited than most to probe the depths of this watery barrier and stepped into the pool, grimacing as the green water rose up to his waist. He prodded cautiously at some slime covered sticks floating, seemingly innocuously, in the gloom but concealing who knows what strange creatures. Satisfied that nothing was lurking in the depths he eventually reached the boulder. Peering through the gap above the waterline he could see nothing and with a struggle he climbed up onto its top. The way on was blocked by yet another boulder more massive than the first, completely barring any progress."*

Forced out of the canyon, take a steep goat track up the hillside on the S just below the barrier cliff and pass through the second col on the left, after which descend a stone shoot on its right, first slightly leftwards then along ledges climbing across basalt columns (Grade 2) back rightwards before dropping down to another pool below a waterfall. Good swimming place! To escape from here climb a pink granite rib on its left, going left up a black wall with the help of a jammed 'Bedouin' log. Continue up until it is possible to descend a rock gully to regain the wadi above a second, higher waterfall and pool. (This section involves Grade 3 climbing.)

From here follow the wadi until the walls narrow again and more climbing still on granite (Grade 3) or wading through a rather green long pool give access to the last section of the wadi. Here, man-made walls are soon seen, indicating the lower end of a paradise of Bedouin gardens with fruit trees, date palms and vegetable gardens. Continue up with care through these well irrigated gardens, probably of Nabataean origin but called The Roman Gardens by the Bedouin, eventually climbing above them to a track below the cliffs on the N side of the canyon where the first signs of Nabataean quarrying will be seen. A good track will eventually be joined in the wadi bottom and before long the tombs of Petra appear in the distance. Just round the corner from here is the first Bedouin cafe and the Forum Restaurant. Another 4k up the track through Petra and The Siq leads to the Visitor Centre.

89. Wadi Maqtal to Petra
This, we are told is one of the old camel routes from Bir Madhkhur. As mentioned above, it starts in Wadi Siyyagh but leaves it almost immediately, ascending the obvious wadi to the right, just E of a long sandstone ridge and below a prominent black summit, with Jebel Harun and its white summit tomb visible in the distance. From the head of the wadi the route then picks up the tracks between Jebel Harun and Petra to the NE. Not checked by the authors, but ask one of the Adventure Travel Companies in Wadi Musa. Map 24.

90. Petra to Jebel Harun
"*Every step opened out fresh interest and beauty in the wild scenery, immense chasms and vast views over strange boundless desert unfolded themselves at each turn of the winding path up the steep mountain; ... the slow advance chills with a feeling of strange solitude the intruder into the loneliness of this bygone world*"
Edward Lear. 13 April 1858 en route to Jebel Harun

A great mountain walk in the footsteps of the Prophets followed by Burkhardt when he 'discovered' Petra back in 1812. The route passes through the heart of Petra then escapes the crowds for the breezy heights of the tomb of Aaron with its superb panoramic views. Camels can be taken to the foot of the mountain. Maps 24, 27 and 28.

Guide necessary if you want go by camel or to enter the Shrine

Moderate trek
11k, 3½ - 4hrs, descending about 100m to the Petra Basin then rising 370m to the summit at 1270m. Allow almost the same for the return journey - or combine the walk with other treks to make a longer trip in this wild and mountainous part of Jordan.

The Route Walk down into Petra and follow the broad track which leaves Petra just past the bend after the Roman Theatre area and rises W over the hill of Katuta to Pharaoh's Column. Continue along the new, wide track, descending into and crossing Wadi Ras Suleiman below Umm el Biyyara, and on towards the Snake Monument which it passes below before curving

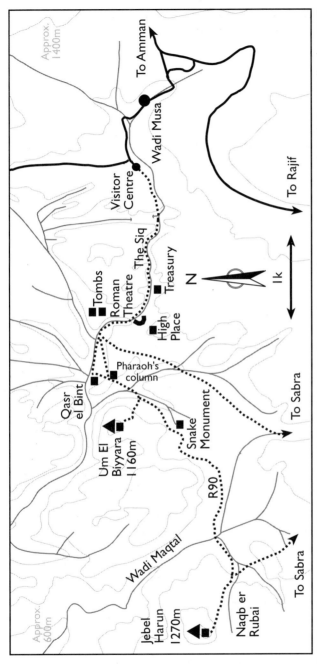

27. Petra to Jebel Harun

back above it near the Djinn Block, to a plateau.

The broad track stops just ahead, at which point Jebel Harun can be seen again. Here, there are three currently occupied caves on the left. Carry straight on, along footpaths crossing the tributaries of Wadi Maqtal (R89), and continuing S, rising up a shoulder, parallel to a branch of the wadi. Carry on, eventually crossing this wadi and following a distinct path round a shoulder and up a gentle valley, before rising up to the saddle on the far skyline. Zig-zag back on a good path winding through cliffs, to a flat area of land below the S side of the summit.

Continue on (ruins on left) turning right at the end with a great view through the gap of Naqb er Rubai to Wadi Araba (see R91). Above is the retaining wall of a huge Nabataean underground cistern with water called Bir Huweimel which is well worth seeing. The path then goes through a gate and across the roof of the cistern then up steps hewn in the rock to the summit. A place perhaps for meditation on the legendary events that took place on this remote mountain top " ... *and the children of Israel whom God had forbidden to fight with Edom or to force a way through his land journeyed from Kadesh and came to Mount Hor [Jebel Harun] ... this mountain is of very difficult and steep ascent, rude steps and niches being cut in the rock to help the traveller. Here Moses and Eleazor, by God's command, accompanied Aaron to the top of the mount, where Moses took off his brother's sacerdotal robes to put them on Eleazor his son, for the high priest's service and life were about to close. And Aaron died there on the top of the mount, and Moses and Eleazor came down from it sorrowfully."*

Palestine Past and Present. L. Valentine. c1918.

The southern approaches to Petra

There were a number of ancient trade routes up to Petra from the S and Wadi Araba to the W. They were documented by Dr Fawzi Zayadine in 'Archaeology of Jordan', 1985, a report which makes interesting reading. It includes the routes already described above as well as those from the S:

91. Ancient routes to Petra

The following is from Fawzi Zayadine's report in 'Archaeology of Jordan', 1985:

The Journey of Sultan Baibars. 1276.

"Looking for the exact route of Sultan Baibars into Petra in 1276, I was able to walk or trace, with help of the Bedouins, six access roads from Wadi 'Araba. To the south, the route Suez-Ma'an ascends by Wadi Gharandal (Aridella) to Sadaqa (Sadagatta). It was possible to travel by Landrover from the village of Garandal through Wadi es-Siq, a narrow colourful gorge, strewn with large boulders, and reach Delagha in two hours (30Km.). At el-Rajef, the explorer can enjoy a most fascinating panorama of the sandstone mountain range of Petra. At 3 Kilometres from Delagha, a road bifurcates to Sadaqa or descends through Tayyibeh to Wadi Musa. Parallel to the Suez-Ma' an route, runs the Suez-Petra track which can reach the Nabataean capital from Wadi 'Araba by Wadi Sabra, Wadi Abu Khusheibeh or Naqb el-Ruba'i, the latter being the easiest for camels (Major C.S. Jarvis had problems with his loaded camels in the ascent of Abu Khusheibeh. See below.) This caravan road was probably described by Strabo as the track from Babylon to Egypt by Petra.

A fifth outlet to Wadi Araba runs through Wadi Musa. A large terraced area, called Roman Garden by the Bedouin, extends at its mouth, west of Qasr Umm Rattam. A water reservoir at the northern side of the tower is fed by a long channel which drains the wadi's water. From there, a steep and narrow track climbs up to Petra by Wadi el-Siyyagh or to Beida by Sleisel. Finally, an easier outlet to the North, can cross to the Negev through Beida, Siq Umm el 'Alda, Namala and Bir Madhkur.

Baibars, who was eager to reach Karak in a short time, had travelled by the shortest way (five days from Cairo to Petra). The last segment of his track had certainly impressed the chronicler:

'And thus, at the break of dawn, he ascended the Mountain, and wondrous high it was, cut with tortuous ravines, and these of crumbling stones, resemblance unto hardened sand, changing in their hues from red to azure and white; thither also were defiles in the mountains admitting the horseman riding through, in which are places as though rising steps hewn in the rock. On this mountain is the tomb of Aaron, Prophet of God, the brother of Moses, son of Umrân, peace upon them, on the left of the traveller whose face is unto Damascus.'

The description of the itinerary by Nuwairi is accurate. Actually, the road which traverses Naqb el-Ruba'i by Jibal Sumr el-Tiyyibeh, ascends Wadi Jarret Salman or Jurf Himar and leaving Jebel Harun to the left, drops down to Petra. In 1940, Major C.S. Jarvis travelling from the Sinai, organised a caravan expedition

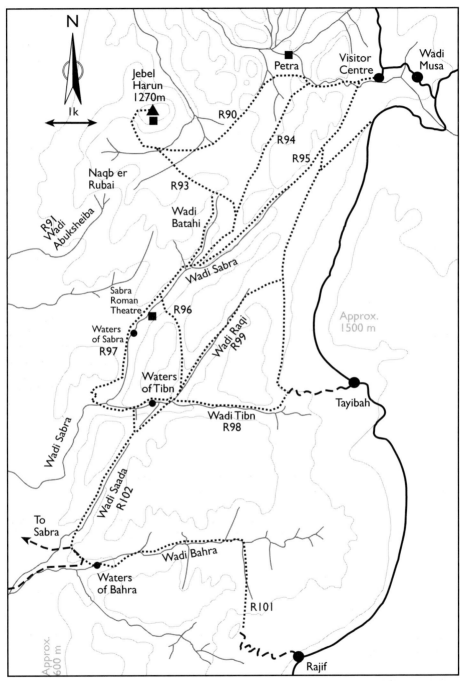

N

1k

Jebel
Harun
1270m

Petra

Visitor
Centre

Wadi
Musa

R90

R94

R95

Naqb er
Rubai

R93

R91
Wadi
Abuksheiba

Wadi
Batahi

Wadi Sabra

Sabra
Roman
Theatre

R96

Waters
of Sabra
R97

Wadi Raqi
R99

Waters
of Tibn

Approx.
1500 m

Tayibah

Wadi Tibn
R98

Wadi Sabra

Wadi Saada
R102

To
Sabra

Wadi Bahra

Waters
of Bahra

R101

Approx.
600 m

Rajif

28. Petra, southern approaches

by camels and horses from Wadi Abu Khusheibeh into Petra. He identified 'the old made track' which leads to the shoulder of Jebel Harun. I followed the same caravan route with a team from Paris, starting from Qasr el Bint, and reached the bed of Wadi Abu Khusheibeh, where extensive ruins are extant, in four hours. Little Nabataean pottery was collected at the ruins called Sayalet Abu Khusheibah, compared to the Late Roman and Byzantine pottery. There is a large water reservoir at the foot of Jebel Harun, known today as Bir Huweimel. At the bottom of Jebal el Farasheh, the slopes are terraced, and barrages built with large boulders extend in Wadi 'Iyal 'Id. No doubt such an agricultural technique was initiated by the Nabataeans. Another rock-cut cistern provided with a drain is at the mouth of the valley. The route passes by Jebal el Barrah, near the Snake Monument where the passage is carved in the sandstone and at the foot of Umm el Biyarah where Arabic graffiti dated 723 H. = 1323 A.D. were recently noticed. Crossing Wadi Farasa the path leads to the Pillar of Pharaoh and Qasr el Bint."

The Adventure Travel Companies in Wadi Musa and Aqaba all organise itineraries at your request on these ancient trails. (See map 28.) Apart from the route over Naqb er Rubai immediately S of Jebel Harun, the key to the S entrance of Petra is the hidden but beautiful valley of Sabra.

92. Ancient trails from Wadi Sabra
"Welcome to Sabra where only Allah and the Bedouin live." A greeting made to us from a small Bedouin camp in the heart of Sabra.

Sabra was the southern caravanserai of Petra and still has the remains of a small Roman outpost and theatre near its S end. From there, ancient Nabataean trails continue to Humeima, Rum and Aqaba in the S, and to Gharandal in Wadi Araba in the W en route to Sinai and Egypt. The route to the W starts about 1k after the Sabra Roman Theatre where a trail takes the right bank onto plains, passing eventually through a carved corridor 24m long. The wadies then merge into a sand-filled tongue, then enter a gorge preceded by an ancient wall and ending after 70m at basins and cisterns. Beyond here is Ras adh Dhawi and its spring and, on the edge of Araba, the 'tower-tomb' made famous by the sketch of David Roberts in the 19th Century, now known as 'Roberts' Rock'.

Also in this area well to the W of Sabra is a Roman copper mine, its chambers supported by columns of rock and called like its counterpart in the Feinan area 'Um el Amad' or 'Mother of Columns'. None of this area W of Sabra has been checked by the authors but, as mentioned above, it is part of the itinerary of local Adventure Tourism Companies.

In actual fact, Sabra is little disturbed by tourism and a great place to wander through or camp in, having some confidence that water will be found at The Waters of Sabra just beyond the Roman Theatre. (See R93 and 94.)

93. Petra to Jebel Harun and Wadi Sabra
A wonderful day in the mountains: pleasant walking, great scenery and lots of historical interest. Go on foot or with camels. Maps 24, 27 and 28.

Guide necessary if you want to travel by camel or recommended if you're going to continue by a different route.

Moderate trek
20k allow 7hrs, first descending about 100m to the Petra Basin then rising 370m to the

summit of Jebel Harun at 1270m before descending almost 500m to the Roman Theatre of Sabra.

The Route Follow R90 to the summit of Jebel Harun (3½hrs). Descend the steps from Aaron's Tomb and follow the path down the zig-zags and out onto the SW saddle, above Naqb er Rubai, then down again in the direction of Petra, crossing a small wadi.

Here, leave the main Petra track and continue down the left (E) side of the wadi across a flat area by a little path and down well worn zig-zags to a bend in the next wadi. Cross this and continue in the same direction into another wadi. Descend this past two juniper trees and cross the next wadi up red sand. Continue still on small paths in the same direction along wadies left of two small domes and up a wadi with terraces and dams to a field. Ahead are small mountains. Continue towards them following a path through fields and up to a saddle above the N end of Wadi Batahi. There are now two options:

a. Contour round to join the Petra - Wadi Sabra track where it leaves the wadi rim to contour round SE between the wadi and the mountains (R94). 1½hrs to here from Jebel Harun, and another 1½hrs down R94 to Sabra Roman Theatre.

b. From the saddle take a path contouring right across a sandy slope, then descending a ridge into Wadi Batahi which leads down to the junction with Wadi Sabra. Continue another 1k to find the Roman Theatre and associated ruins in an area of oleanders and other vegetation.

Springs will be found a little further on down the wadi at The Waters of Sabra.

The usual direct way to Sabra is:

94. Petra to Wadi Sabra and its Roman Theatre
A reasonably easy walk needing careful route finding and combining fascinating history with majestic mountains and wild valleys. If you return to Petra the same day it is quite a long journey, requiring a full day to really appreciate it. Why not sleep out in Sabra? It may be done on foot or with camels which can be hired in Wadi Musa. Map 28.

Guide recommended and essential if you go by camel.

Moderate trek
11k to Sabra, about 3hrs, descending and ascending about 100m before descending 200m again. Alternatively the trek may be extended to include Jebel Harun (R93) or continued through various canyons and valleys up to the King's Highway, down to Wadi Araba or even all the way to Wadi Rum!

The Route Go down The Siq into Petra, turning left round the end of the mountain just after the Roman Theatre. Rise up the hillside and then head S about 100m below the cliffs, past caves and across the old city wall. Pass the entrance of the wadi leading to the Soldiers Tomb and carry on until below some tower-like tombs. Below is a wadi in a small rocky ravine.

Descend and cross it, finding a well trodden path up rainbow rocks on the opposite side. **This path is the key to the route.** Follow it along the right side of this ravine and continue S over a little col and, still on the obvious path, cross the next small wadi to its left side and rise above it through more rainbow red rocks. Immediately after, continue rising through bright white flat rocks (the Jebel Harun tomb is obvious to the right), and carry on towards the distant mountains to the S. **Don't go left through the first valley.**

The path now continues past fields with a wadi on the right (stone dam), to the col above Wadi el Batahi which plunges directly S to join Wadi Sabra after 2k. (Excellent views, 1½hrs from the Visitor Centre.) It is possible to descend this valley (option b. R93). Instead, the main path descends a few m, then contours left towards two rocky hills, then out onto the peninsula between Wadies Batahi and Sabra. From here, it descends by zig-zags (supported by old walls) down to a flat area of land above Sabra.

Cross this by a path on the left side to a rocky promontory where the path goes right along a narrow ridge and up to a small top. From the S end of this little hill, descend into Wadi Sabra, close to its junction with Wadi Batahi. Beyond this point, Sabra is wide and for a while increasingly lush and fertile with running water in springtime. The Roman Theatre is 1k down on the left side - The Waters of Sabra are beyond.

95. Wadi Sabra to Wadi Musa
This provides a pleasant and very direct route back to Wadi Musa, finishing on vague paths with a bit of tricky route finding through the eastern limits of Petra before descending terraced gardens between the entrance to The Siq and The Triclinium. Map 28.

Moderate trek
9k, rising 200m. Allow 3hrs. (20k, at least 6hrs for the round trip starting by R94.)

The Route From the Roman Theatre follow Wadi Sabra back to the NE for about 5k, along paths which occasionally cross the meandering river bed past old walls, eventually climbing up the slopes at the valley head to arrive at a col (1½hrs). (The Petra road is high above on the hillside to the right, with new hotels and unsightly rubble from the new road works visible.)

Continue in the same line, descending through a little valley with ploughed land and rising up and along with domes to the left. Continue still in the same direction roughly NE increasingly close to the domes, rising up to an area with stone walls, and crossing a 4 w.d. track (ignore it). Still in the same line, descend towards a faily large white dome split into three by cracks, with a Bedouin shelter below it.

Go right of this (a few Nabataean steps) and pass through a gap in the domes, then follow a path which rises up past junipers and between white rocks to a ploughed field. Go round the field to reach its far bottom corner and descend a path into and across a valley then follow the path up and along, still heading in the same general direction of NE with domes on the left.

At the top of the rise, there are terraces below, and tombs on the left. Go down the terraces and trend right to join the road to The Siq, at the side of the Triclinium Monument. The Petra Gate is 5mins up the road. (You will need your pass.)

Back in Sabra (and why not, it's a wonderful place to be), this is excellent trekking country and a great place to get lost in! There are various ways on as Fawzi Zayadine's report tells us (see above). If you are with a local guide you can continue on foot or with camels on old caravan routes to Gharandal in Wadi Araba, or 'Robert's Rock' made famous by the painting of David Roberts in 1839 or all the way to Bir Hamad, Humeimah and Wadi Rum. The latter journey takes 5 or 6 days. Contact the recommended Adventure Travel Companies for details.

There are also other routes sometimes requiring one or two days which head out from Sabra towards Tayibah and Rajif on The King's Highway high above, or even alternative ways back to Wadi Musa. To get to the next water source - The Waters of Tibn - there are two ways on:

96. Wadi Sabra to Wadi Tibn via M'zayla Siq
Short and sweet! A typical Bedouin short cut, straightforward in concept but quite complex in detail, always interesting and in wild mountain scenery shown to us by Awad Faraj, a Bedouin who spends much of his time in Sabra. Despite its brevity, good route finding ability is necessary and confidence in the mountains. Maps 28 and 29.

Guide recommended

Serious trek; short but in a remote area and part of a longer journey.
4k to The Waters of Tibn. 1½hrs from Sabra, rising from 800m to the pass at 1000m before descending back to 800m.

The Route From the Roman Theatre in Wadi Sabra go back up the river bed a short way to where it sweeps over to the SE side after travelling in a fairly straight line from the junction of Wadies Batahi and Sabra 1k to the NE.

A careful search now reveals a little path zig zagging up the E side. High above is the huge rock face of Jebel el Jathum. Follow the path up as it becomes more defined entering a narrow ravine which rises up S. Very soon it goes through a small pass to enter a 'hanging garden'. Cross to the right side and go through a gap in the rocks before reaching the end, to enter a parallel ravine. This is the ravine which drops into the 'Roman Theatre' and, so it is said, used to supply water for aquatic games!

Follow this forested valley up, still heading generally S to SE. When it starts to climb more steeply a big black narrow cleft will be seen on the left. 50m inside water will usually be found. Continue up the steepening ravine to the pass and descend the other side, keeping near the right side and eventually passing close to three Bedouin cave shelters. Just below here, the path goes out of the main wadi bed, curving right below a big rock face and passing the head of another wadi. Bedouin steps go down the right side of this and eventually into the bed of the big valley below, which is Wadi el Raqi. Follow this down to the SW for 1k, and the impressive narrow siq of Wadi Tibn will be found gashing the cliffs on the E side almost hidden by oleanders.

100m further down, Wadi Raqi bends sharply to the right (W) and a little way past this bend following a path along the right side of the valley The Waters of Tibn should be found below some large fallen rocks with a fig tree growing from them. Also at the bend in Wadi Raqi another wadi enters from the S. This leads to Wadi Saad which cuts through Jebel Barrat Salama to meet with Wadi el Bahra leading to Rajif, a small village high above on the edge of the plateau (R101, 102). There should be a seasonal pool of water a short distance up this wadi.

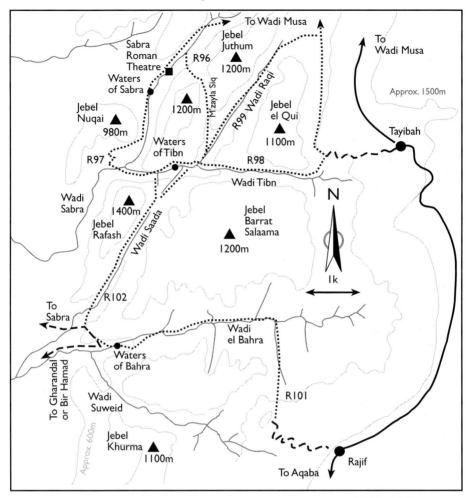

29. Wadi Sabra area

The other way to Tibn is equally interesting with some impressive canyon scenery and its own unexpected route finding problems:

97. The Sabra - Tibn Connection
Despite the fact these two wadies meet downstream of the Sabra Roman Theatre, the way is not quite as straightforward as you might imagine - but then these sort of things rarely are! Like the above alternative it is not so much a route in itself as a way to the next water source. Maps 28 and 29.

Guide recommended

Serious trek; short but in a remote area and part of a longer journey.
5k, 2hrs, descending 100m to 700m then rising again to 800m.

145

The Route Follow Wadi Sabra down from the Roman Theatre, passing the springs of The Waters of Sabra, then going though a narrow white twisting canyon. En route, 1300m down from the theatre a columned building lies in ruins above an S-bend with a pre-historic site above. Continuing down, as the canyon becomes more pronounced about 3.5k down from the Roman Theatre, follow a path along its right bank contouring along a steep cliff. **Don't follow the stream - it continues to descend for a short way then plunges over a cliff into a box canyon!** The path goes along the lip of the canyon for a short distance from where the lower end of Wadi Tibn can be seen below. To reach it, follow the Bedouin shepherd's track as it curves W before descending steeply down the rocky hillside (see R100).

Once in the valley bottom, follow Wadi Tibn upstream passing the box canyon on your left before entering the Lower Tibn Canyon. Scramble up this in rugged surroundings until it opens out a little after 1k into an amphitheatre in the mountains. Continue up the wadi bed passing a wooded valley which goes right (S) to Wadi Saad and eventually Rajif (R102a), until you find The Waters of Tibn seeping out below some large fallen boulders with a fig tree growing from them.

The best is yet to come:

98. The ascent of the Siq of Tibn to Tayibah or Wadi Musa
The Siq of Wadi Tibn winds its awe-inspiring narrow way between steep water polished cliffs, at one point passing below a huge jammed boulder. After rains, it may be necessary to wade through pools (or it may be impassable). During rains it would be extremely dangerous! It is a route well used by Bedouin coming down with loaded donkeys or sheep and goats from the village of Tayibah up on The King's Highway to get to Wadi Sabra and beyond. Don't miss it! Maps 28 and 29.

Guide recommended

Easy Canyon
8k, 3hrs, rising from 800m to 1,360m at Tayibah, or 16k, 5hrs to Wadi Musa

The Route From The Waters of Tibn, go up the path on the left (true right) bank to reach the upper valley of Wadi Raqi almost immediately. Follow Raqi as it bends left into oleander thickets which conceal the unexpected and extremely narrow entrance to The Siq of Tibn on the right.

Follow this up generally ESE in very impressive surroundings rivalling, if not exceeding The Petra Siq, to a junction where the main wadi bed curves left and passes between big cliffs. The best path with 'Bedouin steps' for pack animals is always on the right (E) side, and by-passes obstacles in the wadi bed.

Eventually a yellow scree slope appears to bar the way, but the path continues loosely up it to a col, the wadi being in a narrow siq below to the left. Continue in the same direction (N) along the line of the wadi, following its true left bank and passing two small Nabataean sunken water cisterns cut into the rock. Just beyond, the valley opens out into a pleasant arena surrounded by white rock domes. 100m above to the left a house will be seen built into the cliff. On its right side is a huge concealed water basin. There should be a bucket here, and a rope, to reach the water which is a few m down. This is about 2 - 2½hrs from the start. From here there is a choice of two routes and destinations:

Option I to Tayibah: To the right (E) a 4 w.d. track will be seen descending into the valley. This winds its way up to Tayibah about 2k away, arriving first at the old village which has been tastefully converted to the award winning Hotel of Tayibet Zamman. The new village is above on The King's Highway.

Option 2 to Wadi Musa: *Pleasant walking between domes and along the upper edge of the canyon of Wadi Raqi, most interestingly finished by joining R95, to the Petra Visitor Centre. Otherwise the route follows rather tedious 4 w.d. tracks up to finish in Wadi Musa.*

Directly ahead from the water basin, the main valley of Wadi el Batha continues N. Follow this up, taking the main (right) branch after about 1k, and rising up for another 1k to a gap in the cliffs ahead to reach the tops of the white domes and the E rim of Wadi Raqi (the road from Tayibah to Wadi Musa is about 250m above to the E). Follow the path N along the rim with some minor detours up and down to cross or by-pass the occasional siq, but always keeping close to the canyon rim for about 5k. (About 1½hrs from the water basin.)

Almost immediately after leaving the end of the canyon rim, where the canyon stops, it should be possible to descend the hillside for 150m to join R95 as it emerges from Wadi Sabra. Alternatively, the path meets the end of a 4 w.d. track which rises gradually up the hillside in the same N direction for a further 3½k to meet the road above. Just before meeting the road (telegraph poles visible 100m above) another 4 w.d. track descends gently to the left reaching the outskirts of Wadi Musa village after 1k. From here various paths or roads can be taken directly into Wadi Musa or down to the Visitor Centre (1½hrs from the end of the canyon rim).

99. The Waters of Tibn to Wadi Musa via Wadi Raqi

There is an alternative exit up Wadi el Raqi. Not checked by the authors but local Bedouin told us about a path following the valley to the NE from the lower entrance to Tibn Siq for

Broomrape, south Jordan   *Mary Hartley*

about 3k, and finally ascending to the E rim about 1k before reaching the head of the valley, to join the route described above. The distance from Tibn to Wadi Musa is about 13k. Maps 28 and 29.

Next comes a great trip combining some of the best features S of Petra:

"Imagine you're driving north along the edge of an escarpment: to your right, rolling green uplands are cut here and there by stony ploughed fields sometimes with a black Bedouin tent on their perimeter. To the left, the hillside plunges steeply down past a village of stone-walled, flat roofed houses reminiscent of Morocco or the Himalayas, to a petrified cloud sea of pale rock domes split by dark, mysterious canyons. On the summit of the highest and most distant peak the tomb of Aaron, brother of Moses, brightly reflects the morning sun, already high in a clear blue sky. Far beyond, blue hills shimmer in the heat haze rising from the unseen desert valley of Wadi Araba deep below sea level.

What's down there in those unknown mountains and canyons? Is it as inhospitable as it looks? Is there any water? The area intrigued and tantalised us for years as we passed by on the local bus between Wadi Rum and Petra."

Trekking through Tibn. Howard. 1990.

100. Tayibah to Wadi Musa via the Siq of Tibn, Wadi Sabra, Jebel Harun and Petra

Magic! This is a great trek basically taking in reverse a selection of the routes described above and consequently described here in that direction so the route is more easily followed though it can obviously be done the opposite way with various variations using the above notes. Competence in route finding is necessary. Maps 24, 28, 29.

Guide recommended

Serious trek
33k. It can be done in a day, but far better to split the journey and enjoy the ambience of the surrounding mountains. The route descends almost 800m to the junction of Lower Tibn with Wadi Sabra, then rises about 600m to the summit of Jebel Harun before descending about 300m and rising 100m to reach Wadi Musa.

Approach From Wadi Musa take a bus or taxi 12k S on The King's Highway to Tayibah and walk down to the new hotel complex tastefully created from the old village.

Stage 1. Tayibah to the Waters of Tibn. 8k, 3hrs
Walk down to the lower gate of the Tayibet Zaman Hotel and follow the track slightly downhill above an orchard. After 100m take the left fork and follow the gravel road as it winds down the hill. After ½hr it reaches a picturesque basin and wadi between large rock domes. Across the wadi, hidden in the cliffs, are water cisterns. Up the wadi to the N in a red valley is the track to Petra (R98 alternative finish). Down the wadi to the S is the way to The Siq of Tibn. After 100m the stream bed disappears into a narrow rock chasm. The path goes over the shoulder on its left from the top of which the view abruptly opens out and down into Wadi Tibn.

Carefully descend the long loose slope into the tree filled wadi and follow it for 20mins or so from the end of the road to the first wadi junction where Wadi Tayibeh enters from the left. Continue straight on down the river bed, through the increasingly impressive canyon. Wherever there are minor impasses, a donkey-track will be found on the left bank. After about ½hr the wadi bends right and in another 20mins or so, it goes right quite sharply with a steep tree filled valley entering from the left.

Keep going down the stream bed, taking the donkey track to right or left wherever convenient. Eventually the walls close in until the last section is sometimes less than 2m wide with smooth cliffs on either side, and sometimes passing below large jammed boulders. Suddenly, at the end of the second narrow section, the Siq emerges into Wadi Raqi and widens out. Follow the valley left (SW) for 100m to where another wadi enters from the SW. There is usually a deep pool of water not far up this wadi, but it is often stagnant, being the remnants of winter rains. Though we have not followed this little valley up, it connects with the next side valley of Wadi Saada (Rl02b) at the T-junction with stone walls.

The main river bed of Tibn now swings W. Follow a path along the right side of the valley and about 200m down, just past a fig tree in some large fallen rocks there should be a series of water seepages in the river bed - The Waters of Tibn. These are usually here, but can't be guaranteed. Possible overnight stop.

Stage 2. The Waters of Tibn to The Waters of Sabra. 5k, 2hrs
From the Waters of Tibn, descend the wadi bed. (The second valley on the left goes to Wadi Saada and eventually Rajif - R102a.) Continuing down Tibn, the walls close in again impressively after which a path will eventually be found on the right side, where the wadi changes direction from W to NW. Follow this path along until Wadi Sabra enters through an impressive gash on the right. **Don't bother going up it, it's a vertically walled box canyon!** Instead, go down the main valley which almost immediately widens.

A path will be found on the right at this point, rising up across a rocky hillside - the key to entering Sabra. Follow it along, rising gently into a small side wadi. Scramble up this, often quite steeply (though it is a donkey-path). Where the angle eases the Sabra path goes right on ledges **(don't continue up)**. These ledges (well trodden) emerge directly above the cliffs of the box canyon. Follow them round and along above the stream bed, which it eventually reaches.

Continue along (NE), following the wadi bed for ½hr or so until reaching the little stream of The Waters of Sabra. This cuts its way through some small winding canyons in white rock. Eventually the vegetation in the wadi becomes so dense at an area with a big palm, you are forced onto a track worn into a rocky headland just above. This leads almost directly to the old Roman settlement. The Roman Theatre is a little way further on, cut into the mountain on the opposite side of the wadi. Possible overnight stop.

Stage 3. The Waters of Sabra to Jebel Harun, Petra and Wadi Musa. 20k, 7hrs
Follow Sabra up for 1k to the junction of Wadies Sabra and Batahi, then either go directly up Wadi Batahi or the hillside on its right to find the track of R94 on the ridge between the two valleys. Either way you will eventually arrive at the head of Wadi Batahi after about 1½hrs. Jebel Harun with its white tomb is unmistakable to the W. Cross small wadies and fields heading slightly N of W to reach the track going up to Jebel Harun from Petra (R90). Follow this to the top and return by this route to Petra and Wadi Musa.

The next village S of Tayibah on The King's Highway is Rajif below which two deeply incised valleys can be seen descending into the wilderness of mountains. The S one is the narrow steep walled canyon of Wadi Suweid about which we have no details. The N one is Wadi el Bahra and is a well used Bedouin route to the lower valleys:

101. Rajif to The Waters of Bahra
A reasonably straightforward yet varied trek through some wild terrain. Having reached The Waters of Bahra you still have to get out again which requires care with route finding if you are continuing by another route. We're not absolutely sure you can rely on the water being there in late summer, so take plenty if you're planning to stay overnight. Maps 28 and 29.

Guide recommended if you are planning to walk out by another route

Moderate trek which becomes more serious if you continue on other routes.
10k. About 4hrs from Rajif, 3hrs from the end of the 4 w.d. track, descending from 1,500m to 600m.

Approach Going S from Wadi Musa on The King's Highway one reaches Tayibah after 12k and Rajif after about another 10k. (There are local bus and taxi services.)

The Route In Rajif, take the first major right (W) turn then immediately right again and take the road down through the small village till it becomes a track zig-zagging steeply down the hillside for 3k (2k in a direct line WNW), to some flat ground which then rises gently for a short distance to meet a cliff which bars further W progress (alt 1240m). This point can be reached by 4 w.d. (To the left, a path goes along the foot of the cliff for about 200m to a Nabataean water cistern cut into the narrow ravine above Wadi Suweid.)

To the right (N) is a ploughed field and beyond it a wadi descends towards the hidden valley of Wadi el Bahra. Walk along the left side of the field, below the cliff, to enter the wadi which goes N between the rocky domes of Jebel el Jilf. After about ½hr the wadi drops steeply over small cliffs.

By-pass the obstacle by going up a Bedouin donkey-path on the right side, along a rock ledge below an overhang. (There is a supporting wall on the outside of the path built by Bedouin, to ease access for loaded donkeys.) Follow the ledge round, and across a side wadi, then pick your way carefully down the donkey-track which descends rocky ledges back into the continuation of the wadi.

After 200m or so, the wadi drops over more small cliffs and another path will be found on its right (E) side, contouring along above the wooded ravine and eventually emerging into Wadi el Bahra (approx. 1hr from the end of the 4 w.d. track).

(If you are coming up Wadi el Bahra in the opposite direction this wadi can be identified by a massive projecting rock at the top of the opposite cliff, on the N side of Bahra, vaguely reminiscent of the Sphinx's head.)

From here, the wide stony bed of el Bahra is followed easily W for about 4k passing right of a prominent rock tower beyond which the wadi suddenly narrows, and then becomes filled with oleanders. There is some water seepage here (in springtime). Just beyond this point a stone shelter will be found built into the cliff on the left (S) of the wadi. This marks the place where the donkey-path leaves the wadi and rises up left (SW) to an obvious shoulder above the deep and narrow ravine. The path then descends again to reach the river bed at a (probably dry) waterfall with small shelters built into the overhanging cliff below on both sides of the riverbed. Beyond are an olive grove and gardens, with pools in the wadi (March '98).

From here trails continue downstream connecting with routes to Wadi Araba in the W and with that to Bir Hamad and Humeimah and Rum in the S. (Not checked by the authors.) Or, there is a very direct Bedouin way through the mountains to the N to reach The Waters of Tibn:

102. The Rajif - Tibn Connection
Another essential part of the maze! The discreetly hidden valley and tree-filled ravine of Wadi Saada makes a direct link between The Waters of Bahra and The Waters of Tibn. Maps 28 and 29.

Guide recommended

Serious trek, some scrambling, short but in a remote area and part of a longer journey. 7k, 2½hrs, rising 300m to 900m then descending 100m.

The Route Above the olive grove at The Waters of Bahra (R101) is a concrete water tank and a bulldozed track. Follow this up NW for 0.5k out of the wadi and over a shoulder (alt 640m) then down into the next little valley. (This valley goes back down to join the main valley of Bahra about 0.5k to the SW, whilst the bulldozed track goes W over the next shoulder to an area of low hills S of Wadi Sabra.)

Go up the valley to the NE for 1k at which point it suddenly enters a narrow ravine filled with oleanders, figs and other trees including white broom with (in springtime) sweet smelling blossom. This ravine goes directly NNE. Follow it to its end in Wadi Saada, picking the easiest way on small paths through the bushes. The ravine is about 2k long and varies between 5 to 10m wide. (1½ - 2hrs from the olive grove and about 5hrs from the 4 w.d. track or 6 from Rajif if that was your starting point.)

Exit from the ravine by scrambling up a water worn sandstone chimney to the left (Grade 2) for 10m in easy steps. Beyond is a rocky slope then the open valley of Wadi Saada which rises in 1k up to a pass (alt 900m), the best path being on its right (E) side, past a juniper tree. From the col the valley continues in the same NNE direction for 1k to a hollow with old walls and stone shelters tucked in the small cliffs on either side of the valley. There are now two choices of route, a tree filled valley to the N, or an open valley rising up to a prominent cairn to the NNE:

a. If you take the tree filled valley it descends quite steeply past a large boulder, which can be passed on either side (most easily on the left). Continue down the left side, through trees and boulders, crossing to the right at the valley mouth to emerge at a large juniper. Descend easily into Lower Wadi Tibn. The Waters of Tibn are 5mins upstream at a seepage below a huge fallen block on the N side, with a fig tree growing below it. The way to Wadi Sabra is downstream.

b. The other open valley rising NNE is (we were told by a local Bedouin) the easiest way to reach Wadi Tibn from the hollow. Either way is less then 0.5k. There is a water basin (seasonal) in the right hand valley 200m before reaching Tibn. The Waters of Tibn are 200m downstream of the junction. Although we haven't been this way it is probably the easiest and certainly the best if you are continuing straight on to Tayibah up the canyon of Wadi Tibn.

It would obviously be possible to pick up the Tibn - Sabra - Petra trek here (R100) the whole route being 42k and best spread over two days. It would also be possible to start from Beidah in the N of Petra and continue S by any of these routes making a 50k trek. Or, if you're really into it, why not start at Selah, N of Dana and follow the routes in this guide all the way to Aqaba, passing through:

Humeimah
You are now getting well out of the Petra area, this having been the last important caravanserai on the way S from Petra to Wadi Rum or Aqaba. Humeimah is the largest important antiquity site in this comparatively barren area and is famous for its water systems some of which are still in use. Originally Nabataean, dating from around 80BC, Humeimah was later an important way-station on the Roman Via Nova Traiana. An aqueduct brought water down 19k from the Shara mountains in the NE and there are various reservoirs, underground cisterns and baths - quite an achievement on the edge of the deserts of The Hisma and Rum.

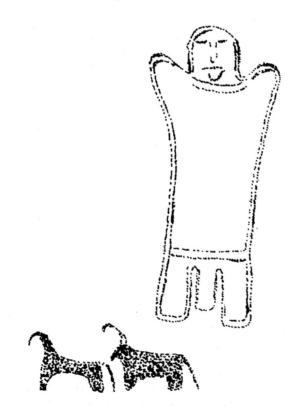

It is situated 11k from the Desert Highway, along a signed track which leaves the road near the bottom of its descent from Ras Naqb. It can also be approached along 4 w.d. tracks from Quweirah, further S along the highway, just before the Rum junction.

103. Trails from Petra to Araba and Rum
The trekking routes to Humeimah and beyond from Petra almost 50k to the N are either down through Sabra and on past the Waters of Bir Hamad below Delagha, or up over the high escarpment from Wadi Musa to meet the same route. There are various ways following Roman roads and old trade routes previously used for carrying precious goods, spices and incense from places like the Orient, Yemen and Egypt. (See R91.)

Rock inscription en-route from Humeimah to Wadi Rum.

Nowadays they are travelled by

adventure travel companies which organise treks, camel and horse safaris. These trips can take anything from 5 - 10 days, continuing past a huge natural rock arch and strange inscriptions to Rum then on to Aqaba via Lawrence's Way (R115). For information contact the travel companies which each have slightly different itineraries or can tailor a trip to suite your requirements. See map 43.

There are obviously almost infinite possibilities for trekking in these mountains and some possibilities for climbing though rock climbing in the actual environs of Petra would seem rather sacrilegious as well as potentially dangerous with so many tourists around. We wouldn't recommend it.

S and E of Humeimah you enter the more barren terrain of the Hisma desert and the southern end of the Shara Mountains ...

THE HISMA
"It was the evening of the 16th of June 1862 ... Behind us lay, in a mass of dark outline, the walls and castle of Ma'an, its houses and gardens, and further back in the distance, the high and barren range of the Shera'a mountains, merging into the coast plain of Hejaz. Before and around us extended a level plain, blackened over with countless pebbles of basalt and flint, except where the moonbeams gleamed white on little intervening patches of clear sand, or on yellowish streaks of withered grass, the scanty product of the winter rains and now dried to hay. Over all a deep silence, which even our Arab companions seemed fearful of breaking; when they spoke it was in a half whisper and in few words, while the noiseless tread of our camels sped stealthily but rapidly through the gloom without disturbing its stillness."
A Year's Journey through Central and Eastern Arabia. W.G. Palgrave. c1868.

Ma'an which is about 120k N of Aqaba and 40k E of Wadi Musa on the Desert Highway is on one of The Haj pilgrimage routes to Mecca in Saudi Arabia. The Shara mountains end not far to the W whilst the great expanse of The Hisma desert starts to the E, including the town of Jafr 60k E of Ma'an and extending across the border 100k away into Saudi Arabia and S to the colourful mountains of Rum and the Hejaz.

At the moment we know of only one adventure travel company doing tours out here between the desert town of El Jafr and Wadi Rum, billed as:

104. 'The Desert in the Sky'
The area got its name due to the many mirages. Nyazi Tours of Aqaba (see the start of this chapter on South Jordan) organise 4 w.d. safaris out here. Lawrence of Arabia crossed it on camels with the Arab Forces and, more recently, Charles Blackmore followed in his footsteps with our good friend the late Muhammed Musa of Wadi Rum. You can read all about it in his book 'In the Footsteps of Lawrence of Arabia', 1986.

The S of this area including the remains of a Turkish Fort at the border post of Mudawarah and the old Hejaz railway (or what's left of it after the raids of Lawrence and the Arab forces) can be visited by crossing the deserts of Rum by 4 w.d. (see R114). There are also other desert journeys in this area though the real desert and mountain experience par excellence is to be found in:

WADI RUM

"three easy marches ... up Wadi Yitm [from Aqaba] and behind the range El Sharra, one day south of El-Ma'an ... The fountains flow in winter, in summer the wells are never dry; the people, especially the Huwaytat, are kind and hospitable."

The Land of Midian. Richard Burton. 1879.

This, one of the world's most colourful and unique landscapes of desert and mountain scenery, has long been inhabited by man. Rock carvings mark the passage of ancient tribes in pre-history. Thamudic inscriptions, burial mounds, ancient megaliths and ruined buildings abound and Nabataean rock carved stairways, dams and temples are still to be found throughout the area. Rum is mentioned in Greek and Roman literature and once there were "vineyards and pine trees" here. Indeed, there are still relict olive trees growing in remote corners of the desert and large ancient junipers close to the summit of Jebel Rum and the other high summits.

The following routes which were shown to us by the Bedouin of Rum, are some of their many traditional ways through the labyrinths of canyons, passing from one desert valley to the next, or up into the mountains - even to the highest summit - for hunting Ibex or for collecting edible plants and medicinal herbs. They are some of the most fascinating walks, scrambles and climbs it is possible to find anywhere in the world. Some of these routes, as evidenced by the inscriptions high on Jebel Rum's Thamudic Way (R106), date back over 2,000 years and must be amongst the world's oldest known rock climbs, though it was not until the late 1940s that 'outsiders' began to explore these mountains.

The first known non-Bedouin ascent of Jebel Rum was in 1947 by Major Henry Coombe-Tennant of the Welsh Guards and Lance Corporal 'Havabash' Butler, Royal Signals, with Major StJohn Armitage (who did not complete the ascent). All were members of the British Military Mission to Saudi Arabia, who were travelling with the Jaish al Badia in Jordan by kindness of its commander and Glubb Pasha. They started their ascent from Wadi Shellaali (R105) though the precise route they took to the top is not clear - it appears to have taken a similar line to an excellent Bedouin climb called Rijm Assaf (see the guide to ' Treks and Climbs in Wadi Rum').

Bedouin camp, Wadi Rum   *Peter Hall*

154

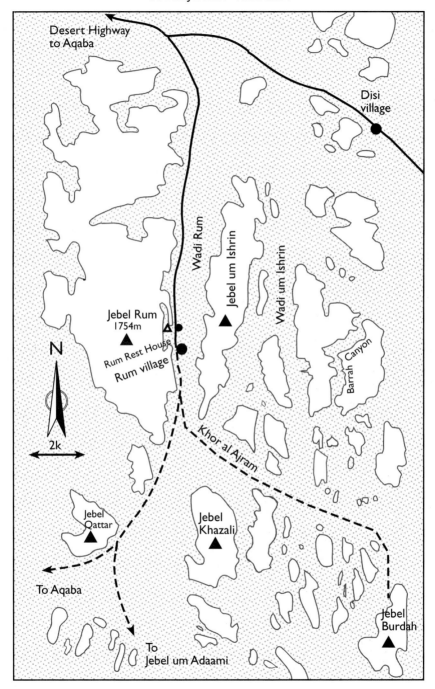

30. Wadi Rum central area

As far as we know, the next non-Bedouin party to explore Rum's mountains were Sylvia Branford and Charmian Longstaff, members of a cartographic team who made an ascent of Jebel Rum from the 'back' of the mountain, up the W side via the impressive Great Siq, guided by Sheikh Hamdan Amad in November 1952 (R107). (Sheikh Hamdan Amad was the father of Hammad and the combination of their eponymous routes has become the classic traverse of the mountain, see R108.) Although other Europeans, usually with military connections, visited the mountains of Rum intermittently over the following years, no effort seems to have been made to record the Bedouin climbs or to further explore these unique mountains until our arrival there in 1984. We have been captivated by Rum and its people ever since!

You too shouldn't miss the opportunity to follow the superb Bedouin routes described below, either up into the mountains, through the canyons, or on foot or with camels or 4 w.d. across the desert; travel and spend some time with the Bedouin - they have given us unforgettable memories and we are sure they will do the same for you.

The people of Rum

For over a century the area has been the homeland of the Huweitat Bedouin, until very recently semi-nomadic, but now mostly based in the rapidly growing villages of Rum in the heart of Wadi Rum itself, and Disi some 20k to the NE. These people, their lifestyle, their black tents and wild desert homeland were made famous by T. E. Lawrence in his book 'Seven Pillars of Wisdom' in which he described the area as "Rumm *the magnificent ... vast, echoing and godlike.*"

The majority of the Rum Bedouin are members of the Huweitat tribe which has links with the great Anaiza tribal confederation of northern Arabia through the Bani Atiya. As their numbers increased the Huweitat spread out from the Aqaba region in various directions, one branch even emigrating to Egypt. Their black "bait sha'ar" tents have been in Rum longer than anyone can remember. Tribal pride is very strong as a legend told by one

Sheikh Atieeg, Wadi Rum　　　*Peter Hall*

of the ancestral Huweitat Sheikhs, Suleiman ibn Jad, illustrates: "The human race was divided at the beginning into three classes: the tent makers, the agriculturalists and the Huweitat!"

During World War 1, the Huweitat fought against the Turks led by their paramount sheikh, Auda Abu Taiyy, who, already a famous fighting man in Arabia, became internationally known through the writings of Lawrence of Arabia. The Huweitat also fought in World War 2 as soldiers in the Arab Legion with Glubb Pasha in the Syrian campaign against the Vichy French. A number of the tribe, led by Shaikh Zaal bin Mutlaq, who had been at Auda's side in WW 1 joined in the fighting of their own accord as irregulars. On one occasion whilst most of them sought cover in trenches with the regular troops, Zaal stood on a hill top in the open, firing at the French aircraft which were strafing them and afterwards complained that war was not as good as it had been in the old days! This epitomises the bold, relaxed and highly confident approach many of the locals have to climbing, which has allowed them to become totally intimate with every detail of the mountains of Rum during their hunting exploits.

The hospitality of the Huweitat is also legendary, as is their anger when crossed! We were advised by them from the beginning "If you are soft with us, we will squeeze you; if you are hard with us, we will break you; if you are straight, you will be our friend." Treat them honestly and openly and you will be welcomed into their homes and desert camps and have a unique and memorable experience.

Accommodation and Hire of Camels and 4 w.d. in Wadi Rum
Camping, including showers, toilets and other Rest House facilities costs 1JD/person or 3-5JD for hire of tents, mattress etc. There is also a campsite at Abu Aina 2k further down the valley run by the Rest House, otherwise you can camp or sleep freely in the desert but if you have to use wood for fuel, use it sparingly: it is the sole source of fuel for the Bedouin out in the desert and as such is a precious and shrinking resource. Far better to bring your own stove.

The excellent Buffet meals at the Rest House vary from 6-9JD dependent on choice or you can choose from the menu. Just so you know, a large beer is 2.5JD. You can contact the Rest House at: tel 03 2018867, fax 03 2014240. There is also the friendly 'Bedouin Cafe' across the road serving Arabic food at local prices.

Vehicles and camels for hire from local people will be found between the Rest House and the village. Dependent on itinerary, prices vary from 6 or 7JD for a short trip through to 20JD / day for a camel (20k limit) or 45JD / day for a 4 w.d. which easily holds 8 people. If you are going climbing or trekking, remember to ask to be met later in the day at a specific time and place!

The RSCN Wadi Rum National Park
The new 'Reserve' centres on the Rum valley in the heart of these well known mountains and deserts and covers an area of approx. 500sq.k. The boundaries enclose the distinctive sheer sided jebels of the Rum area along with some of the typically sandy wadies and the divers vegetated Wadi Rumman, W of Jebel Rum. Elevation ranges from 800m to 1754m above sea level.

Wadi Rum was created in an enormous upheaval that thrust granite and sandstone outcrops through the earth's surface millions of years ago. Looking at the cliffs one sees the colourful phenomenon of ever changing hues, depending on the hour of day. Human habitation dates back

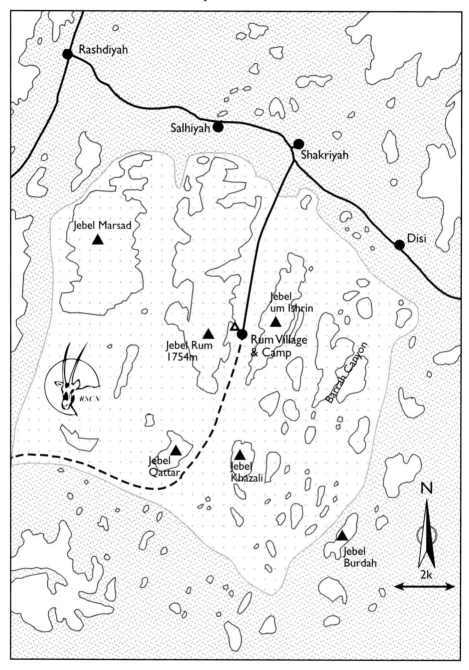

31. RSCN Wadi Rum National Park

8,000 years with numerous sites sand rock drawings bearing witness to this fact. Ruins of a Nabataean temple found at the foot of the great massif of Jebel Rum identifies Wadi Rum as an important centre for Nabataeans in early times.

The new Reserve is one of the few remaining places that harbour remnant populations of large animals such as ibex and the goitered gazelle. In addition, there are hedgehogs, striped hyena, wolves, hare, red fox, rock hyrax and porcupine. Resident birds include mourning wheatear, white crowned black wheatear, Sinai rose finch, the brown necked raven, Tristram's grackle, griffon vultures, the rare Verreaux's eagle and many more.

As Wadi Rum has a well established tourism business, access to and camping in the area will not be restricted as in other RSCN Reserves and the position of the local community and its desert and mountain guides is being respected. The Reserve regulations and compulsory guiding service applicable in the other RSCN Reserves are being adapted to suite the well established traditions of Rum. There is also a move to declare Wadi Rum an IUCN World Heritage Site which would give it additional status and protection.

Guides
At the moment there are a number of local Bedouin Guides in Wadi Rum who are approved by the Tourism Ministry for taking treks and camel safaris in the desert. Ask at the Rest House or adjacent Bedouin Co-operative or at the Bedouin Cafe, or contact the RSCN.

For routes involving climbing, such as that to the top of Jebel Rum, those without sufficient experience will need a Mountain Guide with equipment. At the moment, there are only three residents of Jordan who have been on training courses for guiding and mountain rescue in the UK; these are Sabbah Atieeq, Sabbah Eid and Atieeq Auda, all of whom live in Wadi Rum. They can be contacted via the above mentioned places. Sabbah Eid is also on the phone (tel: 009626 3 2016238). Atieeq Auda, who is younger than the other two, has less experience of guiding but, like the others, he is an excellent natural rock climber and knows the mountains extremely well.

All Jordan's Travel Companies take tours into Rum, on foot, with camels (or sometimes horses) and 4 w.d. Many other European mountain guides and trekking companies also visit Rum.

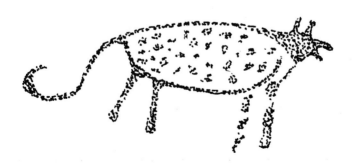

Rum inscription - hyena, at Um Tawagi, near Barrah Canyon

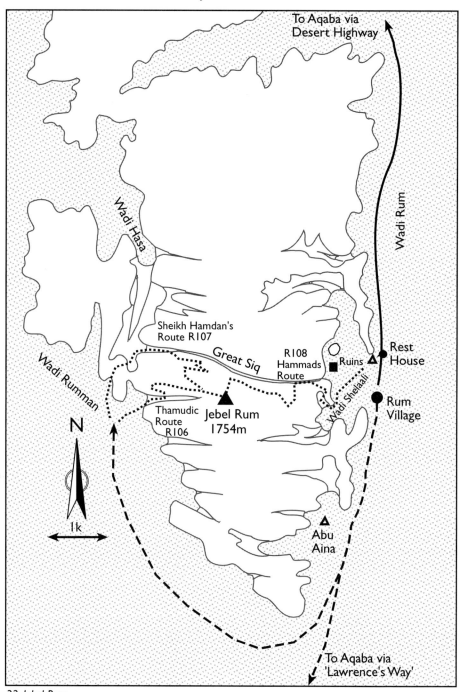

32. Jebel Rum

Jebel Rum

Jebel Rum is undoubtedly Jordan's most famous mountain. Hidden beneath its 500m walls which dominate the Rest House and valley of Rum from the W is one of the most well known sites in the valley (often confused with the well at Abu Aina 2k away at the S end of Jebel Rum which is erroneously called 'Lawrence's Well'):

105. Wadi Shelaali (Valley of the Waterfall) - Lawrence's Spring

A pleasant short walk that may also be linked with a visit to the Nabataean temple immediately W of the Rest House to make a combined 'pilgrimage'.

Wadi Shelaali is the site of Lawrence's Spring about which he wrote so evocatively in The Seven Pillars of Wisdom. It also has a Nabataean stone water channel, much of which is in place, from the spring down to a Nabataean site just S of the temple. The spring is in the shade after late morning and is surrounded by greenery making a pleasant retreat from the heat of the day and the crowds around the Rest House. Here is an extract from Lawrence's description of his visit on the eleventh of September 1917:

"The sun had sunk behind the western wall leaving the pit in shadow; but its dying glare flooded with startling red the wings each side of the entry, and the fiery bulk of the further wall across the great valley. The pit-floor was of damp sand, darkly wooded with shrubs; while about the feet of all the cliffs lay boulders greater than houses, sometimes, indeed, like fortresses which had crashed down from the heights above. In front of us a path, pale with use, zigzagged up the cliff-plinth to the point from which the main face rose, and there it turned precariously southward along a shallow ledge outlined by occasional leafy trees. From between these trees, in hidden crannies of the rock, issued strange cries; the echoes, turned into music, of the voices of the Arabs watering camels at the springs which there flowed out three hundred feet above ground."

On another visit, Lawrence bathed in one of these springs which he described eloquently:

"Its rushing noise came from my left, by a jutting bastion of cliff over whose crimson face trailed long falling runners of green leaves. The path skirted it in an undercut ledge. On the rock-bulge above were clear-cut Nabataean inscriptions and a sunk panel incised with a monogram or symbol. Around and about were Arab scratches, including tribe-marks, some of which were witnesses of forgotten migrations: but my attention was only for

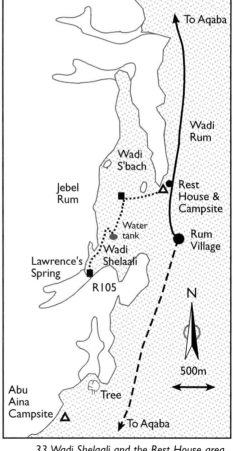

33. Wadi Shelaali and the Rest House area.

the splashing of water in a crevice under the shadow of the overhanging rock.

From this rock a silver runlet issued into the sunlight. I looked in to see the spout, a little thinner than my wrist, jetting out firmly from a fissure in the roof and falling with that clean sound into a shallow, frothing pool, behind the step which served as entrance. The walls and roof of the crevice dripped with moisture. Thick ferns and grasses of the finest green made it a paradise just five feet square.

Upon the water-cleansed and fragrant ledge I undressed my soiled body, and stepped onto the little basin, to taste at last a freshness of moving air and water against my tired skin. It was deliciously cool. I lay there quietly letting the clear, dark red water run over me in a ribbly stream, and rub the travel-dirt away."

Maps 32, 33 and 34.

Easy Walk
2.5k there and back, allow 1 - 1½hrs.

The Route To visit the spring which is SW of the Rest House, cross the desert either directly, towards a white water tank right of the valley entrance or, first, visit the Nabataean temple behind the Rest House.

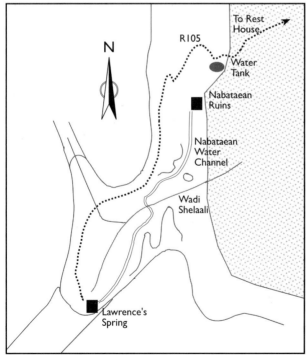

From the tank, a well used track "pale with use" zig-zags up the hillside to a little flat plateau above the valley entrance. From here the path contours round above the valley and just below the cliffs, past the green minty springs of Abu Shleilieh to arrive at 'Lawrence's Spring'.

The canyon of Wadi Shelaali is just above and can be entered from 200m right, up easy ledges. It is blocked after a few hundred metres by the steep cliffs of Jebel Rum.

Around the area of the well will be seen the ancient 'tribal markings' described by Lawrence. From here, along the right (E) side of the valley will also be found the beginning of the Nabataean stone water channel. This can be followed back with care and

34. 'Lawrence's spring', Wadi Shelaali

some detective-work, down the true right side of the valley, across the wadi bed above some smooth granite slabs, then along the other side of the wadi, to the valley floor. Or, of course, one can return by the same route.

Now for something definitely more serious: the next three routes are of Dolomitic or even Alpine proportions and should not be lightly undertaken except by experienced mountaineers:

106. Jebel Rum (1754m) by The Thamudic Way

A truly magnificent day out in wild and beautiful rock scenery reaching the remote summit of Jordan's best known mountain by what must surely be one of the world's oldest known rock climbs. The Thamudic inscriptions in the 'cave' are people's names: "By Kharajat, son of Sa'adan" seems to have been inscribed first, on the left, then at a later date, "By Jahfal, brother of Taym". These inscriptions are so close to the end of difficulties that it is certain these people must have climbed to the summit plateau over 2,000 years ago to hunt the ibex depicted in so many Rum petroglyphs. These animals are still hunted there to this day - let us hope the newly designated RSCN Reserve will protect them for future generations.

Also known locally as The Nabataean Route, and referred to in 'Treks and Climbs in Wadi Rum' Edition 3 as Western Safari, the climb demands ability to climb Grade 2 rock comfortably, the key section crossing steep rock where an un-roped fall would be fatal. Nevertheless the ledges are large and the holds are big so a competent team can climb without ropes, but remember - this is Rum sandstone so route finding is not straightforward and holds should never be trusted implicitly. The route is therefore a serious undertaking for someone not familiar with climbing. If in any doubt, hire a qualified local Bedouin mountain-guide.

The plateau below the summit domes is a great place to spend the night and watch the sun set over the distant mountains of Sinai. Maps 32, 35 and 36.

Special equipment and skills *Rope, harnesses, slings and carabiners, lightweight boots or trainers and confidence to climb in exposed terrain are all necessary as are route finding skill and the ability to abseil in descent, though competent climbers can down-climb both this route and the alternative Sheikh Hamdan's Route. If you're staying the night you will need sleeping bags, food and water. Any fire should be minimal as wood is scarce - better to use a stove.*

Guide required for inexperienced groups.

Serious scramble
1.5k to the summit, 750m of height gain; allow 2½ - 4hrs for the ascent, maybe more.

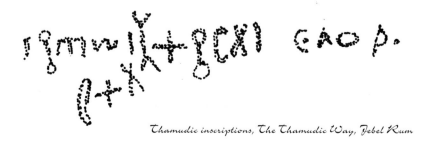

Thamudic inscriptions, The Thamudic Way, Jebel Rum

Approach Arrange the day before for a vehicle and an early start. It is ½hr by 4 w.d. from Wadi Rum village, first to the S end of Jebel Rum then back N up Wadi Rumman to below the entrance to the hanging canyon that leads to the summit. (The Bedouin driver should know the location, but check before leaving the village to be sure!)

The Route Scramble up scree and easy granite slabs to flat ledges on the right (S) side of the entrance to the canyon (½hr).

Now on rocky ledges keep going left with the occasional 2m steep rock step (Grade 2 - 3) rising diagonally into the canyon across its right (true left) side; a confusion of cairns! (Ignore the ones that continue to rise up the canyon wall, they are on another superb but considerably more difficult Bedouin climbing route, called Sabbah's Route - see 'Treks and Climbs in Wadi Rum'.)

The route then goes up through the cliff where the wadi drops down from the upper canyon floor, by easy ledges on its right. The upper wadi floor has a few water basins in it; passing the last one is awkward (Grade 3) to reach the next level of the canyon 2m above.

Continue along the canyon floor with cliffs rising over 200m on each side. A rocky depression is passed on the left

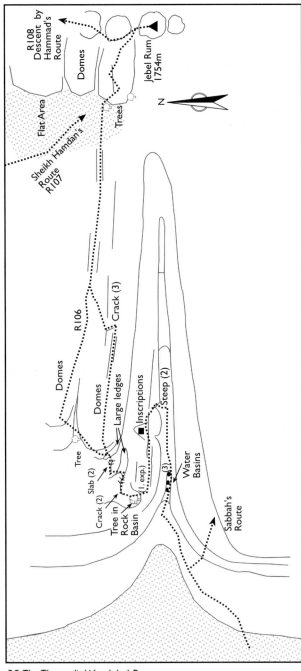

35. The Thamudic Way, Jebel Rum

(N) side in less than 100m and a short distance beyond that another larger depression with scree, also on the left will be found.

Go up the scree a short way then climb rocks above and on the right (good holds and ledges, Grade 2) to just below a hollow with a scree covered ledge. Go left (large cairn), across the gully and out onto ledges. Scramble easily up to the right end of a long ledge with steeper rock above. The wide ledge leads back W along the steep canyon wall. Follow it with care, walking in a superb position to a 'cave' overhang with Thamudic inscriptions about 1hr or so from the desert. Step down a little and continue along the lower ledge until it narrows and an exposed bulge has to be passed with care (Grade 2) before entering a huge rock basin with a juniper tree high above the canyon mouth.

From the back of the basin, scramble up a crack (Grade 2) then up slabs and an easy gully to a big flat ledge. From the ledge, rise diagonally left up pocketed slabs (Grade 2) to another gully line trending right to reach the white rock of the domes.

Go left here and keep rising diagonally left to cross behind a previously hidden but large juniper tree onto the next line of domes to the N. If the correct way is found, the way to the summit is then almost a direct line. (If the tree is missed and a route is taken too far right, it will eventually be necessary to go back left up a short steep crack (10m Grade 3) which will be found on the left, just after emerging from a little siq between domes.)

Back on route, continue heading directly E towards a saddle with a dead V-shaped tree in it, just left of the highest point.

The way rises and falls over domes and through sandy areas until the final domes are reached leading to the saddle - the correct ridge of domes is identified by two small juniper trees just left of the foot, where Sheikh Hamdan's Route joins it from the N. (There are also junipers in a hollow to its right.) The way then goes up a shallow curving groove in the slabs eventually moving left at the top of the groove then, higher, stepping back right to continue up to the saddle. The summit is directly above up a 20m ramp in its N face.

Please don't add to the increasing profusion of painted and inscribed graffiti on the top.

The Descent Allow at least the same time. For competent groups or those with a guide it is possible to return by other Bedouin climbing routes, namely Sheikh Hamdan's Route back to Wadi Rumman (R107), or Hammad's Route (R108), requiring five abseils, down to Wadi Rum, thereby completing the unique and magnificent W - E traverse of the mountain, one of the best adventure trips in Jordan. The ascent of Hammad's Route which is rather more serious than the other routes in this book (with the possible exception of the Mujib Siq!) is described in 'Treks and Climbs in Wadi Rum'.

Otherwise, unless you are very sure of your route finding and climbing abilities, it's best to take the same way back. In this case you will need to have made arrangements to be met at the bottom of the route to be driven back to Rum. If not, it's a long walk round the S end of the mountain!

An equally splendid but slightly harder route to the top is:

107. Jebel Rum by Sheikh Hamdan's Route

A Bedouin classic! A fascinating way to the top of Jebel Rum, with few difficulties and nothing more than Grade 3, but nevertheless requiring a head for heights. The route takes the shaded N facing wall of the Great Siq, utilising a long ledge which rises all the way to the domes, from where, with some Bedouin cunning, all major obstacles are passed by a circuitous but enjoyable bit of route finding which arrives at the col immediately N of the top. For non-climbers this is a route well worth doing with a guide and perhaps spending the night up in the flat area in the domes just below the summit, before returning by the same route.

Although a traditional Bedouin route, the first reported ascent was by Sheikh Hamdan Amad, Sylvia Branford and Charmian Longstaff, November 1952. The following excerpt is from Charmian Longstaff's article in the Ladies Alpine Journal 1953, which gives the only original description of this route:

"We started off up broken scree to enter a wide gully leading into the heart of the mountain. Usually these gullies, so promising at first, end, as my husband put it, inhospitably, but we circumvented this by taking to cliff ledges on our right and traversed along always making height until we reached a narrow cleft which led us still further into the mountain along a level gravelly bed. I remember a few bushes beside which we had our first rest. To the right of us was vertical cliff and to the left, broken rock leading upwards to a red palisade a thousand feet high.

Hamdan climbed with bare feet as surely as a mountain goat. We had gym shoes and were glad of them. I suppose really that it was very easy climbing but it was very exposed.

Sometimes holding one or both of us by the hand, Hamdan led us along horizontal ledges in the cliff face. There always came a time when we had to climb from one ledge to the one above. Once we did this up a small gully that held two tall trees; we found afterwards that they were a kind of juniper. Then there were two vertical pitches and suddenly we were among the gleaming white of the summit domes. The top! cried Hamdan.

We looked round us and saw that although we were indeed on the summit plateau we were a long way from its highest point. 'We must go there', we said, pointing towards it. 'If you go there', replied Hamdan, 'you will be very tired', but by now, the spirit of the intrepid woman explorers was in us and it must be the top and nothing but the top.

'You English women', said Hamdan, 'are as strong as men'. 'You should see our husbands', we replied.

It had taken us about two hours up to the plateau and it took us another hour up and down the complication of white domes to reach the summit. Between the domes were beds of gravel and these must hold moisture after the rare rains, or perhaps dew, because to our surprise we found junipers growing in them up to two or three times the height of a man."

Maps 32 and 36.

Special equipment and skills Ropes harnesses, climbing and abseil equipment will be needed by most parties as well as route finding skill, ability to climb Grade 3 and a 'head for heights'.

Guide required for inexperienced groups

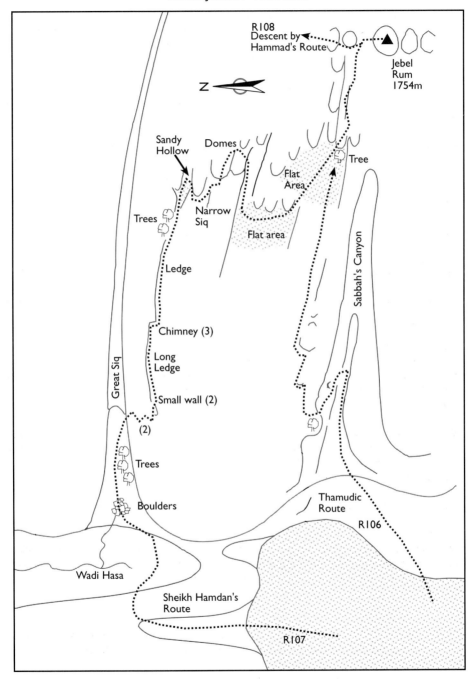

36. Sheikh Hamdan's Route, Jebel Rum

Serious Scramble
2k to the summit, 750m of height gain. 3 - 4hrs for ascent, and the same for descent, possibly more.

Approach As for The Thamudic Route round to Wadi Rumman on the W side of the mountain, to a point immediately W of the summit.

The Route Scramble N up a wadi to a col between Jebel Rum and Jebel Rumman. The entrance to The Great Siq up which the route goes will then be seen across the head of the little valley of Wadi Hassa to the NE. The route enters the Siq and, from its end, ascends its right (S) side in pleasant shade first by steep zig-zags then along a perfectly situated gradually rising rock ledge to the domes with some short sections of climbing including a steep chimney (Grade 2 and 3).

Once on the domes, great care is required with route finding. The easiest way is not obvious and there are a few misleading cairns. There are a couple of awkward little descents of 2 or 3m (Grade 3) if the best route is not found, otherwise there is nothing more than Grade 2.

From the sandy hollow at the arrival point in the domes, continue E another 50m or so, then back-track right (W) onto the next level of domes, returning E again almost immediately through a rock crevasse to reach the next domes. Go up these on slabs, eventually crossing right (S) onto the parallel domes and down them (W) to a sandy desert area. Cross this S, then easily up SE to the next level, to meet the final ridge of domes of The Thamudic Route directly below the N col. There are numerous places to sleep here, with good sunset views.

From here a short climb up the final slabby domes (see R106) leads to the col and thence the top. Please do not add your name to the ugly collection of graffiti that has appeared there in recent years.

Descent Many people take the same way back. If you have a local guide you could also return via The Thamudic Route. For experienced climbers, the best descent is by Hammad's Route to Wadi Rum making a classical traverse of the mountain:

108. The Traverse of Jebel Rum
Rum Rock Rules! A magnificent excursion equalled only by the Mujib Siq for challenge and adventure. The route crosses Jebel Rum from W to E following either of the above Bedouin hunting routes. The descent of 'Hammad's Route' requires abseils where Bedouin traditionally did it up and down without ropes, passing through some stunning rock architecture, first on high domes with unbeatable views of Rum then down into the chasm of the Great Siq - caving without the roof on! Why not enjoy a bivouac on the mountain either on the W side, on the last sandy plateau, or on the E side, on the little desert half-way down. Maps 32, (35 or 36) and 37.

Special equipment and skills Ropes, harnesses, abseil gear, a few slings and carabiners, trainers or lightweight footwear, plus route finding ability, confidence to move with ease on Grade 3-4 rock and abseil experience.

Guide recommended for inexperienced parties.

Serious Scramble

3-5k. Allow 8-12hrs for ascent and descent (possibly more), climbing 750m and descending 850m.

The Route Ascend either R106 or R107 to the summit. Descend by Hammad's Route. From the summit, return to the N col, then follow the N ridge making frequent detours to the right or left to circumvent the many siqs that cut through the ridge. The first main barrier wall is descended near its right (E) end, down-climbing 5m (Grade 3) past a curious hole. The next obstacle is a siq which has to be climbed into (Grade 3) and out of near a tree. The final impasse is another siq approached down the convex bulge of a dome. It is best passed by making a bold leap for the opposite dome or it can be climbed into trickily (Grade 4), escaping out again up a tree!

Beyond, the domes of the N ridge flatten out and a sunken corridor (not really seen until you step over it) leads E just before the final flat-topped dome, down onto an ocean of undulating slabs. Run down grooves in the slabs to reach a sandy wadi at the bottom. After 50m or so along the wadi walk up rocky slabs to the right to reach small domes below a N facing barrier wall. Head E along these passing a large bushy tree and descending to a sandy passage directly under

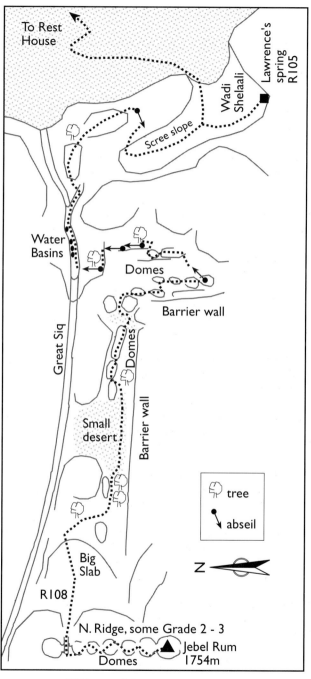

37. Hammad's Route, The Traverse of Jebel Rum

the barrier, continuing E passing more trees to emerge in a small 'desert'.

Still following the barrier cliff, the desert closes again to another sandy corridor. Leave this after 50m or so, at the second tree and go up onto domes on the left. Follow the ridge of domes E, with siqs on either side, eventually descending slightly right (Grade 2-3) to a sandy hollow.

Go left here along a ledge 5m up on the W side of a dome, for about 50m then through a small siq to emerge on the domes above Wadi Rum. Follow these first SE, rising and falling (not literally, we hope!) over the domes and zig-zagging down with superb views (cairns, some steps of Grade 2 - 3). Eventually a 5m barrier wall is reached. This can be down climbed (Grade 4) but there is an abseil bolt above it which makes life easier. After the abseil go out E and up the next domes, then N and down them to another vertical drop. Pass it by a 10m abseil on the right, near a tree, or by continuing a little further and descending into a bottomless concealed chimney on the left (5m, Grade 3). Step out of the chimney onto the ledge below the dome and contour E, to the foot of the above abseil variant, then scramble down to a juniper with the first set of abseil chains nearby. Abseil 20m to a hollow from where the next abseil goes 10m down to a big ledge, past 'Hammad's tree'. (This dead juniper was wedged in place by Hammad to climb the overhang!)

You are now entering the confines of the Great Siq. Walk W down a chimney for 10m to another tree. The next chains are above it for a 40m abseil in unique rock scenery, down into the depths of the chasm. Follow the bed of the siq out E often with water in it, which can be fun: some precarious Grade 2-3 including a 6m descent over a pool! After the last pool and before the siq plunges down to greater depths, walk out right up a corridor and go up left at the end onto a ridge. Scramble E along this (some Grade 2) to emerge on a shoulder directly above the village.

Follow the shoulder S descending in an increasingly exposed position (some Grade 2) to reach a platform on its W side where chains indicate the last 40m abseil down a knobbly slab to a rock pedestal. (Take care when pulling the ropes). From the pedestal, descend NW through large boulders squeezing under or climbing over the last one (exposed Grade 3) to reach a recess. A short exposed traverse (Grade 2) then gives access to a big ledge. Follow this along over a small tower and down a steep ramp (Grade 3) to reach a big scree-filled gully. Go down the gully to emerge amongst the mint filled springs in Wadi Shelaali, 200m N of Lawrence's Spring. Follow R105 down to Wadi Rum for a shower and cold beer!

Rum inscription, ibex hunting

Jebel um Ishrin

Now, safely back in Rum again, you are faced with another equally impressive mountain wall across the desert to the E formed by the W face of the massif of Jebel um Ishrin (1753m). Two massive canyons appear to split it, but they are deceptive: you can scramble into them amongst awe inspiring rock scenery, but you cannot cross to the other side without climbing equipment. The way through is via a remarkable maze of concealed canyons almost directly opposite the Rest House:

109. The Canyons of Rakabat um Ejil

A Magical Mystery Tour! Originally a Bedouin short cut through the mountain, this complex system of canyons now also provides an increasingly popular route through from Wadi Rum to the beautiful orange dunes of Wadi um Ishrin. Route finding is not straightforward and there are some exposed steps of Grade 2. A wonderful half-day in some amazing mountain and desert scenery. Maps 38 and 39.

***Special equipment and skills** A rope for emergencies, ability to climb Grade 2 and a 'head for heights'!*

Guide recommended for inexperienced groups

Moderate scramble
3k from Wadi Rum to Wadi Um Ishrin, 1½ - 2hrs and the same to return S round the mountain.

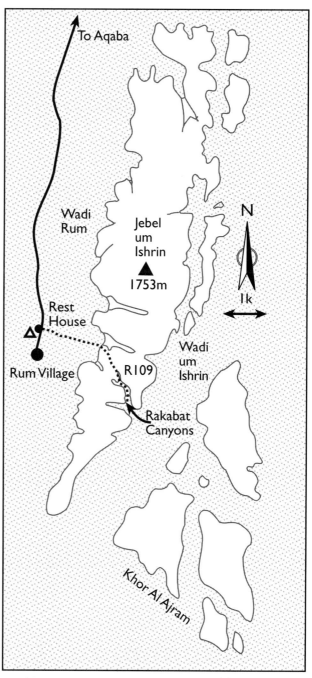

38. Jebel um Ishrin area

171

The Route From the Rest House, cross the desert towards the giant ravine of Kharazeh Canyon. 100m right of the bushy wadi basin below its mouth, a small gully will be seen (not too obvious at first) with a large overhang on its right. This is the 'Goat's Gully' and provides the way in through a barrier of cliffs, to a plateau, ½hr from the Rest House.

Walk almost S along the plateau (bearing 160°) towards the smaller (left hand) of two gullies. Scramble up this, still in the direction of a thumb shaped tower on the distant skyline to arrive in a bay. On the left is a saddle above a ravine which marks the entrance to the Rakabat Canyons. However, they cannot be entered directly. Instead, go left, and down to cross the little stream bed at an S-bend and climb up some smooth pink slabs (Grade 1) on the opposite side. Walk right along their top (exposed) and descend into the ravine above the first barrier.

50m further on is another small steep barrier. Either ascend it directly (Grade 2), or pass it on the left. Continue, until 10m before the end where Bedouin steps lead up left to enter a side canyon. At the next junction, turn right, then almost immediately left and up a narrow ravine (more Bedouin steps) to reach the pass. Descend, down an awkward 5m wall (Bedouin steps, Grade 2), to emerge in the upper Rakabat Canyons at a 'cross-roads'. Here, there are three ways. To the left (N) is the way to the climbs on the W face of Jebel Um Ejil. If this is followed to its end, a 20m abseil goes down into Kharazeh Canyon.

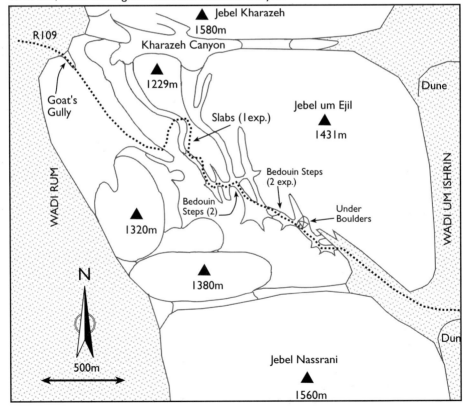

39. Rakabat Canyons, Jebel um Ishrin

Straight on, a narrow cleft goes to a concealed canyon with some rock climbs, while to the right is the way out into Wadi Um Ishrin (this point is approximately 1hr from the Rest House). Go right, keeping to the left side and descending to a lower wadi (the head of which goes back up another ravine into the concealed canyon). Continue down it, again keeping to its very left edge. Rise up over a rock bulge (do not go down the canyon), then through a defile and down steep slabs (Bedouin steps, Grade 2), into the lower ravine.

50m down this, pass under a big boulder and carry on down keeping to the right side through a little defile for the first magnificent view of Um Ishrin's red dunes. Descend the gully from here, squeezing past a jammed boulder onto slabs. Keep right, still close to the mountain, finally descending to the valley floor 10m below, through the lowest little wadi, down smooth rock (Grade 1).

(To find this point from the opposite direction, it is opposite a tongue of rock which descends into the valley from Jebel Um Ejil, and about 50m before the inner end of the valley.) From here, walk out into Wadi Um Ishrin, at the foot of the big dunes. Ascend to their top for superb views.

The return For the walker, it is possible to return to Wadi Rum either the same way, or S down the big red dunes of Um Ishrin, round the end of the mountain and back up the valley of Rum. Either way takes about the same time.

Also, of course, these canyons can be used as part of a longer trek out to the stupendous Barrah Canyon, or as part of a circuit of Jebel Um Ishrin. Either of these journeys takes a full day. (See the guidebook 'Walks and Scrambles in Wadi Rum.') You can also arrange to be met in Wadi Um Ishrin with camels, and so combine a canyon walk with a camel trek.

110. Barrah Canyon
Barrah canyon is a magnificent desert canyon with big dunes which are dwarfed by the immensity of the superlative rock architecture. There are some world class rock climbs here (see 'Treks and Climbs in

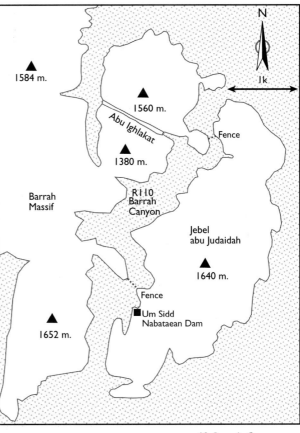

40. Barrah Canyon

Wadi Rum'), but the canyon is also a great place just to walk through and perhaps spend the night in. You can also go through by 4 w.d. or with camels or horses. Maps 30 and 40.

Easy Walk
5k, 1½ - 2hrs

Approach Some people walk it in half a day from the Rest House, perhaps via the Rakabat Canyons, others go by 4 w.d., camel or horse.

The Route Simply head N down the canyon, making exploratory excursions as the fancy takes. (There are fences near both ends. Please leave the 'gates' either open or shut, as you found them - they are to allow or prevent camels from passing through.)

Near the E end of the S fence an old Nabataean dam called Um Sidd will be found in a side canyon, whilst the area inside the N fence is where most of the rock climbs are. There are also some huge dunes here, close to the cliffs on the W side and not immediately apparent. Some of the 'siqs' on the W side hold pools of water for much of the year.

In the same E part of the Rum desert as Barrah, but further S, is what has become one of Jordan's most famous natural landmarks, though it wasn't known to the outside world until 1984:

"October 21. Today whilst gathering wood for a feast at Sabbah's tent, Sabbah and Dayfallah took us out to the south east of Rum. On rounding the end of a mountain they pointed up to the skyline and said with mischievous grins 'Maybe this is of interest?' There, arching across the horizon, almost a thousand feet above the desert was a magnificent natural rock bridge, perhaps the most significant discovery of our trip to Rum."
'A Report on Wadi Rum.' Howard. 1984.

111. The Rock Bridge of Burdah
A truly delightful scramble on good rock, well marked with cairns but sometimes a little 'exposed' and with some moves of Grade 2. The bridge is a 'must' for any fit visitor. The views around the Rum area are superb and even better from the actual summit, though to reach it, 20m of Grade 3 rock has to be climbed just after the bridge (see R112). Most people stop at the bridge. Maps 30 and 41.

Special equipment and skills Safety rope and associated equipment advised, and confidence on exposed Grade 2 rock.

Guide recommended for inexperienced groups

Moderate scramble
1.5k. Allow 2 - 3hrs for the return journey

Approach Take a 4 w.d. for the 15k drive down Rum and the long valley of Khor el Ajram, to the start of the route in a little valley 200m right of the N end of Burdah's W face. (This journey is itself well worthwhile. The driver will wait for you while you climb to the Bridge and will visit the Canyon of Khazali with its rock inscriptions, as well as other sites of antiquity on the way back, if you ask.)

The Route Go E along a pale ridge of rock, on the left side of a little valley, with a broken white rock 'mushroom' marking the start, to the saddle above the end of the valley. Here, trend left (SE) up slabs and over a dome. Carry on in the same direction and descend E for 10m to enter a gully. Go S up this, then down left at a rock barrier to a hollow.

Go up again, in the same direction, then left and right (Grade 1) on a slab to pass a steep chimney, after which walk easily E again, still below the rock barrier, to two big chimneys. Avoid them by going left and across a slab to enter the next parallel ravine.

Follow this up a short way, to 10m before its end. **Don't** go up the square walled chimney ahead but step right and walk back W on a ledge (exposed) passing under a yellow/white overhang and up a black chimney (Grade 1) to ledges.

Now, move up and step onto the left side of the slab above (exposed) and climb right across it (Grade 2) to enter a gully (or reach the gully directly up a well-worn corner with a tree). Follow the gully through bushes and continue E, then go right and zig zag S up slabs and domes above the barrier wall (some Grade 1) to slabs which lead easily up past a rock tower onto a plateau (½hr from start). Go diagonally right to the far right corner and pass the next barrier of cliffs through a small hidden valley on their left, to the next plateau. Here there are three alternatives:

For the climber:
>   a. Cross the little gully and traverse right under an overhang (Grade 1), then go left and up three obvious corners (Grade 3) to reach the bridge.
>   b. Cross the little gully and traverse right under the overhang (Grade 1), then go

The Burdah Rock Bridge, Wadi Rum   *Peter Hall*

diagonally right up a ramp in the slabs (Grade 3) to the bridge.

For the walker:

c.Descend to a flat sandy area, walk S along it then left, and up onto easy slabs. Up these towards the left side of a notch in the skyline, trending right below a barrier wall to enter the gully, when the bridge will suddenly be seen ahead. Follow the gully up, then just before the bridge, climb its left wall steeply (exposed Grade 2) to the big ledge.

NB: In 1984 there were no graffiti near the bridge, while now the rocks are full of carved names. Please do not add to this eyesore. It is a beautiful place - try to keep it that way.

If you want to go to the top, read on:

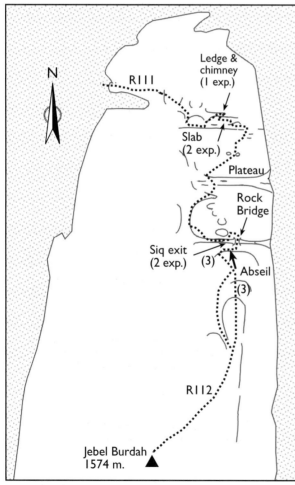

112. Jebel Burdah (1574m) via the Rock Bridge

Well worthwhile and some great views - the crux is the Grade 3 wall just past the bridge. Map 41.

Special equipment and skills. *Climbing and abseil equipment and the knowledge to use it.*

Guide recommended for inexperienced groups

Difficult scramble
2.5k. 3 - 4½hrs for return journey

The Route Ascend R111, then cross the bridge to the barrier wall ahead which is climbed by traversing right (Grade 3) then up and left to easier ground. From here the ridge may be followed directly (Grade 3), or go up the little valley on its W side to regain the ridge above the steep section. The final slopes go up to a superb view point on the summit.

Descent Follow the easiest way down, taking particular care at the steep sections. (Abseil from a bolt to reach the bridge.)

41. Jebel Burdah and the Rock Bridge

Labels on map: N; R111; Ledge & chimney (1 exp.); Slab (2 exp.); Plateau; Rock Bridge; Siq exit (2 exp.); (3); Abseil; (3); R112; Jebel Burdah 1574 m.

South of Rum
The next route goes to Jordan's highest summit, situated in an extremely remote part of the desert, 40k from Rum, and only 2k from the border with Saudi Arabia.

113. Jebel um Adaami 1830m
A great day out! The ascent to the top presents no climbing difficulties and the views are magnificent in all directions, especially S into Saudi Arabia and N across the whole area of Rum. Approach via maps 30 and 42.

Easy scramble
2k for ascent and descent, 2hrs

Approach Allow 2hrs each way for the excellent 40k 4 w.d. journey, which is itself well worthwhile, passing through ever changing rock and desert terrain and past isolated Bedouin camps. The last 3 or 4k are particularly difficult driving up an increasingly narrow and tortuous sandy wadi and require considerable skill. You will need even more time if you want to visit the rock inscription sites on the N and S sides of Wadi Saabit shown to us by Sheikh Mohammad who usually has his camp nearby.

Siq um el Barrid, a narrow and steep walled canyon with carved hand and footprints is 5 - 6k N of Um Adaami. The other location on the NW tip of Jebel Albzouri is about 9k W of Jebel um Adaami. There are some excellent inscriptions near some olive trees belonging to Sheikh Mohammad. You may even find his campsite and be invited for tea and coffee in this remotest corner of Rum.

The Route Simply leave the narrow sandy wadi and scramble up the hillside to reach the ridge which is followed with increasingly fine views to the summit.

Whilst down in this delightful area, you might consider extending your journey by 4 w.d. or with camels or horses to include a great journey to the SE through Wadi Salaada (see below). This is also a good trekking area, in a very quiet and peaceful part of Rum and just N of the Saudi border. To get there you will need a competent local guide and a reliable 4 w.d. vehicle; ideally, make it a 2 day trip and include the scramble to the top of Jebel um Adaami and/or the Burdah Rock Bridge.

114. The Sand Canyon of Wadi Salaada
A wonderful desert drive of 100k or more through a tortuous 'sand canyon' - lots of fun! There are some excellent fossils of worm tubes and other shallow pre-historic marine-life in this area. Do not remove them - leave them for others to photograph and enjoy. Approach via maps 30 and 42.

This is also a great place for horse and camel safari and desert treks.

Guide required. This area is part of the traditional grazing lands of the Zalabia tribal faction in Rum. Consequently all the Atieeq brothers, Sabbah, Eid, Dayfallah and Mazied know the area, as do the other approved guides such as Sabbah Eid and his brothers.

The Route Follow the above route for 40k to Wadi Saabit, from where the route goes E up the rocky pass of Shraif Saabit to M'saiq al Khail and on down the superb 30k Sand Canyon of

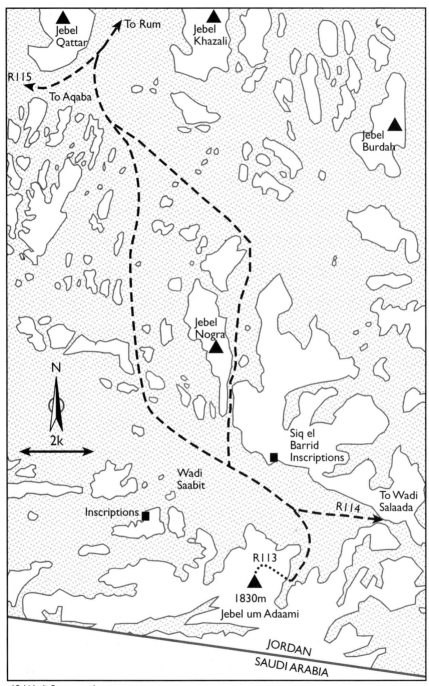

42. Wadi Rum, southern area

Wadi Salaada. The trick is knowing when to leave it to go back W to the low mountains of Um Sahm and so to Burdah. If you miss the way or you really want a long desert journey and go S E you will arrive after about another 50k of remote desert driving at the border post and old Turkish Fort of Mudawarah. Alternatively, 20k to the NNE you will finally emerge on the Mudawarah-Disi track in the area of Abu Suwaneh.

The other classical 4 w.d. trip in the S of Rum is:

115. Lawrence's Way to Aqaba

"In the beginning it was clean sandstone country, of pleasant rock shapes: but as we went spines of granite, the material of the shore, rose up in front of us, and after thirty miles of good trotting gradient we passed, by the southern Itm, into the main valley, just above the well of the surrender of Aqaba. The journey took us only six hours."
Seven Pillars of Wisdom. T.E. Lawrence. 1926.

Assumed erroneously by some to be the way Lawrence and the Arab forces took for their capture of Aqaba, the above quotation makes it clear Lawrence did not follow this route until later. (His original route was down from the Ma'an plateau via Abu el Lissan and Naqb es Shar to the Quweirah plain, thence down Wadi Itm.) This subsequent route is nevertheless a great way to get from Rum to Aqaba, with 4 w.d. involving about 50 - 70k of desert travel, dependent on route. It may also be done with camels or horses or on foot, the time taken ranging from 2 to 5 days. Start of route, maps 30 and 31.

Guide required. Take a local guide or arrange a trip with one of Jordan's Adventure Travel companies.

The Route This takes the desert-track to Aqaba. The start of the route is obvious, out of the village, heading S down Rum valley, past the springs of Abu Aina, then on to the SSW with the steep W face of Khazali 2k to the E, and directly below the SE face of Jebel Qattar with its beautiful 'dripping spring' in a cave once used by Nabataeans. The route continues W and finally NW through Wadi Umran to reach the main highway in Wadi Itm after about 50k, about 15k NE of Aqaba. Alternatively, avoiding the highway, there is a better way which branches SW and then W to reach the Red Sea in the South Beach area. This adds about 20k to the route.

Aqaba
Having arrived in Aqaba you now have the opportunity of some superb snorkelling and diving in the Red Sea before exploring Wadi Araba - for hire of gear, contact any of the hotels such as The Alcazar or take a taxi to the perfectly located Royal Jordanian Diving Centre.

WADI ARABA
Wadi Araba (with the exception of the rich copper-mining district of Feinan) was principally inhabited in ancient times by the Nabataeans, with relatively less intensive occupation during the Roman, Byzantine and Islamic eras.
Antiquities of The Jordan Rift Valley. Rami G. Khouri. 1988.

Wadi Araba is that part of the Great Rift Valley between the Dead Sea and the Red Sea, a distance of 180k. From 400m below sea level at the Dead Sea, the mostly barren desert valley rises for 100k to 280m above sea level near Gharandal, before descending for 80k to sea level at Aqaba.

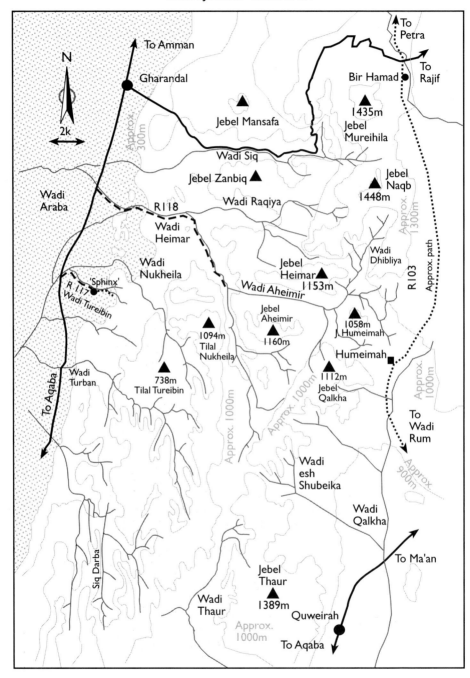

43. Wadi Araba and Humeimah areas

To its E the great barrier of the Shara Mountains dominates the skyline when viewed from Aqaba. Here is the peak of:

116. Jebel el Yitm 1593m
"We all remarked its towering stature and trifid head-piece ... the Bedawin visit it, to make sacrifice, according to universal custom, at the tomb of a certain Shayk Bakir".
Richard Burton. The Land of Midian. 1879.

This summit is probably Beke's Jebel Nur, also referred to by him as Mount Barghir on the east side of Araba and the west side of Wadi Ithm, "overhanging the latter". He rated it as 5,000 feet high and wrote of visiting it with Sheikh Muhammad bin Ijad of the Alauwin Bedouins. Another identification was a link with a notable Muslim saint Sidi Ali bin Alim from Jaffa. Beke's companion and Sheikh Muhammad found sheep skulls and bones on the summit, said to be from sacrifices after which the sheep were eaten.

The peak, also known as Jebel Ahmad el Bakir, the highest of the S Shara mountains, crowns the jagged granite skyline NE of Aqaba and no doubt has excellent views of the surrounding region. Not checked by the authors but should be worth a visit. If you go, let us know!

Moderate scramble
2k from the head of Wadi Mizfir

Calotropis, south Jordan & Wadi Araba   *Mary Hartley*

Approach 12k from Aqaba up the Amman road, in Wadi Yitm, a valley ascends 4k N to a col on the W side of the peak or, alternatively 25k up the road from Aqaba, the wide stony valley of Wadi Mizfir goes 5k W then a branch goes 2k S to the same col.

The Route We have no details so cannot be sure of the route, grade or rock quality.

Taking the other road N from Aqaba, up Wadi Araba, there are a couple of interesting areas for 4 w.d. trips just before reaching the checkpoint and 'Military Zone' sign at about 68k. The first, at 62k is Wadi Tureibin, where you will find:

117. 'Passion in the Desert'!
The location for the film set of 'Passion in the Desert', a film of the Napoleonic era, is hidden away in a quiet little desert valley near an area of large orange dunes. There is a replica of the Sphinx here which provides, if nothing else, a very unusual photo-opportunity and conversation piece! At the moment few people know its location but it was shown to us by Hanna Jahshan of Outdoors Unlimited. (See the section on North Jordan for the address.) The dunes and valley offer the chance of a short walk. Map 43.

Important
It is dangerous to go into the desert on the W side of the Araba Highway as there are reputedly still uncleared mines between here and the border, and the area is a closed Military Zone.

A further 5k N the road crosses a bridge over a wadi - the sign 'Military Zone' is just beyond on the left.

'The sphinx of Jordan'!   Peter Hall

118. Wadi Heimar
To the right, Wadi Heimar can be followed with a 4 w.d. for about 14k up its right side (SE branch) ending in a short Petra-like siq. From here, it's less than 15k up Wadi Heimar to the ancient Nabataean/Roman town of Humeimah. There is reputed to be a trek through, but we have not checked it. Map 43.

Back on the Araba Highway, it's about another 5 or 6k to the bizarre Pagoda left by the Chinese road builders at:

Gharandal
This is 74k N of Aqaba and 50k S of Bir Madhkhur. It is a pre-historic site dating from the Palaeolithic era and one of the few water sources in this part of Wadi Araba. Some of the Jordanian adventure travel companies organise camel safaris down the old routes from Petra to Gharandal which was once a Nabataean/Roman caravanserai (see R91). Also an excellent small road starts here, winding 40k up E through wild and barren scenery to Bir Hamad, Delagha, Rajif and finally Wadi Musa. Map 43.

Continuing N up Wadi Araba, the highway passes W of Petra (the tomb on Jebel Harun - R90 - can be seen high above), before continuing past the turn-offs to Bir Madhkhur then Feinan. It eventually descends a narrow sandy valley to the bridge over Wadi Khnaisser (see R55 and 56). A track goes up this wadi for 1k to a pool beyond which fragmites thickets fill the wadi bed as far as the eye can see - perhaps it continues like this all the way to Jamailha 13k away, the furthest point we reached in our attempt to descend the wadi?

From Wadi Khnaisser, the road makes a gradual descent reaching the new Tafileh road after 4k, at Fifa, then on past Safi at 350m below sea level.

Lot's Cave, Sodom and Gommorah
The Biblical site of Lot's Cave and Monastery is signed just after Safi. This region 5k S of the Dead Sea is also thought to be the location of Sodom and Gommorah.

Beyond is the bridge over Wadi Numeirah (R50). Although the wadi may be dry here, there will almost certainly be water in it ½k to the SE inside the very impressive siq: a great place to escape the sun and sit in the pools and cascades. W of here is:

The Dead Sea
There are almost no convenient places to bathe along the coast, though Jordanians sometimes swim in the Dead Sea below the Hot Springs of Zara (see page 73). However, there are new hotels being built around the northern end where there is also a Rest House with a beach and showers to wash the salt off after the bizarre experience of floating in this amazingly buoyant water.

And there we will leave you - we hope you will have learnt as much and had as much pleasure as we had wandering the hills and valleys and meeting the people of Jordan.

APPENDIXES

RELEVANT READING

Below is some recommended reading in dated order. (Some of the older books may be difficult to get unless they have been re-published.)

Background reading
The Land of Midian. Richard F. Burton. Kegan Paul & Co. 1879. (Oleander Press. 1984)
Travels in Arabia Deserta. Charles M. Doughty. 1888. (Dover Publications Inc. 1979)
Palestine Past and Present. L. Valentine. Frederick Warne & Co. c.1919
Seven Pillars of Wisdom. T.E. Lawrence. Jonathan Cape. 1922, 1935. (Penguin. 1962 also Wordsworth Classics and Castlehill Press.)
A Soldier with The Arabs. Glubb Pasha. Hodder & Stoughton. c. 1930
In the steps of The Master. H.V. Morton. Rich & Cowan. 1934
In the steps of Moses the Conqueror. L. Golding. Rich & Cowan. 1938
Through Lands of the Bible. H.V. Morton. Methuen & Co. 1938
A History of Jordan and its Tribes. F.G. Peake. Coral Gables, University of Miami Press. 1958
Portrait of a Desert. G. Mountfort. Harper Collins. 1965
In the Footsteps of Lawrence of Arabia. Charles Blackmore. Harrap Ltd. 1986

Guidebooks
Petra. Ian Browning. Chatto & Windus Ltd. 1973
Fodor's, Jordan and The Holy Land. Kay Showker. David McKay Company Inc. 1979
Petra - a guide to the capital of the Nabataeans. Rami G. Khouri. Longman. 1986
The Antiquities of the Jordan Rift Valley. Rami G. Khouri. Al Kutba. 1988
Discovery Guide to Jordan. Immel. 1993
Petra - A Traveller's Guide. Rosalyn Maqsood. Garnet Publishing Ltd. 1994
The Birds of the Hashemite Kingdom of Jordan. Ian J. Andrews. I.J. Andrews. 1995
Jordan Blue Guide. Rollin & Streetly. A. & C. Black. 1996
Jordan Revealed. Anthony King. Boxer Publishers. 1997
Landscapes of The Holy Land. Susan Arenz. Sunflower Books. 1997
Insight Guide to Jordan. APA. 1997
Jordan, Syria and Lebanon, Travel Atlas. Lonely Planet. 1997
Jordan & Syria - Travel Survival Kit. Simonis & Finlay. Lonely Planet. 1987, updated 1997
Treks and Climbs in Wadi Rum. Tony Howard. Cicerone Press. 1987, updated 1997
Jordan, Syria and Lebanon Handbook. Ivan Mannheim. Footprint. 1998
Walks and Scrambles in Wadi Rum. Di Taylor and Tony Howard. Al Kutba 1993, Jordan Distribution Agency (UK dist. Cordee), updated 1998
Jordan, Rough Guide. Mathew Teller. Rough Guide. 1998
Wild Flowers of Jordan. Dawud M.H. Al-Eisawi. National Library, Jordan. 1998

SOME USEFUL ARABIC / ENGLISH WORDS

Topographical words

ain	spring (of water)
araqib	ridges
bilad	village, town
bir	well (of water)
birkat	pool
bustan	garden (usually of vegetables)
dhahrat	flat topped hill
ghor	low lying desert
hammamat	hot spring
hudeib	hill
jebel	mountain
khirbat	ruins
maghrar (magharah)	cave
masial	seasonal river
mazar	shrine
mazraa	fields (agricultural area)
qaa	mud flat
qasr	castle
qattar	dripping spring
rijm	cairn, tower
seil	wadi, stream
siq	rock crevasse, narrow canyon
tell	hill, mound
tilal	hills
wadi	seasonal river, desert valley

A few other useful words

water	maya (maa)
here	huna
there	hunak
where?	wayn?
left	yssar
right	yemeen
straight on	dughri
north	shamal
south	jannub
east	sharq
west	gharb
road	tareeq
path	tareeq turabi
where is the path to...?	min wayn el tareeq ila ...?
thanks	shokran
hello	marhaba
how are you?	kayf halik
very well thanks	quais el hamdulillah (m)
very well thanks	quaisa el hamdulillah (f)

Giant fennel, north & central Jordan
Mary Hartley

Glossary

abseil	a method of descending ropes
Bedouin steps	heaped stones or branches to ease ascent or descent
bivouac	sleep out without tent
bolt	drilled fixed protection on a cliff
cairn	a pile of stones to mark the way
chimney	a vertical fissure in the rock wide enough to get into
cirque	a valley closed on three sides by mountains
col	a low region of land between two hills
couloir	see 'gully'
crack	a vertical fissure in the rock narrower than body width
crag	cliff
defile	see 'siq'
gully	a narrow ravine down a hillside
pass	see 'col'
karst	limestone affected by water dissolution
prusik	a method of ascending a rope
rappel	see 'abseil'
saddle	see 'col'
scree	a slope of loose stones
siq	a narrow canyon or rock crevasse
slab	less than vertical rock
wadi	a desert valley or seasonal riverbed

Rum inscription

INDEX

The following list has been compiled to show the number of routes in each grade. They are listed together with important locations, in the order they appear in the book:

Ungraded routes and important locations	*Page*
The Jordan Valley	39
1. Wadi Haramiya (Valley of Thieves)	40
Pella	40
3. The Natural Bridge and Hot Springs of Pella	41
4. Wadi Khusheiba	41
Ajlun	52
Jerash	59
Dibbin Park	59
17. Dibbin Forest Walk	59
The North Eastern Desert	59
The RSCN Azraq Wetland Nature Reserve	60
The RSCN Shaumari Reserve	60
The RSCN Qasr Burqu Reserve	62
The Northern Highlands	42
6. Walks near Um Qais	42
7. The Yarmuk Gorge	42
10. Wadi Shellaleh to the Yarmuk Gorge	45
The RSCN Zubia Nature Reserve	45
The Capital area	62
King Talal Dam Area	63
20. Rumeimin Waterfall	63
21. Walks in The Sumiya Hills	63
Wadi es Sir	64
22. Walks in Wadi es Sir	65
Old Fuheis	65
23. Walks near Old Fuheis	65
The Jal'al and Zai Hills	65
24. Walks in Wadi Shu'eib	66
25. Walks near Tell Hisban	66
Madaba Area	68
26. Walks near Mount Nebo	68
Wadi Zerqa Main	68
Hammamat Zerqa Main	72
29. Roman road, Jordan Valley to Wadi Mujib	73
The RSCN Mujib Nature Reserve	73
34. A short walk to Mukawir	75
Zara Hot Springs	76
35. Roman Road, Mukawir to the Hot Springs of Zerqa Main and Zara	76
Wadi Wala and Wadi Hidan	76
36. Wadi Wala to Wadi Libb and Zerqa Main	77
37. Wadi Wala to Mukawir	77
Wadi Hidan	77

INDEX continued

Ungraded routes and important locations	Page
The Mujib Gorge	81
45. Wadi Shuqeiq	87
The Kerak Area	88
49. Wadi Kerak	91
Kerak	91
Tafileh area	95
51. Wadi Hasa	96
53. Hot Springs of Hammamat Borbita and Hammamat Afra	97
Tafileh	97
The Tafileh - Wadi Araba road	97
The RSCN Dana Nature Reserve	103
Buseira	100
Feinan	108
Shaubak area	111
Mansourah	114
Shaubak Castle	114
The Petra Area	115
Walks in and around Petra	118
The northern approaches to Petra	128
Beidah and Siq el Barrid (Little Petra)	130
The Beidah - Wadi Araba Road	130
80. Jebel Baaga and Wadi Thugra	130
81. Beidah to Shaubak or Feinan	131
The western approaches to Petra	135
89. Wadi Maqtal to Petra	137
The southern approaches to Petra	139
91. Ancient routes to Petra	141
92. Ancient trails from Wadi Sabra	147
99. The Waters of Tibn to Wadi Musa via Wadi Raqi	147
Humeimah	152
The Hisma	153
Wadi Rum	154
The RSCN Wadi Rum National Park	157
Jebel Rum	161
Jebel um Ishrin	171
South of Rum	177
Aqaba	179
Wadi Araba	179
Gharandal	183
Lot's Cave, Sodom and Gommorah	183
The Dead Sea	183

INDEX continued

Easy walks   Page

2. Lower Wadi Yabis from the Jordan Valley 40
5. Jebel Sabarta from Pella 41
8. The Crusader Caves of Al Habis Jaldak 43
9. Wadi Quweiliba, Abila and Wadi es Sijn 43
11. Zubia Village overlook trail 46
12. Zubia Scenic viewpoint trail 46
18. Azraq Marsh Trail 60
19. Burqu Lakeside Walk 62
30. Qaser Riyash Trail 75
31. Mujib Circuit Trail 75
40. Lahoun 80
47. Wadi ibn Hammad 88
59. Rummana Trail 106
60. Dana Campsite Trail 106
61. Dana Cave Trail 106
62. Khirbet Sarab Trail 106
63. Dana Village Trail 106
70. Shaubak to Beidah 114
71. The Petra Siq 120
72. The Hiqh Place, or Attuf Ridge 121
73. Ed Deir (The Monastery) 122
82. Beidah (Little Petra) to 'the three valleys' 131
85. Beidah - Petra via Wadi Muaysra al Gharbiyya 133
86. Beidah - Petra via Wadi Muaysra as Sharkiyya 134
110. Barrah Canyon 173

Moderate treks

14. Wadi Yabis 49
15. Ajlun Castle to Pella 53
27. Libb to Hammamat Zerqa Main 69
41. The Mujib Gorge Trek 82
42. The Upper Mujib Gorge 83
57. Wadi Dhalal to Wadi Araba 101
58. Selah to Buseira and Dana 101
64. Feinan Trail 106
65. Wadi Dana to Feinan 107
66. Dana to Feinan via Wadi Hamra 108
67. Feinan to Shaubak via Wadi Adethni 111
69. Feinan to Mansourah via Um el Amad 112
84. Wadi Musa, Ed Deir, Wadi Ghurab, round trip 133
90. Petra to Jebel Harun 137
93. Petra to Jebel Harun and Wadi Sabra 141
94. Petra to Wadi Sabra and its Roman Theatre 142
95. Wadi Sabra to Wadi Musa 143
101. Rajif to The Waters of Bahra 150

INDEX continued

Serious treks   Page
55. The Canyon of Wadi Jamal 98
56. Wadi Labun - Wadi Jamal - Wadi Khnaisser 101
96. Wadi Sabra to Wadi Tibn via M'zayla Siq 144
97. The Sabra - Tibn Connection 145
100. Tayibah to Wadi Musa via Tibn, Sabra, & Jebel Harun ... 148
102. The Rajif - Tibn Connection 151

Easy Canyons
48. The Canyon of Wadi ibn Hammad 89
50. Wadi Numeira 91
55. The Canyon of Wadi Jamal 98
56. Wadi Labun - Wadi Jamal - Wadi Khnaisser 101
68. Wadi Shaubak to Feinan 112
77. Petra via Wadi al Mudhlim 126
98. The Siq of Tibn to Tayibah or Wadi Musa 146

Moderate canyons
28. The Canyon of Zerqa Main 72
39. The Upper Hidan Gorge 78
41. The Mujib Gorge Trek 82
43. The Lower Mujib Gorge - Wadi Mujib Trail 84
88. Wadi es Siyyagh to Petra 135

Serious Canyons
44. The Mujib Siq 85

Easy scrambles
52. Jebel Tannur 96
54. Selah 97
74. Umm el Biyyara 124
75. Jebel umm al 'Amr 125
78. Petra via Wadi Shib Qays 127
79. Wadi al Mataha & Al Wu'ayra fort from Petra 128
83. Ed Deir to Beidah 132
87. Petra to Beidah via Wadi Abu Ullayqa 134
105. Wadi Shelaali - Lawrence's Spring 161
113. Jebel Um Adaami 177

Moderate scrambles
76. Jebel Khubtha via Jebel umm al 'Amr 125
109. The Canyons of Rakabat um Ejil 171
111. The Rock Bridge of Burdah 174
116. Jebel el Yitm 181

INDEX continued

Serious scrambles   **Page**

106. Jebel Rum by The Thamudic Way 163
107. Jebel Rum by Sheikh Hamdan's Route 166
108. The Traverse of Jebel Rum 168
112. Jebel Burdah via the Rock Bridge 176

Rock climbs

16. Sami's cliffs, Ajlun 57

        Route 1 .... Grade 2 58
        Route 2 .... Grade 2 58
        The Infidel .... Grade 5+ 58
        Saladin's Nose .... Grade 6a 58
        Baldric .... Grade 5 58
        The Red Lion .... Grade 6b 58

Easy Caves

13. The Zubia Cave 46
38. The Cave of Maghrar el Wadid 77
Ancient copper mine, The Canyon of Wadi Jamal 100

4 wheel-drive / horse / camel safaris and treks

46. Wadi el Jarra 88
103. Trails from Petra to Araba and Rum 152
104. 'The Desert in the Sky' 153
114. The Sand Canyon of Wadi Salaada 177
115. Lawrence's Way to Aqaba 179
117. 'Passion in the Desert'! 182
118. Wadi Heimar 183

*The authors with Sheikh Atieeq,
one of the respected elders of
Wadi Rum*